C00 4658885X

D0419526

ES

Glasgow's East End

www.transworldbooks.co.uk

Glasgow's East End

From Bishops to Barraboys

Nuala Naughton

MAINSTREAM
PUBLISHING

TRANSWORLD PUBLISHERS
61–63 Uxbridge Road, London W5 5SA
A Random House Group Company
www.transworldbooks.co.uk

First published in Great Britain
in 2014 by Mainstream Publishing
an imprint of Transworld Publishers

Copyright © Nuala Naughton 2014

Nuala Naughton has asserted her right under the Copyright, Designs
and Patents Act 1988 to be identified as the author of this work.

The author makes reference within the text to websites.
These are separate works and the publishers do not accept
responsibility for any statements on external sites.

A CIP catalogue record for this book
is available from the British Library.

ISBN 9781780576527

This book is sold subject to the condition that it shall not,
by way of trade or otherwise, be lent, resold, hired out,
or otherwise circulated without the publisher's prior
consent in any form of binding or cover other than that
in which it is published and without a similar condition,
including this condition, being imposed on the
subsequent purchaser.

Addresses for Random House Group Ltd companies outside the UK
can be found at: www.randomhouse.co.uk
The Random House Group Ltd Reg. No. 954009

The Random House Group Limited supports the Forest Stewardship
Council® (FSC®), the leading international forest-certification organisation.
Our books carrying the FSC label are printed on FSC®-certified paper. FSC is
the only forest-certification scheme supported by the leading environmental
organisations, including Greenpeace. Our paper procurement policy
can be found at www.randomhouse.co.uk/environment

Typeset in 12/15½pt Goudy Old Style by
Kestrel Data, Exeter, Devon.
Printed and bound by
CPI Group (UK) Ltd, Croydon, CR0 4YY.

2 4 6 8 10 9 7 5 3 1

MIX
Paper from
responsible sources
FSC® C016897

To Cissie Smith, my wonderful mum,
born and bred in the East End

And to my good friend, mentor and researcher, Monty Bryden

EDINBURGH LIBRARIES	
C004658885X	
Bertrams	17/11/2014
	£14.99
BH	DA890.G5

Foreword

*by James Doherty, Proud East Ender and
Head of Media at Glasgow Life*

E ASTERHOUSE WAS A PLEASURE ground, a heady mix of
wonder, a kaleidoscope of fields. My earliest memory is
of living in what was at the time the halcyon promise of
council housing, aged three. In 1977, it must still have been
considered a 'new build'.

Green and safe to roam, we went through a lane to get
to my older brother's primary school. I never noticed the
poverty, the grey or the lack of social facilities. At three,
you're not worried about a lack of shops, bingo or bookies.

But I remember the magic of going home. Home was
Parkhead. Home was reached by going to my granny's house
by way of the number 62 bus. A big, belting beauty of a beast
– better than any Bugatti Veyron – was the Corporation
bus. It transported us to a place where Sandra's Dairy had
pies and peas that would make Nigella Lawson weep – but
only when adorned with vinegar, loads of vinegar, salt (from
a cellar, not milled) and gravy.

It was the way to travel: at the top of the bus, my ma

puffing away on her Kensitas Club King Size, and me and my brother looking down the periscope at the driver's baldy napper – and 'oooing' and 'ahhhing' every time we went under a bridge. It was the stuff of legend; a journey that set the standard for the East End day out, which we were still to encounter, when the delights of the Inner or Outer Circle on the 89 or 90 bus could see a family outing around the city, with a picnic of Barr's American Cream Soda, made up with ice cream, and a couple of spam sandwiches (pan, not plain bread, if you were going posh). Such an outing would take in myriad exotic sights, such as Maryhill, the 'SooSide' (Southside) and treasures like that of Kelvingrove – and it was the only bus journey that took in Ibrox, Celtic Park and Hampden football stadia.

But we'd always return to Springfield Road. This Holy Grail of a poor man's Clockwork Orange would always wind its way home to Parkhead. Granny Alice and Auld Jimmy, my granda, lived in a six-in-a-block grey tenement, not the lovely blonde sandstone much desired today. Two bedrooms, top floor, but even then distinctly over-crowded, and all within the shadow of what, for my family at least, was Paradise – Celtic Park, just a stone's throw away.

There was a coal bunker on the ground floor and there was one on the landing. There was coal, which was harvested from old engines in the scrap yard across the road (a playground of immense proportions, both in size and opportunity, not least for jumping into a hollow steam chamber, with little chance of getting out, but the chance to create your own echo cavern, which could easily rival that of the Grand Canyon). There were screaming matches when someone was accused of stealing a few lumps of the black diamond from someone else's bunker.

There was a three-legged dog.

There was my great granny, who lost a leg to gangrene and her wits to dementia.

For my ma and da, Easterhouse was just too far from the action. The Mecca Bingo Hall at Parkhead Cross was the prize for my ma, and the fitba' and egregious action in Flynn's Bar and the London Road Tavern was the calling card for ma da.

We moved back to Parkhead and our first 'bought hoose', a wee tenement flat overlooking the Bowling Green. Ma da was a wholesale butcher in the Duke Street slaughterhouse – a pig boner, whose claim to fame was being featured in *Butcher Weekly* or whatever the magazine for those involved in the meat trade was called. My ma was a cleaner and auxiliary at Belvedere Hospital. I used to marvel at the prosthetics department from London Road, where occasionally you might catch sight of an arm or a leg through the window.

School was Our Lady of Fatima in Dalmarnock. The 'belt' – a punishment that could sting like a hornet and, for many, was a badge of honour – had been declared a violation of human rights and no longer were teachers sanctioned to carry out the painful admonishment. We sang hymns and were looking forward to the visit of Pope John Paul II – but I was much more interested in reading and numbers.

In later years, I would go to St Michael's in Parkhead. There, the parish priest, Canon Lyne, used to terrorize the children every Monday, demanding to know what details of the gospel had been described in chapel the previous day. Nine year olds don't decide if they're going to mass on a Sunday and my family were not exactly enamoured by the Church. I had watched as my granny was forced to go into the bedroom when the priest came to call – he was apparently offended by the fact that she was a Protestant in a Catholic home. I was offended by his lack of grace and kindness. Sometimes it felt like being Catholic wasn't very Christian.

Of course, sectarianism was rife. On various weekends, you'd see the 'walks' (annual marches associated with religious affiliation), both Orange and Republican: women in bowler hats and wearing sashes on one side, folk dressed in balaclavas and pretending to be pseudo-paramilitaries on the other. There would be bunting and flags draped throughout Bridgeton, and running street battles in the Calton and the Barras after every Old Firm match. Indoctrination started young. When I was asked what team I supported, I always said I supported my ma, not the nonsense that helped create the Old Firm – sectarian hatred that allowed the business of football to thrive, even during the Great Depression.

Fitba', religion, turf wars. All provided at least for a sense of tribalism, community and cohesion in a society that was under attack by Thatcher and her policies. It would also provide the defence when the effects of her government were most keenly felt, as drug abuse and the scourge of heroin decimated countless families. However, the biggest attack was on an industrial base that had made Glasgow great. The wholesale closure of heavy industry did for Glasgow as the Great Fire did for London – but while they rebuilt from the ashes, there was no great desire from the Tories to do the same for the once proud Second City of the Empire. The East End was hit badly. People wanted to work, but there were no jobs – to keep the unemployment figures down, many were put 'on the sick' and many would end their days on benefits. Generations were affected by poverty: a new industry in and of itself. I remember asking one of my neighbour's kids what he wanted to do when he grew up. His response: 'Go on the buroo [the welfare system] and go to the bookies, like my da.' Poverty of expectation is the most insidious of threats to communities.

In the early '80s, my family became a victim of the Thatcher years. My brother and I woke up frightened and worried in a van, in the dark, somewhere in a motorway service station. We were doing an moonlight flit, but this time the destination was London. My da had already been there for six months, paving the way for our arrival. My ma quickly got a cleaning job. We stayed in a wee flat above shops, just across from King's Cross Station. I was a rent-boy at a very early age; sent, as we were, to pay the landlord the weekly dues, with a warning from my mother that we 'were not to speak to any of the women', the light in the district being decidedly red. It wasn't long before we were in another East End, moving to Mile End and what, for Glasgow boys, seemed like another world. We had a maisonette, the neighbours had cars and there were street parties and barbecues – we'd never seen a barbecue, let alone enjoyed food from one.

London was bright, bold and brash. My brother and I became fluent in Cockney within weeks, changing back into broad Glaswegian whenever we approached our house.

I'm sure my new pals were completely mystified whenever I rocked up shouting, 'Ma, gonnae gie's a piece 'n' jam?'

We frequently went home, first on the misery of the night bus and later, when the cash situation improved, by rail on the sleeper. We would invariably be going back because there was a big match on – but no matter how much drink was consumed on the journey, someone would take out the bulbs from the roof, allowing me and my brother the opportunity to sleep on a hammock, styled from the webbing of the luggage racks, without fear of being burned. No sleeper beds for us.

For economic migrants like us, the draw back home was always there. Family, friends, the fitba', the bingo. I was at an age where I realized there was real potential for me growing up in London. I could see the opportunities and I was none too chuffed when after a few years in the Big Smoke we were wrenched back to our own East End, back to Parkhead, to Lilybank, a scheme that was once described as the worst in Europe (the BBC did a documentary on the place).

Glasgow had changed. So many people were on the buroo. Jobs were thin on the ground and the attack on communities was in full flow. 'Glasgow's Miles Better' was the city slogan, but it didn't feel that way. Thatcher's policies had created a post-industrial wasteland. We used to go scrapping for copper and lead, stripping out wires and melting them down for a bit of extra cash. I used to have a pitch outside my granny's, where I would watch the motors every time there was a game on at Celtic Park. 'Hey, mister, can I watch yer motor?' was what we cried out. The new 20p coin was the usual reward; sometimes as much as 50p a motor could be had. It was lucrative stuff and many a turf war erupted when someone strayed onto another's pitch. It wasn't unusual to see a grown woman fighting on her kid's behalf. Of course, we didn't watch the motors – something I regretted once when I went to a black hack to collect: 'Hey, mister, I watched yer motor.' The taxi driver was a little jaded: 'That right, son? Well, you didnae dae a bloody good job ae it.' I still had my palm upturned as he showed me the window that had been smashed.

I was lucky in that my ma and da always seemed to be able to find work. My eyes had been opened to opportunity and ambition, and education was a prize I valued. I loved school, St Michael's and later St Mungo's (by this time it was a comprehensive, not the grammar school of old). The Mungo was still great. I'd had the chance to go on a scholarship to private school St Aloysius, but, making my first socialist decision, was determined to go to our local school and get the same qualifications right there, with my friends. That first day in our first year I perhaps regretted the decision when it became obvious that one of the rituals was for the older kids to gang up and beat the new boys. Fear was the name of the game. Still, I got stuck in to school life. Many of the teachers had come from the old school and there remained real pride in what could be achieved. A lot of my peers had no interest in learning, so I received almost one-on-one tuition. Of course, it meant I was branded a 'snob' and a 'poof' – the latter being a most accurate description of me, albeit one they could never have foreseen.

On our days off, we did everything we could to have fun on not a lot of cash. Day trips to the Barras were brilliant.

We would go to get knock-off tapes and games for our new computer consoles, the ZX Spectrum and the Commodore 64. It could take up to half an hour to load a basic game of ping-pong that today's youngsters would barely thole.

But a day at the Barras was brilliant and was always topped off with some freshly fried doughnuts, dipped in sugar, from the wee shop on the corner of the amusements on London Road.

Other fun was made up of fishing trips to the Clyde, just further than Belvedere Hospital and close to what was Celtic's training ground. We'd head down with our bikes (BMXs were all the rage) and get out some tawdry fishing lines and bait. The most you would ever catch would be an eel or two, with which you could have endless hours of fun throwing at passers-by.

On sunny days we would run, what seemed like miles, to the zoo. It wasn't much of a zoo, not compared to Edinburgh, but watching the polar bears sliding in and out of the water, catching food and doing tricks was something foreign and distinctly different. It was a world of wonder on our doorstep at a time when wonder was a rarity.

The best fun to be had, however, was when it was really hot, the kind of heat that had the tar at the side of the road bubbling up. On those days, we would track down the one person in the scheme who had the best key in the world. He was the man (his name and location changed frequently, so as to avoid detection) who had the water hydrant key. He was the man who knew the best location (Methven Street, Lilybank, just across from the community centre) to unleash a geyser that was our Niagara Falls. The torrent would easily reach the third floor, with superb strength and enough flow to ensure that water pressure elsewhere was nothing but a trickle. But we didn't much care for the risks. It was an East End water park that could rival anything you could find on the Costas. All I needed for my *pièce de théâtre* was the metal binlid. With that, I could fly at the torrent, shield in place around my bum, then be launched skyward as I hit the water. A waif of a child, I would reach a dizzying height, delighting everyone in attendance. Of course, what goes up, must come down and there was more than dented pride when I injured myself, as I invariably did. We also made a few bob by washing passing cars, using the same principle.

Of course, our memories are often rose-tinted. There was pain, real pain. In my family, there were stabbings, serious crime, premature death due to heroin abuse, and children left orphaned because of the same. The women in our family were incredibly strong – they had to be. The East End was built by men but run by women. I've no doubt that continues to be the same to this day. From my granny working in Beardmore Forge making munitions during the war to my ma holding our family together through thick and thin – this aspect of Glasgow remains the same.

I wanted to get out of the East End. I was a young gay guy in an area that, on the face of it, would never tolerate such a thing. It was still a place for hard men and tough reputations. In my mind, I had to get educated and get out. Of course, when I was outed on Hogmanay at the age of 18, everyone was fantastic about it. My ma simply said: 'Ye are what ye are, son, and if naebody else likes it, then fuckum.'

It was a good, solid piece of East End advice and part of a

response that showed that community and compassion were still very much alive in our part of the city. I have many gay friends from much wealthier parts of Scotland whose friends and families shunned them when they came out. Perhaps in middle-class areas there is much more of a desire to keep up appearances; in the East End, people liked you for being yourself.

I would later go on to write for the hit series *Brookside*, then at Channel 5 and for our very own *River City* on BBC1 Scotland. But it was in Glasgow that my career would evolve, as a writer on a small newspaper, the *East End Independent*, based in Bridgeton Cross. There, I was able to go into communities, understand the hardship people faced and provide a voice for them in their battles with power, both local and national. There, I truly understood what it means to be part of the East End diaspora: those who have left the area, but have an opportunity to help improve it through the work they do.

I soon moved to the *Big Issue* in Scotland, where again I was able to investigate wrongs and hold the powers that be to account. I have interviewed various politicians in my career, from those in the City Chambers to those holding the reins of power at the national level, whom I interviewed later while at *The Scotsman* newspaper. I finished each and every interview with a question that, more often than not, had nothing at all to do with the earlier subject matter: 'What are you doing for the East End?' Many didn't have an answer, and those who did talked about the establishment of the GHA and improvements to housing.

It's almost ten years since I moved to the dark side,

managing the PR for City Services. I was able to see for myself the plans that were put in place for rebirth and regeneration, whether we won the Commonwealth Games or not. In Easterhouse, the old, damp-ridden homes were pulled down, with new, low-rise homes put in their place. Who would have thought the National Theatre of Scotland would choose Easterhouse as their home? There is a huge amount of work to be done, but right across the East End real, positive, lasting change is arriving.

I still can't quite believe that there are new-build homes in Dalmarnock and Parkhead that are being sold for more than £200,000. But, more than that, I'm proud that the city is investing in quality social housing that rivals in quality much of what is being provided by the private sector.

My brother was destined for the scrapheap when he was in his late 30s, as he had been out of work for a long, long time. He was able to benefit from the Commonwealth Games, through a scheme that ensured work would be offered first to the people of the East End in positions like his. Contractors had to commit to employing local apprentices and offer support to those who had been out of work. Public agencies are delivering training schemes to give people the skills and confidence they need to change their lives – and it's working; I've seen many a life transformed as a result of the work that's ongoing. There is still a huge amount to be done and massive problems to be faced, but at last there is hope.

I'm incredibly proud when I visit the £113 million Emirates Arena. This massive sports complex, which has an indoor sports arena, and gym and spa facilities, as well as the stunning Sir Chris Hoy Velodrome, sits just across

Foreword

from Celtic Park. I go into various rooms, looking out of the windows and remembering the six-in-a-block grey tenements that were such a part of my youth. I visualize where we used to watch the motors, or see the three-legged dog try to avoid the contents of my great-granny's piss pot being thrown from her bedroom window. But what I always remember is that no matter how grave the adversity, nor the attacks, either social or political, the incredible and indelible sense of community fighting back is at the heart of our part of the East End.

That community remains: it is stronger, more proud and contributing to the next chapter of the East End's story, one that I've no doubt will provide hope, equality and prosperity for many more, as our great city continues to evolve.

Introduction

THIS BOOK BEGAN AS a social and oral history of Glasgow's East End inspired by the many stories – some hilarious, some tragic – that I'd heard from my mother, my aunts and uncles, and their friends, who all grew up in Tollcross and went on to marry and raise their kids in the nearby districts of Shettleston, Parkhead and Carmyle.

When I went on to interview other East Enders myself, I found most of their stories almost mirrored those told to me about my family's upbringing: going to the Barras market on a Saturday; doing the 'wahshin' at the Steamie, all bundled up in a bedsheet and packed in the wean's pram; the weekly or twice weekly trek to the public baths for a hot bath in a private cubicle or, for the younger kids, a tin bath in front of a roaring fire at home in the living room of the 'single end' or butt-'n'-ben.

I spoke to men and women about their war years of 1939–45 and wanted to learn more about the First World War of 1914–18.

The further back I went, the more fascinated I became with the origins of the East End. I was being transported through time to the Victorian era, to its tobacco lords and ancient architecture, then further back to the bishopric, whence evolved the diocese and archdiocese of Glasgow, with its churches, dominant buildings, agriculture, great battles and great legends.

I was somewhat stymied when my research time machine seemed to falter a bit around the period going back from the tenth and eleventh centuries. I could find little available to the non-academic or non-ecclesiastic reader.

Eventually, I arrived at the sixth century and the story of St Mungo and his mother, and the founding of what became known as the Necropolis, City of the Dead, and birthplace of Glasgow.

Of course, Glasgow's history goes back to more ancient times, with relics from the Bronze Age being unearthed in excavation projects.

Small boats, possibly canoes, were discovered on the banks of the River Clyde, indicating that a Stone Age fishing community had settled along the riverside, which was much shallower than it is today and was easily forded.

The small mound that St Mungo chose as the first burial site and upon which he founded his church is believed to have been an earlier place of worship and ceremonial rites for Celtic druids. St Ninian, at least a century before Mungo, is also said to have consecrated this same site.

Glasgow, or Cathures, as it was known in early times, was also settled by the Romans around the late first century Anno Domini.

I had to stop somewhere in my research and begin the writing of the book itself. So, it turned out I had researched the book back to front.

There is so much out there, from ancient and academic texts to tales and legends, all of which put a different spin on certain events and even offer conflicting dates. And, of course, there are some outright fairy tales. I've tried to sift through many of the anomalies and myths, miracles and misinformation. Far be it for me to make any judgements, but, if you take much of the early stuff with a pinch of salt, you'll probably enjoy the book more.

I don't claim in any way to be an expert or a historian, and this book is not a hefty academic tome. It is intended as a light-hearted read that will appeal to those who wouldn't normally pick up a history book but are happy to learn some interesting and entertaining things about the city's past. It is my version of Glasgow's history, told through a wealth of anecdotes and oral legend. I'm sure I'll feel the wrath of many an academic who will have his own, no doubt far more fastidious, version of historic events and legends.

There are so many stories about the evolution of the East End and its communities that I just couldn't fit everything into this book. So I've mainly picked ones that I find interesting and, hopefully, you will too. If you enjoy my rambling, maybe they'll let me write a second volume.

As for the subtitle, 'From Bishops to Barraboys', I know it's non-PC to only mention the Barraboys – indeed, I found that many of the hawkers, stallholders and social traders were female – but I plead artistic licence on this since 'Glasgow's East End: From Bishops to Barraboys, Girls, Men and Women' or 'Barra*persons*' is a bit of a mouthful.

I also appreciate that much of the legendary past is

probably bollocks – but it's our bollocks and, if we choose to perpetuate a completely ridiculous myth or legend, then we jolly well will.

I appreciate that I've taken a somewhat loose approach to the ancient history, but I have included some excellent books, papers, texts and translations in the 'Recommended further reading' section for those who may want to delve deeper and explore events in more detail. Indeed, we are indebted to the scholars and historians who have uncovered and translated ancient texts and for their painstaking attention to detail, where detail could be found.

Glasgow's development was inevitable, given its predisposition. It had, after all – or before all – the three main constituents of settlement, according to architect and professor Frank Arneil Walker: 'a safe or sacred hill, an easy river crossing, a good harbour'.

While I was fascinated and sometimes totally gobsmacked at what I learned of the ancient history – that poor woman who gave the world St Mungo was put through merry hell before giving birth to her illegitimate son – it really was the oral history that I held dear and didn't want to lose.

How I wish I'd recorded all my mother's and aunties' hilarious stories, and I'm grateful to social historians and fiction writers for keeping many precious memories alive.

Glasgow's East End

Saints and sinners

I'm embarrassed to admit that I have grown up happily ignorant of the story behind St Enoch. To me, it was the name of a municipal square and a metro station in Glasgow's city centre. Only while researching this book did I learn not only that St Enoch was a woman but that she was also the mother of St Mungo, sometimes known as Saint Kentigern, the patron saint and founder of Glasgow. Neither was I aware of the harrowing fate that befell her at the hands of her peers when her pregnancy could no longer be concealed.

My own ignorance of things pagan or biblical and saintly left me somewhat adrift in understanding the logic of a young girl's fervent desire to conceive a child out of wedlock, given the dire consequences of her condition.

Even her own status as a pagan princess could not protect her from the laws surrounding 'fornication' out of wedlock.

Not only was the girl to be thrown from the top of the highest nearby mountain or cliff top; the law decreed that the father of the child be beheaded.

Similar laws pronounced that an unmarried woman who willingly conceived a child under her father's roof should be buried alive and her seducer be hanged above her grave or tomb.

But the devout young girl believed she had a greater calling. She was by some accounts so fanatically devoted to Mary, the mother of Jesus, that she desired to emulate her in every way possible, not least to conceive a child who would grow up to perform great deeds – miracles – and be remembered for his saintliness throughout the lands.

The fervour with which she believed in her preordained destiny, and that of the child she would gift to the world, strengthened her resolve to not only bear the child but keep secret, on pain of death, the name of her lover. In this regard, she bore the wrath of her father, who tried to force her to name the unborn child's father.

She proclaimed time and again that she didn't know who the father was, believing herself to have been impregnated by immaculate conception in the manner of her heroine, Mary.

Nevertheless, it has been suggested that the father of St Kentigern was in fact Owain Mab Urien, a legendary warrior whose exploits were celebrated in numerous poems. Some accounts suggest that he raped her.

Being the daughter of a Brythonic king and a member of a pagan community, she said her prayers to her Christian God in secret. She prayed to the Lord that she should be impregnated as a virgin mother.

So, how she came to be with child remains a matter of debate. Was she overheard in prayer by a lustful young man happy to oblige her wishes? If she genuinely was unaware of how her prayers had been answered, might she have been the victim of an ancient type of date-rape drug?

Drunk and capable?

This notion is not as difficult to get one's head around as one might think. Bear with me on this.

Early writings bear witness to incidences of strong potions that had the effect of inducing paralytic drunkenness. Stories abound of people being given doses of a fortified wine or stout, sometimes called Letargion, under the influence of which grown men were so knocked out to be unaware of acts of violence, stabbings and burning carried out upon them. Even the removal of private parts was visited upon them without their being in the least awakened from their oblivion, according to one medieval scribe.

Some analysts claim Letargion could possibly have been an early form of anaesthetic.

And far from being the victims of incestuous abuse, the daughters of Lot in the book of Genesis are said to have been so keen to carry on their father's name that they used such a strong elixir so that they might take advantage of his stupor to impregnate themselves.

Lot lived for a time with his daughters in a cave far from civilization and the book of Genesis claims the two girls got their father drunk and lay with him on consecutive nights without his knowledge. Now, we've all heard of 'brewer's droop', which makes this conjecture somewhat difficult to swallow.

Of course, I wouldn't be so bold as to suggest the author or authors of such an important religious text may have succumbed to personal bias to steer believers away from the idea of incestuous relationships between Lot and his daughters.

And incestuous marriages were not uncommon in ancient times. There are many instances of inter-familial marriages: brother to sister; mother to son; uncle and niece; and cousins.

Born with the given name 'Denw', Kentigern's mother was originally named in sainthood as St Taneu. Her name has been corrupted through the ages, from Saint Tenew, Saint Thenaw, Thenew, Thaney, Teneuch and finally Saint Enoch.

So the young Denw was dragged to the top of a mountain to be thrown with such ferocity from the highest precipice to her almost certain death that she would be torn to bits as she tumbled over rocks before taking her final breath.

On the mountain, she offered up a heartfelt plea to the Virgin Mary, asking her to intervene, to ask her son Jesus to spare her from this fate so that she might live to propagate the Christian faith – an act of defiance that would have infuriated her accusers, not least her pagan father.

But Denw did not die that day.

A bird in the hand?

The story goes that she 'flew like a bird', as if carried in the hand of the Lord himself, and was set down unhurt at the foot of the mountain. For many, this was seen as a sign of divine intervention. It was initially decreed that she should be free from further punishment and the dark stain of dishonour be lifted from her name.

No sooner was this judgement passed by worshippers of the Christian faith, however, than the pagans declared her some kind of witch – that the wondrous outcome owed more to black magic than divine virtue. They invoked her father, the King, to renew the judgement against his daughter and punish her further.

Both factions embarked on a furious war of words: the non-believers had their way by virtue of there being strength in numbers.

The frenzied and bloodthirsty mob led Denw to the harbour intent on setting the pregnant girl out to sea in a small boat – probably a coracle made of leather in the style of the times. To ensure that she met her newly decreed fate of 'death at sea', she was led onto a large ocean-going vessel, taken out to the deepest sea and lowered in her little coracle without oars.

When her persecutors returned to the waiting crowd, they announced that justice was done and the 'evildoer' had met her fate, joking that her God would not save her this time.

Again, in what many consider to be the second miracle of that day, Denw, with her unborn child, praying all the time to her saviour, survived the rigours of the stormy seas and was carried safely ashore near Culross.

Exhausted, she came across some glowing embers of an almost spent campfire and began to build it up, basking in the heat of the fire. There, she finally managed to fall into a fitful sleep.

Mother and child

By dawn, Denw's time had come. She gave birth alone in the woods to her baby boy. The story goes that she was discovered, with babe in arms, by shepherds who had been watching their sheep through the night, protecting them from the attentions of wild animals who would view their young lambs as a succulent and tasty meal.

These 'Good Samaritans' brought the two to the house of Servanus, also known as Saint Serf, who taught the Scriptures in those parts.

Nurturing the mother and child, he took the earliest opportunity to anoint with holy water the baby boy, whom Servanus named Kentigern, and at long last his mother, whom he renamed Taneu.

Servanus took the boy under his wing, teaching him the Holy Scriptures, among other disciplines. The two became very close and often Servanus would call Kentigern by the pet name Munghu, meaning 'dear one', which explains why today he is known equally as Saint Kentigern and Saint Mungo.

According to some accounts, this close relationship made him the subject of jealousy among his peers. Thus, his fellow students gave the young Kentigern his first miraculous deed.

Servanus had a small bird that would come to him and rest on his lap or shoulder. The old holy man would feed it tasty morsels while gently petting it. One particular day the little redbird, believed to be a robin, was caught by the students, who taunted it to death. Some accounts are less accusatory; in them, the story is told slightly differently, with the boys playing with the bird and it meeting with an accidental death. Whichever way we read it, the solution was the same.

The dead bird was brought to Kentigern, the boys intending to blame him for its demise. Kentigern cupped the lifeless creature in his hands and prayed over it. After a short while, the bird was coaxed back to life.

The young scholar was later credited with bringing back to life the monastery's cook – after the man had been consecrated and buried. Far-fetched? Well, I did warn you.

Kentigern's envious enemies continued to try to thwart his good work and sully his good name until eventually the boy left the monastery and his beloved Servanus.

Moving on

It is believed that St Mungo first visited Glasgow to bury a holy man named Fregus, or Fergus, who clung on to life until Kentigern visited him. The holy man was to carry out Fergus's dying wish, to have his body carried by cart (or 'carted') westward by two great and unruly bulls. Kentigern was then to leave the bulls to their own path and bury Fergus wherever the beasts came to a halt.

The bulls traversed many miles towards the west before they stopped upon a mound within a grove encircled by fir trees. It is understood that the place had previously been used as a pagan altar, possibly by Celtic Druids.

Fergus was the first to be buried there. This was around 540 AD, when Kentigern would have been in his early teens.

He is believed to have been born around 527 AD, although there are many contradictions within sources describing the significant chronology of Kentigern's life.

And in that tranquil place, with the nearby clear waters of the Molindinar (pronounced *moll-in-diner*) burn, Kentigern settled and made it his home, building a spartan cell, which marked the beginning of the evolution of the bishopric of Glasgow.

Between a rock and a hard place

According to Bishop Jocelyn of Furness, who was instructed by his elder – also Bishop Jocelyn – to write Kentigern's biography, there were already two brothers living near the burial site.

Jocelyn writes with almost obsequious evangelical zeal and much of his story is believed to be inaccurate, but hey, why let a lack of provenance spoil a good story?

Bishop Jocelyn writes that the brothers Telleyr and Anguen were as different as chalk from cheese. Anguen warmly welcomed the newcomer, while Telleyr wanted nothing to do with the interloper.

Anguen was pleased to serve and learn from Kentigern, while Telleyr thwarted him at every turn. And, it may be argued, they both got their just deserts.

Anguen and his family were blessed with greatness throughout consequent generations, as the small Christian community evolved. Not so for Telleyr. He embarked on a smear campaign to discredit Kentigern, reinterpreting his good deeds and putting a negative spin on his every move, slandering him and his faith at will. He argued every point and openly challenged him to his face.

Relying on his great size and strength, he tried to bully the holy man, growing ever more furious when his acts of malice seemed to have no impact on the man of peace. Often he would show off with feats of burden, lifting and carrying impossibly heavy rocks and trees.

Just as Anguen was rewarded for his faith and obedience, Telleyr was soon to get his comeuppance.

One day Telleyr was felling trees when he misjudged his own capabilities, lifting a tree to his shoulders that was far too heavy, even for him. As he carried his load, he tripped on a rock and fell, still with the huge tree on his back. No one was around to save him and he was crushed to death by his load.

As they say, pride comes before a fall.

Far from being relieved at the demise of his persecutor, Kentigern was distraught when he heard the news and lovingly cared for Telleyr's grave.

Grave circumstances

The burial site was eventually named the Necropolis, or 'City of the Dead'.

Since ancient times, the Necropolis has been both a tourist attraction and a pilgrimage site, not least for the magnificence of many of the gravestones, wells and monuments that populate the site where Kentigern carried out the first Christian burial and so laid the foundations of the city we know today.

The name Glasgow (Glasghu) has long been known to translate as 'dear green place'. However, it has also been argued by enlightened scholars and linguistic experts that the true meaning might be 'the place of the grey rock', based on the premise that the birthplace of the city was the mound of grey rock where Fergus's body was laid to rest in the mid-sixth century.

I would suggest that the 'dear' is represented by the last three letters of the early spellings of Glas*ghu* and Mun*ghu*, but I'm no scholar of ancient tongues.

The site is also reputed to have been the very spot where Aymer de Valence and John de Menteith met to plot the downfall of Scottish hero William Wallace in the late 1200s.

And, in more modern times, it was by no means a grave-yard for the hoi polloi. Rather, over time the mound on the hill became the burial site for the movers and shakers of the city: gentry, merchants, tobacco barons and civic leaders.

Even in death, it seems, the eminent citizens of Glasgow were determined to outdo one another, building grander and grander monuments. So much so that only the most expert stonemasons, designers, architects and sculptors were contracted to create stunning stonework. As such, Glasgow's leading architects would vie for coveted commissions. For example, visitors can see works of art at the Necropolis by Charles Rennie Mackintosh or Alexander 'Greek' Thomson, who would contract only the best stonemasons and sculptors to carry out their designs.

But I digress.

Kentigern adopted and consecrated the nearby holy waters of the Molindinar, which he began to use to baptize newcomers to the Christian faith. As his flock grew, his followers wanted to bestow upon him the unofficial accolade of Bishop of Glasgow.

Despite the modest holy man's objections – not least that, being only 25 years of age, he was too young to be elevated to such high echelon – the growing congregation persuaded Kentigern to succumb to the post and, as was the custom of the times, a bishop was invited to ordain him. Some texts suggest that this would have been a flawed ordination, as it was the custom of ordination for such an elevated position that three bishops were present, not just one.

Kentigern lived a life of austerity and abstinence. Texts claim that he shunned a comfortable bed in favour of a stone slab with only a large boulder for a pillow, and that he bathed in the cold Molindinar waters, reciting all the psalms in their entirety before retreating to the nearby hill for further contemplation.

The year 560 AD is often quoted as the one in which he ordained his first bishop.

The bird, the tree, the bell and the fish

Glasgow's coat of arms commemorates four of Kentigern's most famous miracles. There are many variations in the telling of these legends, but this is my version, based on the most convincing of the surviving texts.

The first miracle was saving Saint Serf's (Servanus) tamed bird, reviving it after Kentigern's fellow students had killed it. *'This is the bird that never flew.'*

While still residing at Saint Serf's monastery, Kentigern

was given the task of watching over the holy flame, which was to be kept burning constantly. But the young boy fell asleep during his watch and the flame of the holy fire expired. Devastated, Kentigern grabbed a branch from a nearby hazel tree. The branch was frozen but, in the hands of the boy, as he prayed over it, the fire was rekindled. *'This is the tree that never grew.'*

While on his travels abroad, Kentigern visited the Pope in Rome, who is believed to have given him a hand bell. It is not known what eventually happened to this bell, which was to be rung during funeral services and other ceremonial rites, however it is believed to have still been in existence in the late fifteenth century. It is recorded that a replacement bell was commissioned by the Magistrates of Glasgow in 1641 and this bell is preserved, but not rung, in the People's Palace Museum in Glasgow's East End. *'This is the bell that never rang.'*

My own interpretation of the story of the ring and the fish goes like this: The King of Cadzow saw that one of his knights was wearing a precious ring that the king had given to his queen. He was livid and demanded that the knight return it. So furious was he that, on his way back to his castle, the king threw the ring into a nearby river, probably the Clyde, which was much cleaner in olden days – people could even fish for salmon from its banks.

Believing his wife to have strayed with the knight, the king demanded that the only proof he would accept that she had remained faithful was to show him the ring. This, despite him knowing it was actually swimming with the fishes.

Helpless, and with the king's threat of death looming over her, she implored Kentigern to help her. He bid one of his brethren to go forth and bring back the first fish that he caught. The fish was presented to the king and gutted in front of him. Inside was the ring. *'This is the fish that never swam.'*

There are similar tales of yore from around the world. This 'fish' story is retold by Hans Christian Andersen as *The Steadfast Tin Soldier*, which tells of a flawed tin soldier with only one leg. He was thrown into a river and reappeared at the dinner table inside a fish.

In ancient times, Glasgow had no city motto; it was granted leave to register one by Lord Lyon in 1866. When a coat of arms for the city was commissioned around 1868, Kentigern's preaching of 'Let Glasgow flourish by the preaching of His word and the praising of His name' was the inspiration for the city's motto, albeit contracted to just three words: 'Let Glasgow Flourish'. These same three words were reintroduced in recent times as Glasgow's motto by the City Council. In the early 1990s, 'There's a lot GlasGOwing on' replaced 'Glasgow's Miles Better'. In 2014, the motto is: 'People Make Glasgow'. The coat of arms preserves the miracles of the bird, the tree, the bell and the fish.

Out and about

As his followers grew in number, communities began to come together and the geography expanded further afield. Kentigern would often set out on his travels, calling more and more to the faith. Indeed, while many would like to claim St Mungo as exclusively Glasgow's, he travelled throughout the land and stayed a while in Wales. As a result, many towns and villages have churches dedicated in his name.

When he returned from his travels, seeing how the burgh was growing, he set about dividing his flock into parishes with set boundaries and ordaining more clergy.

Kentigern's first church might have been little more than a wooden shack, but his reputation spread far and wide, and he was becoming somewhat of a cult figure, attracting many visitors as his church grew as a place of pilgrimage. So much so, in fact, that it is believed the young holy man was blessed with a visit from St Columba.

Although the burgh had not yet formally been awarded the status of diocese, the church was developing and Kentigern was educating and consecrating more clergy and bishops to preach the scriptures to the various communities and settlements that were emerging.

Kentigern encouraged communities to till and farm the land and endeavour as far as possible to be self-sufficient.

He lived to a ripe old age and, by the time he died in his eighties, around the first decade of the seventh century, he had laid the foundations of an important and respected ecclesiastical centre second in size only to St Andrews.

His saint's day falls on 13 January, nominated as the date of his death.

Burgeoning burgh

Comparatively little is documented of the ensuing years. However, we do know that, as each century passed, the community blossomed, despite the many battles and several plagues that were to visit the growing town.

Dirt paths were mapped out as settlements began to flourish and trade began to grow. Buildings were erected alongside these paths: the first 'streets', connecting the main areas of business and residences.

The presence of such a successful ecclesiastic hub would have been excellent for the local economy, attracting traders and visitors alike to serve the bishops and other clergy and their followers.

The second St Mungo's cathedral was built near the site of the Necropolis at the brow of the hill, which would become High Street, possibly the oldest proper street in the city. It was a far more substantial stone building.

While Glasgow was not a king's burgh, with its associated privileges and trading rights, it was an important mini-metropolis, with a thriving overseas trade.

This was strengthened when it was awarded a 'Burgh of Regality' in 1450, which made it a king's burgh in all but name, and then in 1453, when Glasgow's first provost, John Stewart, was appointed.

But it could have been a different story. Ancient stones and artefacts found in the district of Govan indicate that the area may have been one of the earliest seats of Christianity on the other side of the Clyde. There a school of thought that suggests the oldest church in Govan would have played a key role in the kingdom of Strathclyde. And that, when the Vikings raided the town of Dumbarton in circa 870 AD, Govan's chieftains played a major role in resisting the Vikings, possibly shifting focus from ecclesiastic development to the business of war.

Surprisingly (to me, at least), Glasgow wasn't officially recognized as a city until well into the twentieth century, although it had been referred to as such since at least the 1700s and maybe earlier.

The first recipient of the honour of Freedom of the City was His Grace the Duke of Hamilton in 1800, despite having no official recognition. In England, early conferring of city status relied on a number of criteria, the first being that it had its own diocesan cathedral, but this was not the case in Scotland.

City status did not confer any special privileges, and it would have been approved only by royal decree and 'letters patent'. When the royal burgh of Inverness applied to be appointed city status in 1897, during Queen Victoria's jubilee year, the application was rejected. Some say the main reason for this was that the monarchy didn't want the embarrassment of the revelation that many more existing 'cities' didn't have official charter. This had been highlighted in 1889, when Dundee was granted city status.

Even as late as 1929, Aberdeen, Dundee, Edinburgh and Glasgow were constituted as 'county of cities', meaning that the burghs were still not recognized as cities. By 1975, when the status of 'burgh' was abolished across the land, these four burghs – while still not recognized officially – were at least listed as cities in the Local Government Scotland Act 1973.

In fact, it wasn't until as recently as 1996 that the four cities were established officially.

Building upon strong foundations

St Mungo's importance in founding the burgh of Glasgow and developing it to become a respected ecclesiastic centre was underpinned with the erection of a new stone cathedral dedicated to the saint and accommodating the holy man's remains. It was consecrated in 1136, with King David I attending the ceremony.

The cathedral has been in various stages of repair and disrepair ever since, and was reportedly all but destroyed by fire in the late 1100s, possibly 1189.

The current cathedral was constructed on the site of the older building and was consecrated in 1197.

It has been argued that it was Bishop Jocelyn of Furness who really put Glasgow on the map.

He was also key in influencing the establishment and formalization of the Glasgow episcopal diocese in 1145.

After King William I signed the Treaty of Falaise in 1174, which relegated the Scottish monarchy and Church to subordinate status under the English, Jocelyn displayed his political nous with an elegant finesse. He travelled to Rome for a special audience with Pope Alexander III and emerged from the meeting with his trump card.

Jocelyn had pled the case to the Pope to issue a special charter – a papal 'bull' – declaring the bishopric of Glasgow as a 'special daughter' of the Catholic Church.

This was about two years after the Treaty of Falaise and,

while a new king, Henry II, now sat on the throne, the treaty was still in place.

When Jocelyn was called to stand before the king to proclaim the subordination of the bishopric of Glasgow to the Archbishop of York, he played his trump card of special daughter status, thus avoiding the terms of the treaty.

Pope Alexander III cemented Glasgow's unique status when he also issued a decree that everyone within the diocese of Glasgow – which stretched from Argyll to Ayrshire – would be obliged to make an annual pilgrimage to the shrine of St Kentigern.

Fair play to them

Jocelyn was also instrumental in negotiating an annual fair in Glasgow. Originally an eight-day event, the Glasgow Fair Fortnight we enjoy today surely evolved from this. The yearly event would attract more trade and visitors from further afield, thus the East End as we now know it (but which originally was the centre and hub of Glasgow) came to be granted permission to hold a weekly market close to the area that would become Glasgow Cross – where High Street extends towards the Clyde to Saltmarket and crosses with Trongate and Gallowgate. This is roughly where, centuries later, the Barras market stands today.

Links were forged between the disparate settlements, as the fishermen on the banks of the Clyde – which was rich with salmon and trout – would venture inland to sell their catch at the market.

Thus there developed two separate hubs, one centring

on the ecclesiastic community at the top of the hill, where Glasgow's Catholic cathedral and its neighbouring Bishop's Castle dominated; the other, down the hill in the market square.

Jocelyn was a charismatic man and so politically astute that he became possibly the most influential man in the country, having the ear of the Pope and many of Europe's leaders. It was he who negotiated a royal charter for Glasgow around the late 1170s, which allowed the bishopric similar privileges to those of a royal burgh.

He may have been viewed as the original 'town planner', being credited with much of the early building development, not just the more substantial version of the Catholic cathedral, which went on in various stages of construction for one and a half centuries. This was partly due to its difficult situation on a steep hill, restoration after lightning strike and new extensions being built over time.

Streets ahead

Jocelyn's hand is seen in the building and infrastructure around Glasgow Cross and the lower town, with the emergence of streets such as the one leading to the wooden bridge over the Clyde at Bridgegait, or Briggait.

In these times, 'gate' or 'gait' would translate not as we now know it but meaning 'the road to'. Thus, the Gallowgate was not the place where hangings and other punishments were carried out; rather, it was more like a signpost to where the gallows proper resided. At one time, the city's first public park, Glasgow Green, was used as

The magnificent and imposing Glasgow Cathedral viewed
from the Necropolis. It has been a place of battles and
bloodshed almost as much as prayer and sacrament.

public grazing for cattle and for public executions.

To add to the confusion, the burgh had four ports, or gates, that served as tollbooths. Visitors would have to pay a toll to enter and trade within its confines. This served to fill the coffers of the bishopric.

Street development followed the routes of well-trodden pathways over centuries and dwellings and other buildings were erected along these routes, named for their geographical location – the Gallowgate, Trongate, Drygate, Mercat (Market) Square, et cetera.

Later streets were named after key religious or political figures, and many of the rich merchants would name the road leading to their mansion after themselves or members of royalty: Queen Street, Glassford Street, Hutcheson Street. Others, such as Virginia Street, would be associated with the tobacco trade – the American states that dominated tobacco cultivation.

And there are – or were, since a lot of them have undergone name changes or simply no longer exist – streets named after famous battles, such as Salamanca Street, after the British victory over the French in Spain; and Alma Street, from the Crimean War.

An influx of Roman Catholic immigrants from Ireland in the late 1800s fuelled the fire, not only because of religious differences but also because they were viewed as 'scabs' who broke strikes and worked for lower wages.

One street in the East End was unofficially named Scabby Loan, as it housed foreign strike-breakers. Eventually its nickname was made official and a new street sign replaced the original – and is still there today.

Stockwell Street is mentioned in the tales of a prolific storyteller known to embellish historical accounts in highly entertaining yarns. 'Blind Harry' tells of the Battle o' the Bell o' the Brae, when William Wallace rid the Bishop's Castle of pesky English who occupied the holy place and were terrorizing the townspeople. He split his army in two, ordering them to carry out a 'pincer' style attack, rounding the garrison from front and back, thus hemming the enemy in. He freed the castle and ordered his men to cut off the enemies' heads and stuff them down a well near High Street. 'Stock it well with Englishmen,' he cried and, so the story goes, the name stuck: Stockwell Street.

Keep the faith

The sacking of Glasgow by Somerled of Argyll, alongside the sons of King Malcolm IV, in 1153, witnessed many 'right-eous' men slain. It is also recorded that Somerled persuaded the allegiance of foreign armies, including an Albanian con-tingency. Church buildings and the cathedral were all but razed to the ground 'by fire and sword'; rigs and farmland were laid waste. Those clergy who could, fled Glasgow and few remained to mourn the passing of the recently enjoyed prosperity of the burgh. In fact, it has been suggested that only one wounded cleric, Brother Mark, remained to pray for retribution.

It has to be said that Bishop Herbert was conspicuous by his absence during all this.

The lone cleric prayed to Kentigern, imploring him to intervene and plead for retribution. After some time it was clear that the people's prayers remained unanswered. Thus Kentigern's credibility came into question: it was felt that he had forsaken the very Church he had founded. As the years passed, it became clear that his reputation was in need of some public-relations crisis management before confidence in his power and sanctity could be restored.

Faithful followers of Kentigern seem to have been made to wait another decade before they could believe their prayers had at last been answered.

Bishop Herbert, at that time, was given some credit for this. He is believed to have led a holy army to face Somerled, as he landed near Renfrew intent on ravaging the whole kingdom. Somerled was defeated in this battle of 1164 and, to some extent, St Kentigern's reputation was restored.

Confirmation of this came when the bishops produced a statement in the form of a poem on both battles, declaring that 'the Scottish saints must surely be praised', thus suggesting that St Kentigern should come in from the cold and continue to enjoy the praises and fidelity of his flock and of the monarchy.

Lest we forget

While St Kentigern was glorified, and his tomb and cathedral were sacred places of pilgrimage, his mother, St Enoch, was not forgotten. She was also venerated and the two are often spoken of as the 'co-patrons' of Glasgow.

She was finally recognized in 1295, when a chapel was built and consecrated in her name.

Legend has it that this was also the site of her burial and

was a place of pilgrimage whereupon successive chapels were built on the same sacred site, the last of which is believed to have been demolished in 1926 and this, sadly, marked the beginning of the end for the memory of the mother of Glasgow's founding saint among the general populace.

Few people today who live along the broken pathway of St Enoch's burn have any idea that they reside within the route of the stream named for St Mungo's sainted mother, although there are some fabulous maps, blogs and forums on that very burn. It's well worth checking out hiddenglasgow. com and urbanglasgow.co.uk (the Wee Burn Adventure).

It is understood that the current St Enoch's Square hides her grave. It is strange to think that, as we run down the stairs at St Enoch's metro station to catch the underground train, we are possibly treading on sacred ground or almost literally treading on the founding mother's grave.

There is also mention in the book of Genesis of another St Enoch, son of Jared. This St Enoch is said to be the great grandson of Adam, the father of Methuselah and the great grandfather of Noah.

Some sources attribute this saint as being commemorated at St Enoch's Square in Glasgow; however, its association with the mother of Kentigern is more widely accepted.

At the tollbooth at Glasgow Cross, St Enoch's memory is prominent only to those in the know. The Trongate and Tron Kirk, nowadays the home of the Tron Theatre, were originally named after St Tenus, which is another variation of her name.

The Provand's Lordship exterior, above. The etcher Robert Bryden depicts
contemporary bill posters advertising Oxo and 'Absolute Temperance'.
The interior, below, shows the life of austerity that clerical leaders in medieval
times were expected to live, following the lead of their founder, St Kentigern – a
far cry from the plush arrangements of today's clerical hierarchy. It was built in
1471, commissioned by Bishop Muirhead, whose original coat of arms can still
be seen engraved on an outside wall, and is the oldest dwelling house
in the city, now in the curatorship of Glasgow Life.

Last house standing

While they were not paid a stipend by the Church hierarchy to carry on their work, clergy were given the privilege of a prebendary. They were allocated some of the revenue from rents or tolls and other income, as well as their food and accommodation.

Over time, there were to be 32 prebendary manses built in the upper burgh – of which only the Provand's Lordship remains. The house of the Lord of the Prebend became known as Lord of Provand, the Provand's Lordship.

The Provand's Lordship may have been the last of such prebendaries, built by Bishop Andrew Muirhead around 1471, originally as part of St Nicholas's, a small charitable hospital for the poor, still proudly displaying the bishop's coat of arms today.

The house escaped the zeal of new-town planners during the reign of Queen Victoria in which many, or most, of the beautiful Georgian buildings were demolished.

It may be argued that Glasgow needed a makeover, wider streets and a new sewerage system to serve a post-Industrial Revolution society.

The little Provand's house escaped the radar of the council's architectural raiders until way into the twentieth century, when a new wave of town planners seemed hell-bent on razing the old city to the ground and building anew in the name of modernity and 'progress' in the 1970s.

It is now a popular visitor attraction, thanks to the fore-sight of the Provand's Lordship Society, which took over custody of the small 'random rubble' building in 1978.

Building bridges

While the bishops didn't own the land, they were extremely influential and were empowered to manage the tolls and land, and interpret the law in their courts.

They were the ecclesiastical law-keepers, part of a trinity of courts, the other two being baronial and royal. Bishops had the power to banish or imprison people who had trespassed a church law. Heresy was their favourite.

The old wooden bridge that had been constructed over the Clyde river around 1286 played a significant role in the movement of goods and people into Glasgow. It was replaced by a far more substantial stone structure that could withstand heavier traffic around 1345, although some sources put this nearer to the end of the century.

This new bridge served as recognition of Glasgow's growing stature as a market town, with more farmers and traders making the journey to the weekly market, which, in turn, contributed greatly to the burgh's income. Over the next century, Glasgow was truly flourishing, with an enviable overseas trade.

Keep off the grass

By the start of the 1400s, Glasgow's developing community of 1,500 or so citizens enjoyed far greater respect than its neighbouring royal burghs, such as Rutherglen. And, indeed, it punched above its weight economically.

Royal burghs would pay a certain amount of their income back to the king. Therefore, it is clear to see the influence of the Glasgow bishops, when, around 1450, they were granted full jurisdiction over their property and other assets.

In that same year, King James II granted land in the lower town for use as common grazing ground. Glasgow Green was the first of many common grounds for public use. It runs from the Saltmarket at the High Court, across to the Calton and Bridgeton districts, and is bordered by the River Clyde to the south; it was more recently used by the women of the East End for drying and bleaching their linen and clothing, which they had washed in the nearby wash house.

Before the wash house, women would hitch up their skirts and tread the washing in huge half barrels of soapy water and lay them out to dry on the lawns.

This so fascinated tourists, one of whom wrote home to his family:

The women generally to us seemed none of the handsomest. They are not very cleanly in their houses but sluttish in dressing their meat [clothing their bodies]. Their way of washing linen is to tuck up their coats and tread them in a tub.

The washing greens were still widely used well into the 1970s and some of the poles used by the women to hang their clothes out to air can still be seen today near the former Templeton carpet factory.

Sporting events were popular throughout the year despite a prohibitive bye-law, introduced in 1819, banning sports activities such as golf, tennis, bowling, football and cricket. Swimming Fleshers' Haugh was another regular pursuit; the site hosted a gathering by Regent Moray and the army of Mary, Queen of Scots at the Battle of Langside in 1568.

Bonnie Prince Charlie also mustered troops there in 1746, causing resentment among the anti-Jacobite population of the East End of the city.

And the power of the East End people was brought to the fore in 1821 when Milton Iron Works was given permission to mine for coal on the Green, prompting an irreverent 'hands-off' song dedicated to Auld John, referring to John McDowall, the mine works company director.

Plans to erect a railway viaduct through the Green were also thwarted by the local people, and motorway development in the 1970s and '80s was fiercely contested.

Executions, demonstrations and public speeches have all taken place on the Green, with the last public execution that of Dr Pritchard, who murdered his wife and mother-in-law.

Temperance rallies and religious and political events have all vied for the attentions of East Enders.

When the right to the electoral vote was extended by the Reform Bill in 1832, more than 70,000 gathered on the Green to celebrate.

Public outrage was again provoked by an attempt to ban public speaking by councillors, who sought to silence those wishing to talk on subjects that didn't meet with their approval. One of the fiercest opponents was the anti-parliamentarian and anarchist Guy Aldred, whose opposition in the mid-1900s on the grounds of freedom of speech was taken up and followed by rioting in the city and the eventual repeal of the restrictive law in 1932.

Monuments commemorating those such as Queen Victoria and Horatio Nelson have been erected on the Green. The Doulton Fountain and the McLennan Arch were restored recently, as was the Collins Fountain, erected in honour of temperance supporter and renowned publisher Sir William Collins, whose most enduring publications have been the Collins dictionaries.

Probably the most important leisure activity associated with the Green is the Glasgow Fair, which from the early 1800s was held near the High Court building. The start of the fair saw thousands of East Enders make their way in droves to the festivities hosted at the Green.

The fair originally included sales of horses, cattle and the hiring of servants. In the nineteenth century, it began to attract amusements such as travelling theatre companies and circuses.

The area has long been associated with the people's struggle for reforms and justice. As at Speaker's Corner in London's Hyde Park, the Green became the place to listen to religious and political speakers debating causes such as electoral reform, trade-union rights and women's suffrage.

If Glasgow Green could talk, the tales it would tell.

Having been steadfastly protected from predatory developers by successive generations, the Green has brought people together in community activity since its early role as common grazing land. In fact Cow Lone, now Argyle Street, was the main thoroughfare for the town herd, who would call in his cattle on his way to the Green or Drygate.

The Green has been the destination for many walks and rallies – for example, the Orange Walk, and until very recently it was the final destination for the marches that took place on May Day. Thousands of trade-union members would meet at Blythswood Square on 1 May and walk through the streets of Glasgow, banners held aloft, towards Glasgow Green. While there would inevitably be political speakers – almost always from the Labour and socialist parties – organizers would invite likeminded entertainers such as comedians, singers and bands, making for a fun family day out.

The Green hosts the World Pipe Band Championship every year.

The park was prone to flooding and work on redesigning the layout began in 1817 to accommodate the re-channelling of the Camlachie and Molindinar burns underground. Much of the hard labour would have been carried out by unemployed weavers and other craftsmen, cast aside as the Industrial Revolution ploughed on. Many of the cottage industries were rendered redundant by the introduction of power looms and mass production machinery.

Power to the papal

It was Bishop Turnbull who pursued a charter from King James II that bestowed upon the bishops the right to appoint provosts, baillies and other offices, which had previously been elected posts. This gave enormous power to the clergy in terms of fiscal and legal responsibilities.

By the end of the century, the bishops were allowed to collect and retain their taxes, or customs, levied on goods such as wool, leather and agricultural produce, as well as rights to export and import. These privileges are hugely significant in that it was usually only royal burghs that enjoyed them.

Then in January 1492, the crowning glory came: the see, or diocese, of Glasgow was elevated to the status of archdiocese, with jurisdiction stretching further afield, from Argyll to Galloway.

King James IV, who described the cathedral in a letter to Pope Innocent VIII as surpassing other cathedral churches in its 'structure, its learned men, its foundation, its ornaments and other very noble prerogatives', may have encouraged its elevation to archdiocese. The papal 'bull' was granted, declaring the see to be 'metropolitan'. The Pope died only a few months later.

His naming Robert Blackadder as the town's first archbishop would have been one of the Pope's last official deeds. Blackadder's importance was demonstrated by the construction of an extension to the cathedral in his name, which became known as Blackadder Aisle.

Not Catholic but catholic

The episcopalians didn't claim religious exclusivity. While there had been a separate Bishop's Castle built adjacent to the cathedral, the burgh attracted other religious orders. As well as the Dominican Order, the Blackfriars, around 1240, the Franciscan Greyfriars laid down foundations nearby, building their monastery also on High Street in 1476.

The Tron Theatre building was originally a church,

founded in 1525, at the bottom of High Street, the area now known as Trongate.

Founded by James Houston as the Collegiate Church of Our Lady and St Anne, it underwent a change of use as a Protestant place of worship after the Reformation and became known as the Tron Kirk.

Ich protestiere!

Around 1517, a new era of Reformation was knocking on the door – quite literally, with religious Augustine monk and great scholar Martin Luther reportedly nailing his controversial theses to the door of a church in Wittenberg, Germany. They ran to a hefty 95 theses.

It was a feisty act of protest, whence his new interpretation of biblical scripture became known as Protestantism and was to split the church into two factions – Protestant and Catholic – still fiercely contested today such was the enormity of this religious divide.

Perhaps it was inevitable that a scholar of the school of St Augustine should take such radical action against the established church since the controversial Augustine himself was not averse to orchestrating a breakaway schism within his own scope.

This bold action got him summoned to the Diet of Worms, an assembly of the Holy Roman Empire. There, he refused to recant and Emperor Charles V declared him an outlaw and a heretic, such was the power of the ecclesia.

It was in this same year that the boy who was to become the last episcopalian archbishop of Glasgow, James Beaton, was born. Ironically, at the height of his career, he would become a victim of the new Protestant movement.

Battles royal

Around this time, the original town's wooden dwellings were being replaced with more substantial stone-built housing.

While it is difficult to say exactly when the Bishop's Castle was built, it was certainly *in situ* around the middle 1500s; it may have been erected as early as 1438–40. Other sources place its construction in the 1300s.

The castle was besieged in 1544, during a series of battles that resulted from the Scots parliament's rejection of the English proposal of a marriage between Prince Edward, son of Henry VIII, and Mary, Queen of Scots, as agreed by the Treaty of Greenwich. The rejection of the treaty was seen as a snub, as the young Mary had been promised to the English prince, and their marriage underpinned a commitment towards a Union of the Crowns.

In March 1544, the armies of Scottish Regent James Hamilton (2nd Earl of Arran) and Matthew Stewart (4th Earl of Lennox) clashed, the latter supporting the English proposal of marriage. On this occasion, the spoils of the day went to Hamilton.

A second battle in May 1544 between the earls Arran and Glencairn at Glasgow Muir, just a mile to the east of Glasgow, saw Hamilton the victor once again.

These battles sparked an eight-year-long war between England and Scotland that would be dubbed 'the Rough Wooing'.

Holy moly!

There was a lot of blood shed in Glasgow in the summer of 1544, but an altogether different war broke out the following year between two rival archdioceses.

The story goes that on 4 June the then archbishop of St Andrews, Cardinal David Beaton, sought to determine the supremacy of his archdiocese over that of Glasgow's archbishop, Gavin Dunbar.

Beaton and his entourage embarked on a display of peacockry with his processional cross held aloft as he and his clergy marched right into the cathedral on High Street to make their point.

This so infuriated the Glasgow clergy and attendants that a brawl of 'rammy' proportions broke out within the cathedral's hallowed walls.

One cannot help visualizing this incongruous punch-up in the form of a cartoon, with cassocks flying and rosary beads swung overhead like lassos, seeking a random neck to throttle.

By all accounts, it was a no-holds-barred affair during which both ceremonial crosses were broken.

Their bitter enmity came to an abrupt end with Beaton's assassination two years later.

Keeping bishops in check

By the end of the 1500s, the population had grown to 4,500. Pathways were well stepped out at the rear of dwellings, where long narrow rigs of land were attached for cultivation.

Basic housing was constructed along the rigs near the dirt paths and new districts of Glasgow were incubating.

While the Catholic bishops would have been loath to relinquish their powers, they were astute enough to pick their fights carefully. They knew that Glasgow was, indeed, flourishing – as St Mungo had preached – and that, for the economy to grow, the common people, traders and merchants would need an incentive to put themselves behind it.

The bishops would have to cut the laity some slack to keep them on board. So they agreed to hand over the administration of income, for example from rents and tolls, in exchange for an agreed annual payment, a stipend of sorts, paid to the bishops. Thus, the townspeople took hold of the purse strings, though the bishops retained a major role in the town's administration.

Some of the first baillies who answered by this time to the 'provost' were clerical officers. The provost would continue to be appointed by the archbishop, so it was prudent to keep on close terms with his trusted advisors.

Incomes were credited to the general coffers towards 'the common good'.

The town held its own court, with magistrates presided over by the provost, or Lord Provost. As the title suggests, this was initially an appointed post, usually occupied by a member of the local gentry.

Glasgow was growing up, taking responsibility for its own administration, shaping a new future in which religious and secular boundaries would be redrawn.

The Reformation movement had taken hold and the Protestant–Catholic tug of war dug in.

Seeing the writing on the wall, James Beaton, the last Roman Catholic Archbishop of Glasgow, fled the country and took refuge in the French capital, taking with him a swag of church records, religious icons and treasured relics.

It's a shame that this act has come to almost define the man. In truth, he saved the mace and other icons and books for posterity. Yet, ironically, much of the swag was destroyed during the French Revolution. The mace was recovered and handed over to Glasgow University, where it continues to reside.

And it makes sense that Beaton would seek succour in France since he was educated there, and Avignon, in particular, was the seat of many fourteenth- and fifteenth-century bishops.

As Archbishop of Glasgow, Beaton was a trusted advisor to Mary, Queen of Scots, who appointed him Royal Ambassador to France. According to some reports, for the decade from 1551 he held the post of Chancellor of the University of Glasgow, albeit *in absentia*, since he remained in France during this time.

Some sources suggest that he fled to France as late as 1560, which seems more likely, since that was also the year that the Protestant Reformation was formally accepted by the Scottish Parliament after 'the five Johns' – led by Scotland's first and best known Reformist, John Knox – lobbied parliament, and was later instrumental in instigating Scotland's first Presbyterian General Assembly.

In Glasgow, the secular or civic leadership's grip tightened, with traders, merchants and artisans quickly taking up the reins and leading the town towards a greater civic power.

Of course, this had to be formalized by the monarchy, to which jurisdiction automatically passed in the absence of its clerical leadership. So the bishops really had no option but to suck it up and be grateful for what crumbs of power they were left with.

Thus, in 1611, by the royal charter of King James VI, Glasgow was granted the status of free burgh, relegating the powers of the bishops and elevating the merchant leaders towards a new self-governance.

This had been a long time coming, as individual trades and crafts had been formally incorporated as far back as 1516; but it was almost a century later, in 1605, that changes in the city's governance allowed a hierarchy of 14 recognized trades to come together as a single incorporated entity.

And when I say 'hierarchy', I mean it quite literally, as there was some snobbery among certain craftsmen as to which had a greater standing. The final draft ranking of Incorporation of the Fourteen Trades was drawn up in 1605, though there was apparently some argy-bargy way into the next century, with the coopers arguing that they should be ranked higher than the Fleshers in terms of 'immemorial useage' in 1752. The coopers won the argument after a search of ancient records and the necessary switch in rank was agreed. But it was yonks before the outcome of this dispute and a finalized ranking was ratified, as late as 1777.

This was the first manifestation of a trade union.

Friendly fire

One of the earliest examples of trade-union collectivism in action came about in the aftermath of the Protestant Reformation. Tragically, much of the medieval housing, and many public buildings and churches which were associated with Catholicism, were raided, burned or completely demolished by Protestant zealots intent on wiping out all connection with the Catholic faith.

While St Mungo's cathedral was the epitome of Catholicism – and despite falling into disrepair – it survived many an occupation by warring armies. While it represented so much of Glasgow's ecclesiastic history, it also held examples of the fine workmanship of glaziers, sculptors, architects, wood workers, metal workers and stonemasons. As a result, the cathedral was saved from post-Reformation destruction by tradesmen, who rallied together in its defence in 1579.

This was probably the only example of friendly occupation of the cathedral, as tradesmen took up arms and temporary residence, threatening anyone who raised an axe against the building, saying: 'He who would cast down the first stone will be buried under it!'

'Watt do ye mean, "No"!?'

Trade guilds were formed to raise the standards of certain trades and to monitor those who worked in certain specialist crafts.

Membership of a trade guild was worn as a badge of honour, as the recruitment process of most guilds was a rigorous affair, often requiring applicants to create a piece of work demonstrating their skill.

In other trades incorporations, membership depended upon applicants providing proof of their ability, such as a certificate of completion of an apprenticeship.

While some trade bodies – the bonnet-makers, for example – were pretty toothless, others carried weight, and had the power to decide who should and should not be allowed to work or carry on trading in their specific craft. The revered engineer and inventor of the modern steam engine James Watt was forbidden from running a workshop on his return to Glasgow in 1756 after a year's apprenticeship in London because he hadn't 'served his time'.

This clearly illustrates the 'closed shop' in trade-union terms, where, until very recently, no one was allowed to work in a trade without becoming a member of its union.

Yet, admission to a formal guild or incorporation wasn't a shoo-in. Tailors, for example, had to audition for membership of their benchmark body. According to one account, to pass muster apprentices were locked in a room and instructed to produce a tailored coat, waistcoat and breeches in the latest fashion trend; for women, it was a trendy gown and petticoats.

The Trades House versus the Merchants House

If the cathedral buildings, manses and the university represented the ecclesiastic heart of the city, the merchants on the one hand, and the craftsmen on the other, were her lungs, breathing new life into the city streets and spreading urban landscape with an influx of Irish, French, Spanish and Dutch craftsmen.

Glasgow's Trades House website lists the Fourteen Trades like this (and note that the coopers got their way):

Hammermen: Founded in 1536, the Incorporation of Hammermen of Glasgow originally comprised craftsmen associated with metalworking – traditionally, 'men who wielded the hammer': blacksmiths, goldsmiths, lorimers, cutlers, armourers, sword-makers, clockmakers, locksmiths, pewterers, copperworkers and tinsmiths, among others.

Tailors: The tailors were formally incorporated in October 1527 to uphold the standards of the garment-making industry in Glasgow. New members had to pass an entrance test by producing in a locked room 'for men one upper coat, one waistcoat and a pair of breeches according to the fashion or for a woman a gown and a petticoat according to the fashion . . . or a pair of stays, if he is a staymaker'.

Cordiners: In old Glasgow, boots, jerkins and other leather goods were provided by a group of tanners, curriers, barkers and souters. They adopted the single title of cordiners (from 'Cordoba workers', i.e. those who worked with the best Spanish shoe leather), while in due course their ranks were augmented by craftsmen from the Netherlands and France to replace those 'slain in the wars'.

Maltmen: Today's maltmen represent an ancient craft that goes back to prehistoric times in Scotland. By the seventeenth century, perhaps the heyday of Scotland's old burghs, maltmen or brewers were well established in every town. Their craft symbol of malt shovels and sheaves of corn can still be found on gravestones all over the country, as indeed can those of the other crafts.

Weavers: The weavers of Glasgow date back to the Middle Ages, when members of the craft were those entitled to make and sell woven clothes within the ancient burgh. The craft became incorporated by a charter from the Archbishop Gavin Dunbar, as feudal lord of Glasgow in 1528, but is known to have been in existence at least as far back as 1514. Its 500th anniversary fell on 9 March 2014.

Bakers: The exact date on which the Incorporation of Bakers was founded is uncertain, but it is known that the incorporation existed prior to its first official mention in 1556.

Skinners and Glovers: The Incorporation of Skinners claims to be the oldest of the fourteen Incorporated Trades of Glasgow, incorporated on 28 May 1516 by the burgh of Glasgow's feudal superior, Archbishop James Beaton, then also Chancellor of Scotland.

Wrights: In order to recognize the craftsmen who were helping to build Glasgow Cathedral at the beginning of the eleventh century, King Malcolm III of Scotland granted the craftsmen a royal charter in 1057. The effect of this was that the governing structure of the crafts was from then on officially recognized by the state.

The families of wealthy craftsmen would commission extremely elaborate monuments in keeping with their elevated status. They are more ornate than commoners' gravestones and showcase the stonemason's expertise. Top left, a blacksmith's stone; top right, a farmer's; bottom left, a grisly gravedigger's; bottom right, a simpler 'clype' monument to a covenanter, pointing the finger of blame for posterity.

Coopers: The incorporation originated along with the wrights in the ancient craft of the masons. In 1569, the coopers separated from the masons and wrights and were granted their own charter.

Fleshers: The fleshers became an incorporation in 1580 to regulate the affairs of those who provided meat for the growing population of Glasgow.

Masons: The masons, along with the wrights and coopers, claim to have been first incorporated by King Malcolm III of Scotland in 1057. Since its origin, craft members have been closely involved with the buildings of a city whose Victorian heritage in particular is now ranked among the foremost in Europe. Whilst still very much associated with Glasgow's thriving building and architectural community, the masons no longer, of course, exercise their medieval monopoly.

Gardeners: The Incorporation of Gardeners of Glasgow, with its motto, 'Gardening, the first of arts'. Around 1605, a number of 'practical gardeners' got in on the act by promptly applying for a charter from the burgh of Glasgow, conferring the usual rights and privileges, just in time to be included as one of 'the Fourteen'.

Barbers: The honourable craft of the barber can be traced to the earliest times and the motto of the Glasgow craft, 'Munda hæc vigebat diebus Josephi patriarchæ Jacobi filii, Aegypti præfecti', translates into English as 'This elegant art flourished in the days of Joseph, son of Jacob the Patriarch, Governor of Egypt'.

Bonnetmakers and Dyers: When the town council of Glasgow awarded a charter – or, as it's known in Scotland, a Seal of Cause – in 1597 to the voluntary association that had hitherto been supervising the bonnetmakers trading in the city, the craft of bonnetmaking received official recognition in Glasgow. The effect of the charter was to completely transform the unofficial and weak association of craftsmen who made bonnets, woollen socks and wylie coats (flannel undervests or petticoats) into a legally recognized craft with important powers, privileges and liberties.

The craft incorporations or guilds comprised the trades rank of burgesses under the leadership of the deacon convener, who also held a seat on the town council. This is no longer an elected post, rather an invitation to attend as an observer to keep the tradespeople in touch with town council business and vice versa.

Now then, if there was a snobbery among the trades and guilds, this was ramped all they way up to 11 by the merchants of Glasgow, who thought they were the dog's bollocks, being wealthy, well-positioned and with a firm grip on the running of the city, holding all the top posts of civic authority. They were the decision-makers, the 'city fathers'. (I couldn't resist that little nod in the direction of Spinal Tap.)

In the same year, 1605, the merchants of Glasgow came together as a lead body and became incorporated as the Merchants House, although they had formalized their collective stature probably as far back as the middle 1500s.

The Trades House and the Merchants House met in

various accommodations around the East End of Glasgow until they eventually moved to their own premises – the Trades Hall at No. 85 Glassford Street and the Merchants Hall, which, after two further incarnations, eventually took up residence in George Square on the corner of West George Street.

Merchants Hall

The first to acquire their own permanent residence were the merchants. The original Merchants Hall was built in the early 1600s as a meeting place, but it also served as a charitable organization, to help members who had fallen on hard times. It was rebuilt in the 1650s to a design by Sir William Bruce of Kinross, architect to Charles II.

In 1817, it was proposed that the hall be moved from the Bridgegate, or Briggait, closer to the centre of business, where the grand residences and elegant commercial buildings of George Square were being developed.

In due course, the Briggait building was sold, with provision for the retention of the steeple, which remained a landmark of its original address. There appears to have ensued more than two decades of argy-bargy over where the new hall should be located, during which time the merchants would meet at the Chamber of Commerce premises.

It wasn't until 1843 that the new hall was opened in Hutcheson Street; it played host to many a grand ball and on 27 September 1848 the Polish piano virtuoso Frédéric Chopin made it his only Glasgow gig on a whistle-stop British tour – tickets half-a-guinea, doors open half past two.

Chopin had been very ill with tuberculosis and it was obvious he was a dying man; his Glasgow concert received mixed reviews and it was thought the tour may well have been his swansong. Indeed, he managed to live out another year before taking his final bow in the small hours of 17 October 1849.

In 1870, the Hutcheson Street building was bought by the town council to accommodate the growing civic administration.

Since 1813, the Merchants House had been participating in the scheme to develop George Square and in 1877 its new hall was complete. The design by John Burnet included offices for the Chamber of Commerce.

Trades Hall

At first the Trades House and Incorporated Crafts held their meetings in Tron Kirk, or at times in either public houses or in one of the cathedral houses. Their first proper meeting place was in the upper floor of an almshouse on the corner of Cathedral Street and High Street at the Barony Hall of Strathclyde University.

Sometime in the latter half of the 1700s, they decided to close the almshouse, which accommodated only a few members who had fallen on hard times. Much of their work was in granting pensions and other charitable grants, and it was felt that there were other more practical ways of administering funds.

The Trades House was growing up and needed a home of its own.

In 1791, the esteemed architect Robert Adam was instructed to build the present hall on Glassford Street. Adam didn't live to see his work completed; it was his two younger brothers who brought the building to fruition in 1794.

The Adam family, father and sons, were incredibly talented engineers and architects whose work dominated much of Glasgow's streetscape, as well as immense country mansions.

Trades House today is a wholly charitable organization that awards grants and prizes for 'any good and pious use which may tend to the advancement of the *commonweal* of the Burgh'.

These were no namby-pamby do-gooders, though. As well as fighting among themselves and together against the merchants, who thought themselves socially superior, the traders took their fighting spirit overseas. This included, in 1777, subscribing funds to raise a battalion to serve in the American War of Independence and in 1803 raising a battalion of volunteers to fight in the Napoleonic Wars.

Crime and punishment

As far as criminal activity goes, women were certainly the greater victims of sexism à l'extreme. For example, note the distinct lack of male witches in history and the special 'crime' of 'gossiping', which was, apparently, committed only by the fairer sex.

Adultery, fornication, whoredom and slander were, by all accounts, almost exclusively women's failings for which the bishops, baillies and provosts – all male appointments – would mete out various punishments.

Ironmongers were commissioned to fashion an iron head cage and collar, with a metal tongue-piece, often with jagged spikes, to be placed in the mouth to hinder speech. But that was just the start of the punishment; the women would then be dressed in sack cloth and paraded through the streets – usually on a Monday, which was market day, thereby exposing the errant women to a bigger crowd – then dragged or 'carted' to the gallows, where they would be introduced to the scaffold.

There was even a special pulley system erected on the Clyde for the purposes of 'ducking' in the water.

Hangings and other forms of punishment and ridicule were very public affairs. Whether it was to serve as a deterrent – and whether or not it worked – is a matter for debate, but it certainly was a popular form of entertainment.

Women would bring their knitting; kids would steal rotten tomatoes to throw at the miscreants; and many men would no doubt be thinking: 'There but for the grace of God go I.'

For petty criminals, the practice of 'lug-pinning' was another punishment that would draw the crowds, especially the kids, who would tear down the streets to the Tolbooth at Trongate to laugh and point at some poor miscreant having an ear literally nailed to the tollbooth door. This may be the origin of the practice of chastising naughty children by pulling them by the ear.

Just as progress was being made towards greater civic involvement in secular matters in Glasgow in the early 1600s, religious leaders of the Protestant faith continued to wield a double-edged sword of repression and dominance over

Catholics. (Don't get me wrong, the Catholics were just as bad when theirs was the chosen faith.)

While the royal pendulum swung in favour of one faith or another, practising an out-of-favour faith was a dangerous business.

And while city leaders, merchants and traders sat around the table discussing issues of business, law and the welfare of the poor, others were being paraded through the streets towards the gallows for various crimes, many of which would today be considered misdemeanours but in bygone days carried much heftier sentences, especially if you were a member of the great unwashed, without gentry credentials to wield.

Under the new Reformist movement, Catholics were persecuted and driven from their homes. Those who persevered in their faith would meet secretly in darkened rooms, where a priest would say a clandestine mass.

One of the most revered holy men of this time, the martyred John Ogilvie, was arguably the most famous Catholic convert. He was born into a wealthy family in Banffshire and raised as a Calvinist. Ogilvie was sent to complete his education in Europe, where he chose to follow the Catholic faith. He spent time in Germany with Benedictine monks and in Eastern Europe with the Jesuits. He was ordained into the priesthood in Paris in 1610.

His burning ambition was to return to Scotland to save the diminishing Catholic faithful in Glasgow. It was a brave move, as Catholics were being tortured and persecuted for their faith. The high standing of his Calvinist family would provide no protection when, within a year, he was caught and tried for treason.

Ogilvie refused to betray his fellow faithful, enduring untold torture in an attempt to get him to reveal the names of other closet Catholics; nor would he proclaim the supremacy of the monarchy over the Church.

He was hanged and publicly disembowelled at the gallows near Glasgow Cross on 10 March 1615. He is the only post-Reformation saint in Scotland.

Phoenix nights

While many of the town's dwellings had, by the mid-1600s, been rebuilt using more substantial stone and rubble, the majority of housing for the town's residents was still made of wood and thatch.

The town had been devastated over the centuries by battles, riots, religious persecution, fire and plague, and in 1652 the city suffered another devastating blow. What became known as the Great Fire of Glasgow – 14 years before the Great Fire of London – wiped out at least 1,000 homesteads and rendered thousands homeless.

At least one source lays the blame at the house of James Hamilton in High Street.

The fire occurred on 17 June and swiftly spread in all directions from Mercat Cross as far as Saltmarket and along Trongate, Gallowgate and Briggait to the south.

Glasgow did not have a public fire service, so a fire engine was dispatched from Edinburgh to help the stricken town. The firemen would have passed streets lined with citizens forming a human chain, passing bucket upon small bucket of water to appease the angry blaze.

The fire raged for up to 18 hours before it began to tire, lighting the night sky for miles around. From a bird's eye view, it would have drawn out a giant cross of fire, growing ever larger as it made its way out in four directions. Yet it was another four years before Glasgow had its own fire wagon.

The devastation caused by the fire would have influenced the town council's decision in 1658 to expel businesses that carried out what was deemed to be dangerous trade.

Among the refugee businesses to be relocated out of town were at least four candlemaking factories. They took up residence on land just beyond the town's boundary to the west, occupying one or more rig of land. This hub of enterprise became known as Candleriggs and is today a bustling hotspot at the centre of the area now known as the Merchant City.

The town was spared another attack by large-scale fire for almost 20 years, then in 1677 a disgruntled apprentice blacksmith allegedly set fire to his master's premises on the corner of Saltmarket and Trongate, destroying up to 130 properties and, in the process, possibly becoming Glasgow's first arsonist.

As in many forests around the world where massive naturally occurring fires pave the way for new wildlife habitats, it was this last fire that prompted the town council to formally regulate urban construction and building restoration, decreeing that all houses and business premises should be built entirely of stone 'frae heid tae foot back and forrit', using slate rather than thatch as roofing.

A second major arson attack came in 1793, when members of the notorious Hellfire Club invaded the Tron Kirk Session

Left, *The Trongate, with its magnificent steeple, at Glasgow Cross.*
The Tron Kirk Session House was burned to the ground in a 'prank' that
went horribly wrong, but the steeple remained intact. Right, the original
Merchants Hall and steeple at the Briggait.

House while the civic guard was out doing his rounds. The Session House was where the Presbytery of Glasgow held its meetings, as well as several other organizations that didn't have their own premises. It was also used as a base by members of the civic guard, who patrolled the streets at night.

On 15 February at three o'clock in the morning, drunk as skunks, the young men sneaked into the premises and, seeing a small brazier, began to stoke the embers. Before long, they had a blazing fire going and were daring one another to see who could withstand the heat the longest.

Fuelled by drink and daredevil, they embarked on a frenzied indoor bonfire fest, throwing everything that was flammable into the fire – wooden beams, curtain panels, even hay. The fire raged on through the night, by which time the louts had fled the scene. Only the steeple, dating back to 1637, survived the attack.

Still in their infancy, fire brigades were pretty much run by insurance firms whose agents would etch their mark on a household or business indicating that, in the event of fire, the premises were fully paid up and entitled to be rescued.

This private enterprise was never going to work as a long-term concern; it was inevitable that the town council had to take matters into civic hands and carry out firefighting as a public service, free to all.

Learning new tricks

One year after Glasgow Green was opened, the burgh's clout was ramped up another notch, as it was decreed that Glasgow was to have its own university.

The University of Glasgow was founded in 1451 at the top of High Street alongside the cathedral, under the auspices of Bishop Turnbull. This is of great significance, as it made Glasgow highly visible internationally, despite having only nominal numbers of students and academics at the time.

The university led to a further increase in activity around High Street: as students and lecturers arrived, there was a consequent need for trades and services to accommodate the growing community.

Turnbull had travelled to Rome to petition the Pope, Nicholas V, to obtain a charter for the founding of a university.

From its humble beginnings, occupying accommodation in and around the cathedral and at Blackfriars monastery, the university campus grew. First a building was added, later to become known as the Auld Pedagogy on Rotten Row; then the faculty was forced to rent a larger tenement building east of High Street from the then Lord Hamilton, who was to bequeath the property and some land in 1459, with the proviso that the faculty and students should say daily prayers for his soul and that of his wife and family.

Yet, by the third quarter of the sixteenth century the university had fallen on hard times, eventually shutting its doors for a time due to lack of students and a pittance of funds.

By the time of the appointment in 1574 of the respected scholar and theologian Andrew Melville as principal, the university was in serious decline, with the whole faculty of students and 'regents' numbering little more than a baker's dozen and an annual income of a measly £25.

Melville was the 'new broom' who would sweep away the cobwebs of academic lethargy and spark a renewed verve among students and lecturers, very quickly attracting a growing international student body.

Fresh from a stint in Geneva, Melville embarked on a programme of renewal designed to expand the curriculum and enhance the university's reputation. He had witnessed the influx of droves of religious refugees to the Swiss city, as they fled one of the biggest religious massacres in history, occurring in Paris and the French provinces on the feast day of St Bartholomew, 1572. This time it was the Catholics who were the persecutors, attacking and killing tens of thousands of Protestants in a protracted mob frenzy that lasted for weeks.

Melville's efforts were boosted by Church properties and acreage conveyed to the university, which had been granted to the magistrates and council of Glasgow by Queen Mary.

By 1577, the university had received a formal royal charter for new 'chairs' of learning that Melville had introduced, including science, languages, philosophy and divinity.

He is credited with introducing 'specific subject' specialist lecturers over the outmoded one-teacher-fits-all approach.

His reforms breathed new life into the university and he continued its governance until he was invited to work the same kind of magic at St Mary's College of Divinity at St Andrews university.

Having studied at St Andrews as young man, he returned in 1580 as principal. However, his reforms and even some of his new doctrines, such as the non-infallibility of Aristotle, brought him into collision with other teachers in the university and the wider academic and ecclesiastic community.

He became Moderator of the General Assembly in 1582, but troubles arose from the attempts of his court to force a system of episcopacy upon the Church of Scotland.

Melville's prosecution of Robert Montgomery, one of the 'tulchan' bishops, was another affront. Tulchan was a derogatory term, used against post-Reformation bishops to indicate that they held only titular posts and that many were unqualified for the appointment.

For this action, Melville was summoned before the Privy Council in February 1584 and had to flee south of the border with charges of treason ringing in his ears. After an absence of almost two years, he returned to Scotland in November 1585, and in the following March he resumed his lectures in St Andrews, where he remained for twenty years.

Melville became rector of the university in 1590. During his tenure, he jealously protected his church from royal or governmental interference. He refused to accept the monarchy's superiority over the Church, which eventually became his downfall. His labelling of the king as 'God's silly vassal' wouldn't have helped his case either.

In 1599, he lost his position as rector. In 1606, Melville was one of eight clergymen summoned to London and eventually imprisoned in the Tower for four years. On his release, he was exiled and banned from returning to Scotland, whereupon he accepted an invitation of a professorship at the University of Sedan, France, where he lived until his death, aged 77, in 1622.

In Glasgow, the Bishop's Castle was left to fall into disrepair after the Protestant Reformation and was finally demolished to make way for the Royal Infirmary, a hospital designed by revered architect Robert Adam. The original hospital building remains today, albeit modernized over time.

The university was relocated to its current situation in the West End in 1870, largely because it had outgrown its humble beginnings. As new 'chairs' were added and faculties

Glasgow University gatehouse. It was carefully dismantled, along with its impressive back staircase, at its original site beside the cathedral at Collegelands and meticulously reconstructed at its current home on Gilmorehill in the West End.

were taking over many of the buildings around the cathedral, the special area around High Street was practically bursting at the seams.

Some sections of the ancient buildings were dismantled stone-by-stone to be re-erected at the university's new site – Collegelands' loss was Gilmorehill's gain.

Nowadays, the area around High Street and Cathedral Street is overcrowded with various colleges, universities and university campuses, so it continues to flex its academic muscle.

Early coalmining was the pits

By the time Oliver Cromwell made a triumphal stopover in Glasgow in 1650, following his defeat of the Scots at Dunbar, Glasgow was the third most-populated of all the Scottish burghs. Cromwell is said to have lodged at the home of a local well-to-do, at Silvercraigs House in Saltmarket.

It was around this same time that a number of coal pits were discovered on the outskirts of Glasgow, the first being found in the Gorbals. This discovery would add to the already extensive list of commodities being traded out of the burgh.

But for those on the coalface it was hard and dangerous work. The newspaper of the times, the *Caledonian Mercury*, would report on the many accidents and deaths, not least those occurring at the pit at Tollcross, where, in 1773, a man was killed when he fell from rubble, and at another Glasgow pit a 14-year-old boy was thrown from a wayward coal bucket and killed.

In 1785, another 'melancholy accident' occurred when a beam fell on a pit owner with such force that, the report said, it 'knocked out his brains'.

That same day at a pit in Camlachie a falling scaffold killed two miners. In that same mine a year later, the newspaper reported the death of a young man who was crushed 'in a manner too shocking to relate'.

The news of the all-too-many accidents and deaths prompted one reader to write to the editor offering a piece of advice, with an anecdote that could possibly mark the first recorded use of mouth-to-mouth resuscitation – or 'the kiss of life' as it became known. The reader told of an Alloa surgeon, Mr W. Tossach, who, in 1732, had seemingly brought a miner who was suffocated after ingesting toxic fumes from a coal seam back to life.

When the man was brought out of the mine, he was not breathing and the doctor could feel no pulse 'in his heart or his arteries'. To all appearances, the man was dead. Yet, the doctor had the rescuers lay him down on his back, he 'applied' his mouth close to the miner's and blew as strong a breath as he could manage. Finding that the breath simply came back out through the nostrils, the doctor tried again, this time holding the man's nose closed.

Though it took some time before the man was fully recovered, the writer closes with the suggestion that this method of recovery 'may be not ineffectually applied to the recovery of persons seemingly killed by lightning'.

Cafe society

Much of life was lived in the streets and wynds of old Glasgow. Gatherings, protests, punishments, market days, hawking, dating (or 'walking out') and street-corner deal-making were outdoor pursuits.

And while the important decisions of law and business were carried out by the town council, and issues of the day were hammered out by lowlier men in the inns and taverns, or on Speakers' Corner on Glasgow Green, there was emerging a new platform for the temperate, who would never darken the doorway of a drinking den.

While some sources credit temperance for the introduction of the first cafe in Glasgow, as an answer to the drunkenness that pubs and taverns bred, I beg to differ.

Glasgow's first coffee shop was opened at the corner of Trongate and Saltmarket. At least one source suggests that it was introduced to Glasgow in 1678 by Colonel Walter Whiteford (or Whitford), the son of Bishop Whiteford. Others say 1673.

It seems absurd to me that some historians would suggest that the first cafe in Glasgow was introduced as a dubious antidote to alcoholism; in fact, coffee houses were popping up in all the major cities of the world as centres of debate, philosophy, art and even trade.

Cafe society is not a recent phenomenon. Kiva Han, located in the Turkish city of Constantinople (now Istanbul), is the first recorded public place serving coffee, dating back to 1475. Coffee was a prized commodity; the Turkish version being strong, thick and black.

By 1529, Franz Georg Kolschitzky had opened his coffee house in Vienna, supposedly claiming bags of coffee left behind by the Turkish Army as the spoils of war. It was he who created the trend of sweetening the brew with cream and sugar.

In 1530, Damascus opened its first cafe, and by around 1645 coffee culture had made its way to Europe – Poland, Ukraine and Italy – by way of trade links with the Ottoman Empire.

It was a London merchant with trading links in Turkey who introduced coffee to England, albeit indirectly. It is said that two servants in the merchant's household recognized a good thing when they saw it. They left their master in 1652 to start the Turk's Head Coffee House.

It's probably not surprising, however, that the university town of Oxford lays claim to the first coffee house, The Angel, in 1650.

Cafe owners were astute enough to realize that if they sold newspapers and journals on the premises, they were sure to attract customers who had an ear for more than simply showbiz gossip.

Coffee houses played a key role in polite society. They were nicknamed 'penny universities' after the price of a cuppa. These cafes became a hub for creatives and thinkers alike. They were hotbeds of gossip and political protest; even some duels were fought in cafes.

It is claimed that an English coffee house first coined the word 'tips'. A jar with a sign reading 'To Insure Prompt Service' sat on the counter. You put a coin in the jar to be served quickly – pretty much, paying to jump the queue.

The oldest cafe in Paris, where philosophers Henri Voltaire and Jean-Jacques Rousseau held court of an afternoon, was opened in 1686 and became the place to see and be seen on the Rue de L'Ancienne Comédie.

While Paris cafes played host to celebrated writers, artists and philosophers, the cafes frequented by a trio of friends in Ireland – Whistler, Shaw and Wilde – came somewhat later. I don't know why I'm tickled by the mention of two early cafes in Dublin: The Cock on Cook Street and Dick's on Skinner's Row.

But cafes were more than just places for clever dicks to contemplate their navel or pontificate loudly. Tontine Coffee House in New York, which opened in 1793, became the centre of trade in stocks and commodities, giving birth to the first New York Stock Exchange.

The world famous insurance firm Lloyd's of London began as a coffee house where sailors, merchants and ship owners would gather for the latest shipping news.

In Glasgow, the first coffee house was adjoined to Glasgow's first hotel, or *hottle*, as the original word was spelled. The Tontine Hotel building was the original town hall, having taken over from Merchants Hall as the go-to place for talk and trade. It was a regular hangout for Glasgow's wealthy tobacco lords and, like its New York counterpart, became a centre of news and gossip, as well as a platform for trade in commodities, stocks and shares.

This was the birthplace of the Glasgow Stock Exchange, which was to become the only UK stock exchange outside of London.

As the town gradually developed westward, the Tontine

appeared to sit outside the new business boundaries that were being informally drawn, with George Square and its surrounding streets morphing a new town centre onto the local map.

The new stock exchange took up residence off Queen Street in the house of the extremely wealthy tobacco lord William Cunninghame. The basement rooms housed the central exchange for the National Telephone Company – Buy! Buy! Sell! Sell!

The pear orchard and gardens were pulled down to accommodate a picturesque square named Royal Exchange Square. In 1848, just a few weeks after Chopin's recital in Merchants Hall, just a few hundred yards away, the square was besieged by a throng of starving and angry citizens in what was to become known as the Bread Riots.

Royal Exchange Square was renamed Nelson Mandela Square in 1986 by Glasgow City Council, responding to anti-apartheid lobbyists.

It's interesting to note that the city's stock exchange was born out of a common ménage (pronounced 'minnoj' in Glasgow vernacular). This is an arrangement whereby a group of people contribute a set sum to a common fund, usually in regular weekly payments – if there were 20 contributors, the ménage would last for 20 weeks, with each contributor in turn receiving the total weekly fund; no one really wants to be first because that means they get the first payment but have to continue paying for the duration of the arrangement.

The tontine effect

A tontine, named after Neapolitan banker Lorenzo de Tonti, who invented the system in France in the 1600s, was a way of raising funds for speculation; it was a long-term investment by which members made a contribution to group funds to be invested over the course of their lives. The funds would be used for ventures such as hotels or other business. Usually members were paid an annual dividend from the profits of the business, the capital investment remaining intact throughout the term of the contract.

It was a rather macabre set-up: as each member of the syndicate met his maker, his funds would be redistributed among surviving members. It wasn't a case of passing on the share to the deceased's heirs.

Any profits an investment brought to the pot would increase as the membership diminished. The stakeholder who lived the longest got the spoils, by which time he or she probably needed the extra income to pay for care in old age.

Such arrangements were risky in the first place, but when only two or three of the original contributors remained alive, it was not unheard of for them to resort to murder, if the stakes were high enough.

As it became clear that the only surviving investor in a tontine was generally too old to enjoy his 'winnings', it became common practice for families to invest on behalf of their healthiest-looking child. This wasn't without its risks, as child-mortality rates were far greater then than they are today.

Governments would soon get in on the act, too, though

when de Tonti first pitched the idea to the French parliament in 1653 it wasn't well received.

The idea was later re-interpreted by Louis XIV's advisors, who implemented tontine funds in 1689 to finance military operations. Ironically, the British government first issued tontines in 1693 to fund a war against France.

A version of a tontine arrangement was used to sell life insurance policies.

Glasgow's first hotel was born of just such an arrangement.

According to James Cleland, author of *The Rise and Progress of the City of Glasgow*, published in 1820, the first Tontine Society in Glasgow was instituted in 1871 – a good 200 years or more after the first cafes came into being – when it acquired a hotel and coffee shop. The building was originally built as the town hall by Allan Dreghorn in 1737–60, and became known as the Tontine Hotel.

The first contract involved 107 shares of £50 each. Each 'shareholder' would receive dividends from rental of the society's property until his or her death, whence the shares would be transferred to the society and divided equally among surviving shareholders.

The hotel was destroyed by fire in 1911, by which time all the clever money had relocated to Royal Exchange Square.

The hotel was redesigned in 1781 by William Hamilton. It retained the original facade, and a series of 'grotesques' were carved into the stonework of the building's arches, dubbed 'the Tontine Heads'. These heads now reside in the People's Palace at Glasgow Green.

'The peasants are revolting!'

As the Clyde and all the riverways and burns flow through the city, so the fighting spirit rushes through the arteries of its people. From battles royal to Red Clydeside, it's in the blood. If they weren't executing internecine battles, they were abroad fighting someone else's war.

If good fences make good neighbours, Hadrian's Wall was a waste of time. There was certainly no love lost between the Scots and the English. While the battles of Scotland's great warriors have been told and retold from the school-room to the multiplex cinema, Glasgow's townsmen, women and children's fights against invasion and injustice are just as worthy of an audience.

The power of prayer

All through history, it seems, where there's a bishop, there's a battle. Scotland's clergy rarely ran shy of a punch-up. And their frocks or beads were no deterrent to their congregation, either.

When in 1637 the English King Charles I tried to impose a new Anglican prayer book upon the Presbytarian Church of Scotland, it was never going to be pretty.

When the Archbishop Laud was instructed by the king to read from the controversial new Book of Common Prayer from the pulpit of St Giles in Edinburgh, he sent *haun'ers* (back-up) of an entourage of bishops, being in no doubt that trouble would kick off.

And it did. As soon as he opened his mouth to read from

the book, he was shouted down and pelted with the prayer books. His bishops were no match for the women in the congregation, one of whom picked up her prayer stool and lobbed it at the archbishop on the pulpit.

In Glasgow, one minister was reportedly 'torn to shreds'. The Bishop of Brechin read from the pulpit with a cocked pistol in each hand.

Malt Tax Riots

In 1713, the Westminster government introduced a malt tax across the UK, though when the taxmen tried to collect it in Scotland they were given short shrift and didn't fancy trying again. It was talked down, but not forgotten.

Whisky and beer were among Scotland's biggest exports, with a thriving home market. The malt tax was seen as a punitive measure – there were even talks in Westminster of tearing up the Treaty of Union.

In 1725, a more determined government managed to pass an Act that made it clear the tax would be enforced with vigour. When the excisemen turned up in Glasgow to collect from the maltsters, they were met by an angry mob, armed and ready for a fight. The tax collectors were easily brought down, but the Glaswegians were only just getting started. Acting on a rumour that the Glasgow MP to Westminster, Daniel (or Duncan) Campbell, had voted in favour of the tax – which added 3d to the price of a barrel of ale – it seemed like the whole town was out in force as they rampaged through the streets, amassing at Campbell's mansion house on Glassford Street.

The building was the epitome of luxury and opulence, and was reputed to be the most elegant building in the burgh, if not the west of Scotland. By morning, it was a heap of rubble.

Frenzied rioters completely destroyed the building, setting fire to its sumptuous drapes and furniture, and taking hammer and axe to dismantle what couldn't be set ablaze.

Troops were sent in from Edinburgh to quell the mob, but Glasgow's magistrates, fearing more bloodshed, advised the troops to hold fire. Unaware of this, the townsmen set about the dragoons, who were ordered to flee the scene and retreat back to Dumbarton. The crowd chased after the troops, however, who turned and fired on them, killing nine men before they reached the outskirts of town.

Each riotous onslaught was heralded by the beating of drums and ringing of bells.

The next day, the government deployed a suite of armies. Deloraine's Regiment of Foot comprised eight dragoon troops, including an army of Highlanders, to overcome the rioters.

In the aftermath of the battle, warrants were issued for the arrest of Provost Miller and five of his baillies, who were accused of complicity in the affair. They were released on bail and returned as heroes to be met with a jubilant guard of townspeople.

In a wry irony, Campbell appealed for compensation from the government and was awarded damages of between £6,000 and £9,000 – which was recovered from Glasgow's malt taxes.

Campbell used the money to buy the islands of Islay and Jura.

Taxes were always a contentious issue, as they are today, mainly because they were imposed on those who couldn't afford them by those who could.

Evenin' all . . .

Unemployment and high taxes are a dangerous mix. In 1800, starving townspeople embarked on a looting frenzy of grocers, butchers, fishmongers et al., arming themselves on their way through the streets by breaking into a gunshop and helping themselves to an arsenal of weaponry.

Again, troops were called in, but Glasgow has always had a sense of social justice and the threat of military force was little deterrent to a town bursting at the seams with starving immigrants and unemployed refugees of the industrial age.

So it's not surprising that, by the summer of the same year, the government had introduced the Glasgow Police Act. It was the first police force in the UK and, it is claimed, the first and oldest in the world.

Calton Weavers' Strike

By the tail end of the eighteenth century, the weavers of Glasgow had become highly respected for their quality of workmanship and commanded higher than average wages for their expertise. The weaving community in Glasgow and Calton was the largest among the 20,000 weavers in the west of Scotland. Their relationship with merchants and manufacturers was enviable and long established.

Bales of raw material would be delivered to or collected by

the workers, and a price negotiated for the finished pieces.

With the introduction of the power loom and other methods of mass production, along with cheaper materials, mainly from India, manufacturers were feeling the pinch. Competition was hitting the industry hard, and the weavers were being forced to accept reduced payment for completed work.

In the summer of 1787, following a number of wage decreases, the weavers met on Glasgow Green to hammer out ways of combating the ever-diminishing returns for their labour. This meeting is considered to be the incubator of the modern trade-union movement and the forebear of Red Clydeside.

The workers agreed that, together, they would make a stand against the manufacturers and refuse to accept work at the latest price cut. However, not every member of the weaving community complied with this decision and some continued to take on work. These were the original 'scabs', undermining the strike action and prolonging the dispute, which dragged on for weeks.

They changed tack and decided to confiscate materials from the houses of the scabs and intercept the deliveries of others, in both cases returning the bales to the manufacturers. But as the weavers grew more desperate, they upped the ante.

Instead of returning the materials, they gathered the bales together and burned them in a public bonfire. Then they marched the strikebreakers through the streets to publicly name and shame them.

When the authorities turned up during one conflagration,

they were met with a volley of stones and bricks, and quickly retreated.

The dispute went on for more than two months before troops were called in and quickly dispersed the throng.

But not for long.

Within hours, the weavers had regrouped and were marching on the cathedral. By the time they reached the Drygate, the troops were on them once more. Bricks and stones were no match for the military's firepower and three strikers were shot dead almost immediately. Others were wounded, some fatally.

James Grainger was arrested as a ringleader, publicly whipped and exiled for seven years. Many more were charged and imprisoned for 'illegal combinations'.

Grainger returned to Scotland after his exile and was involved in a later strike in 1811–12, which lasted for three months and led to strike action being declared illegal in Scotland. This was retracted in 1824.

Bread or Revolution!

In 1838, campaigners for social reform came together as a growing movement. They called themselves the Chartists after the People's Charter, introduced in the same year. In the main, these were political lobbyists whose modus operandi was to organize large-scale petitions signed by thousands, and even millions, of people followed by public mass meetings of 'working-class men' to apply pressure on politicians and at Westminster. Though the movement lasted little more than a decade, it had a radical impact on modern-day politics.

Chartists campaigned for the rights laid out in the People's Charter, which called for the right of working men over 21 to vote – with the exception, of course, of criminals and lunatics. It proclaimed that voting should be done in private and that representation in parliament should not be the prerogative exclusively of the rich and landed gentry.

The fly in the ointment was a small group of radicals who sometimes took their fight to the streets in violent protest, which may have led to the Chartists' downfall.

While support for Chartism was strongest in England and Wales, it had its followers in Glasgow. Chartists were good at gathering huge numbers of people behind a cause and, in Glasgow, they flexed their muscles in a people's protest against poverty and unemployment.

With thousands of Highlanders and Irish immigrants coming to the city in search of employment, a food shortage was inevitable. The situation was worsened by problems in the supply chain from Europe, which had been debilitated by a series of revolutions. Cue the Chartists to mobilize the poor and starving.

At Glasgow Green, the protest began with at least 3,000 people. As the march took legs through the streets towards Exchange Square, which housed the Royal Bank of Scotland, more and more people joined the seething mob, with shouts of 'Bread or Revolution!'

The Exchange and the bank represented the wealth of the merchants: with rumblings of a town uprising, many of the city's rich had deposited expensive silverware and jewellery with the bank for safekeeping, hoping its stronghold would be impenetrable to the 'rabble-rousers'.

As the mob progressed towards its goal, shops were looted, not just of food but also precious metalware and fine jewellery.

While the riots were expected, thousands of civilians were sworn in as special constables; before they arrived at the scene, however, the regular police were overwhelmed and began firing at will. A number of rioters were killed by the time the unofficial police arrived. They pushed the attack back towards Gallowgate, but it took an army of troops to finally put a stop to the sorry affair.

It marked the beginning of the end of the Chartist movement in Scotland.

Many of those arrested during the riots were prosecuted and deported.

Suffrage

In the same year as the fateful maiden voyage of the luxury cruise ship *Titanic*, women in Glasgow were embarking on the first major battle in their titanic struggle for the right to vote in elections.

The suffrage movement had been a rising current for some time, with high-profile campaigners such as Emmeline Pankhurst, who gained infamy by staging dramatic stunts such as chaining herself to the railings of No. 10 Downing Street.

The right to vote became such a fundamental issue in the lives of women that it crossed the great divides of social and economic class, embracing women from well-to-do families, the wives, sisters and daughters of politicians and businessmen, and many more who could barely write their own name but had a very persuasive turn of phrase on the podium.

In Glasgow, thousands of women took up the hammer – sometimes literally – against male social and political dominance, including three East End sisters, daughters of timber merchant and local Liberal councillor, baillie and Justice of the Peace John McPhun.

Window-smashing, among other stunts, was a regular protest used by militant suffragettes, as they became known, invariably resulting in jail sentences for the most prolific activists. Others sacrificed their jobs to the cause when they refused to desist from their struggle under threat of being sacked. Two of the McPhun sisters, Frances and Margaret, were highly distinguished graduates from the prestigious University of Glasgow.

Frances had a degree in psychology, while Margaret specialized in political economy; both took part in a major window-smashing spree in London, for which they were sentenced to a term of hard labour.

Along with their younger sister Nessie, the sisters joined the Women's Social and Political Union, as well as being members of the university suffrage union. Their organizational skills were legendary.

During her time in prison, Frances confided her hardship by letter to a friend, who kept the worst of her suffering from her family. In one letter, she wrote:

Today is Monday, the sun is shining and here I am in this stuffy den and I had such a night my bones are aching with the plank bed.

I was shivering with cold! I asked the doctor this morning if I could get another blanket so I have got one . . . Mrs Crawford (fellow activist) sneaked me this writing paper but I am in terror the wardress looks in the inspection hole of my cell and finds me writing and takes it all away.

Some of them are callous in the extreme. I was out in the yard today and spied Miss Hudson at her cell – she is still on remand so is allowed 'papers. She asked me if I would like *The Standard* and threw it down to me. Imagine! The beast of a wardress saw me saving it and took it away from me.

Oh, it seems so long to be here for two months – still 57 days to do! The other suffrage prisoners are all so nice; sometimes, I exercise a little with Mrs Crawford. She receives me with tears in her eyes. She is lucky, only got one month to go.

Not having hard labour, she gets out twice and can get books and fruit sent in. Then, she had the satisfaction of doing 10/- [ten shillings] worth of damage while I only did a quarter of 9/-.

I wish I had smashed the whole place and Mr Curtis Bennet's head into the bargain! I wish I were near Margaret. She and Mrs John are together in E wing. I haven't had a bath and no hot water and I have been here one week tomorrow.

I have only a few hairpins left and I forgot nail scissors and I shall look quite prehistoric in a few weeks!

When the women went on hunger strike in protest against the treatment of Mrs Pankhurst, violence and force-feeding methods were used against them, a graphic account of which is found in another letter to Mrs Underwood:

> On the third day of the fast . . . a doctor and nurse and helpers rushed in; a sheet was thrown around me. I was held down in a chair and two pints of milk were poured down my throat . . . it was only the feeding cup they used. I didn't feel equal to the nasal tube.
>
> They give you the choice: 'Will you take it through the nose?' they say. Miss Allan . . . made a brave fight – she barricaded her cell and it took three men with iron bars three-quarters of an hour to break it in! Miss Hudson, I hear, nearly lamed the wardresses. She (fiery spirited) scorned the feeding cup and, using her head as a battering ram, she kept them at bay for some time and when she was fed at last it was under difficulties – the fat nurse reposed on her tummy; a wardress on each foot, the doctor supporting her head between his knees!
>
> Even then, with the tube in her nose she managed to tell them: 'It's wonderful what dirty work a doctor would do for £500 a year!'
>
> One girl [a young suffragette] was so hurt her nose bled and she was unconscious for some minutes. Mrs Parker had a tube also – she turned sick after it and was taken to hospital.

Because of the brutal treatment meted out to them in prison, working-class women were not encouraged to take part in militant action. Gentry ladies were less likely to be brutalized to the same extent.

The suffrage movement was used in advertising campaigns; Gorbals glazier James Caldwell made an ad that read: 'Suffragettes may break windows, but I am the wee boy that can put them in.'

The action was stepped up again after 1912, with telephone links being cut and bombs thrown to disrupt communications; bottles of acid and Molatov cocktails were used with impunity.

The McPhun sisters were benefactors of a number of causes in later life and donated a grand house in Callander as a holiday retreat to the Guild of Aid in the Gorbals. They were instrumental in forming the Women Citizens Association and sat on the executive committee of the Glasgow branch.

The suffrage movement crossed geographic boundaries in Glasgow, too: East End women travelled to the gentrified West End to support militant action.

In 1914, a doctor from Dennistoun, the wife of Reverend William Chalmers-Smith, was arrested for arson. Many red pillar boxes in the city had been set alight or had had acid poured into them as part of the protests, but Dorothea and an accomplice, Ethel Moorhead, upped the ante when they sneaked into an empty house in the West End of Glasgow and set it ablaze. They were caught red-handed, still with fire-starting equipment in their possession, and arrested and brought to Duke Street prison. They jumped bail, however, and went underground, causing havoc where they could. Hunted down as fugitives, they were finally tried for the crime and sentenced to eight months in prison. At their trial, the judge was pummelled with apples by supporters.

This was the last straw for the Reverend William. Presumably, the idea that his wife might end up in Calton jail while he preached in his Calton parish church was too cruel an irony for him. The pair split and shared the children, she taking the girls and he taking the boys.

Moorhead was a real firebrand and her weapon of choice was a flaming torch. Originally from Dundee, she moved to Edinburgh and almost immediately appointed herself peripatetic arsonist for the cause. She spent time in Holloway for her part in London protests in 1913.

Those who took part in hunger strikes and other inmates who became ill in prison were released, but only until they were well enough to withstand more brutality by wardens and doctors. This measure was brought in as part of a cruel Act of Parliament, the Prisoners (Temporary Discharge for Ill-health) Act 1913, dubbed the Cat and Mouse Act.

Under this Act, Moorhead was released from Holloway on temporary discharge and went on the run again. This time, she was caught in Peebles and imprisoned in Calton jail, whence she began a triple protest – hunger strike, refusing liquids and self-imposed sleep deprivation. While there was for a time a jailhouse, or Bridewell, in Calton in Glasgow, Moorhead was incarcerated in the Calton prison in Edinburgh.

She became so weak that she was taken out of the hands of prison authorities and transferred to Morningside Asylum in Edinburgh. This was certainly not a move for the better.

It was in the asylum's 'care' that she was subjected to force-feeding. This, despite her weakened condition, she would not have taken lightly. Her fighting spirit no doubt made matters worse. She fell seriously ill with double pneumonia when food got into her lungs.

She holds the dubious honour of becoming the first victim of force-feeding in Scotland. The Scots had initially rejected the practice used in jails in England, proclaiming it an act of brutality.

Whilst enjoying one bout of freedom, she famously lobbed a rotten egg at Winston Churchill at a public meeting in Dundee. He represented the city between 1908 and 1921.

Other prominent Glasgow suffragettes include the household maid Jessie Stephen. She was educated at North Kelvinside School after moving to the city from London. When her father, a tailor, lost his job at the Co-operative Society, she turned down a scholarship award and left school at 14 to find work.

She took a position as a maidservant to a family in the West End and, in 1912, she began to organize other domestic workers, eventually co-founding the Scottish Federation of Domestic Workers. She is credited with organizing an army of domestics who attacked Glasgow's red pillar boxes with fire or acid.

There are so many stories of Glasgow's suffragettes, whose acts of militancy led to such brutal treatment for what we today consider a basic right. I recommend the Women's Library in Bridgeton and the People's Palace at Glasgow Green for those who want to explore their history further.

Yet, while much is made of the heroics of the militant sisterhood of suffrage, there were many more who preferred to pursue peaceful negotiation and diplomacy towards their goal and these women contributed greatly to the cause.

Women had been fighting for equal rights, equal pay, equality of status and the right to vote long before the turn of the twentieth century.

Suffrage for working men and women was a cause championed by the Chartists between 1838 and 1848, when their influence was at its peak.

And it was a female weaver who had raised the issue publicly in 1838, arguing that women were as capable as men to reason, work and pay taxes and should therefore be equally entitled to vote.

The National Society for Women's Suffrage was founded in London in 1869.

Today, we obviously know the outcome of women's enfranchisement, but it was still a somewhat straggly victory.

In pre-industrial Britain, only landed gentry with a certain income had any say in parliamentary affairs. It took three versions of the Reform Act to extend voting rights to all men with a property of a certain value, including farmers. This, however, cast adrift a vast body of returning soldiers who had survived the First World War and had fought valiantly for their king and country.

The 1918 version of the Representation of the People Act opened up voting for all men over 21 and did away with the requirement of property ownership. This turned out to be an advantage to the women suffragettes who were fighting for their own voting rights.

In this same Act, women were 'allowed' to vote as long as they owned property and were over 30. While it wasn't ideal, it was a major breakthrough for women and was celebrated across the land.

In Glasgow, an oak tree was planted on land alongside the Kelvin Way in the West End in commemoration of this momentous political victory. The Suffrage Oak remains today.

The struggle for voting equality continued, and when the Act was amended in 1928 to give women equal voting rights to their male counterparts, this automatically excluded the requirement of property ownership.

Rent strike

One of the most successful social protests was the rent strike of 1915.

With the onset of war, men were leaving the city in droves, taking the king's shilling, the nominal incentive to sign up to fight in the First World War. The war effort needed skilled engineers at home, too, particularly in ship-building and munitions. Glasgow saw another surge in the population, adding to the already untenable overcrowding in the slums and unkempt tenements.

And landlords, far from easing the hardship of the women and families who were left behind, took the opportunity to impose hikes in rent of up to 25 per cent. They ignored pleas to carry out repairs and threatened eviction for those who refused or couldn't afford to pay.

With the men at work and at war, it was mainly down to the women to lead the fight against rent increases and to campaign for better social housing.

Families were being thrown into the streets with not a care by ruthless landlords who knew that those who could afford to pay a higher rent would move in at a moment's notice.

Activists have been at the forefront of campaigns for decent living conditions since the late 1800s. There was no such thing as council or social housing back then: the landlords ruled the roost.

The Glasgow Women's Housing Association was founded in 1914, with the aim of improving tenement housing for working-class families.

A mere 2,000 or so tenement buildings couldn't fill the demands of almost 70,000 people.

Landlords were quick to act, giving little notice of eviction, and the women were quick to react. Resistance began in Govan but very quickly crossed the water to the East End.

In Ireland, the Tenants Rights Association, which became the Tenants' Defence Association, was founded to uphold the rights of tenant farmers. Glasgow adopted its own Tenants' Defence Association, which was chaired by Mary Barbour, the wife of a Glasgow engineer. She was the kind of charismatic leader that people automatically followed.

Barbour, like many political activists in Glasgow, was a member of the Independent Labour Party and a founding member of what became known as Red Clydeside. She quickly rallied her 'women's army', setting up lookouts who would watch for baillies or landlords intent on forcibly evicting non-payers.

Throughout the streets, lanes and wynds, hand bells, drums and even football rattles were used to rally her 'troops' to action.

Sheriff officers and Messengers at Arms would be met

with a blank wall of women packed into the closes that were targeted, so that no man could pass.

Barbour organized a 'papering' of windows with notices declaring 'We're not removing' and other slogans. Women paraded outside vulnerable tenement closes with placards calling for fair rents and decent 'municipal' housing, which would take the monopoly away from unscrupulous land-lords. Other posters warned sheriff officers to enter at their peril.

Eviction notices could also be accompanied by a *'poinding'* letter, which allowed for the removal and sale of a tenant's *'goods and chattels'*. This punitive and humiliating practice later became warrant sales and, until the 1980s, these notices would be advertised in Glasgow newspapers to attract would-be buyers.

Warrant sales were only abolished in 2001, when another charismatic leader, Tommy Sheridan, led his own social army to fight against such injustices.

Mary Barbour's Army fought not with rifles or guns but with balls of flour and wet peasemeal, rotten fish and veg-etables.

The war years placed a ban on strike action by workers, to ensure the manpower for shipbuilding and armaments essential to the war effort, so men weren't in a position to leave their place of work and support the women.

And it looked like the women weren't doing too badly on their own.

But the situation was coming to boiling point; at one stage, an estimated 20,000 households were part of the strike action.

By November 1915, the men could no longer play a passive role and the trade unions brokered the support of their employers to put an end to the troubles.

On 17 November, almost 50 tenants were simultaneously served with eviction citations. This time, thousands marched on the City Chambers in George Square and the Glasgow Sheriff Court. Shop steward Willie Gallagher issued a statement to the effect that the mood of the men was such that they would 'not hesitate to not only prevent evictions but to influence Parliament by any other means in their power'. This was clearly threatening mass strike action and management got the message.

The management of John Brown's and Beardmore's shipbuilders couldn't afford to have a mass exodus from their site and issued a joint statement urging a resolution to the stalemate.

By December, parliament had rushed through a Rent Restriction Act, freezing all rents to pre-war levels.

Battle of George Square, 1919

At the close of the First World War, probably the bloodiest and most intense exchange between civilians and police turned the elegant and picturesque George Square into a battlefield of frightening proportions on a social level.

This was not a fight for bread or against tax hikes.

What transpired and brought about a police baton frenzy, followed by armed troops storming the square and the deployment of tanks and a howitzer, was a proposal by trade unionists to implement a shorter working week.

A committee of trade-union shop stewards had petitioned the City Council during a meeting at the City Chambers.

Men were returning demobbed from the war. Unemployment was ballooning. The unions came up with a solution to the problem.

An honest wage for an honest day's work for all. Rather than offer overtime to those lucky enough to be in work, why not shorten the working week from 54 hours to 40 and expand the workforce, thus reducing unemployment figures. The working day would begin at 8 a.m. rather the usual 6 a.m.

The group presented their proposals to council leaders and asked the Provost to put their case to parliament.

These were the formidable Red Clydesiders. These were members of the Independent Labour Party.

These were reasonable men.

They didn't advocate taking up arms, but they left the town councillors in no doubt that 'drastic action' would be considered if their demands weren't met. This would be a threat of strike action.

The workers committee returned on Friday, 31 January to hear the Lord Provost's response to their request.

While the men sat round the conference table in the plush City Chambers, there was movement afoot outside in the square. People were gathering to hear the outcome of the talks.

They faced a small army of police. Tensions were running high. The crowd swelled to more than 60,000 demonstrators keen to put on a show of support for the 40-hour week.

It was the golden age of 'flying pickets', whereby members

of other trade unions would rally to support strike action by one union or another.

The square was packed tight with engineering workers, shipbuilders, electricity workers, a massive deputation of 36,000 miners from across Lanarkshire and a battalion of ex-servicemen.

In such a situation, it doesn't take much for things to seriously kick off.

Nerves were taut like a coil.

It's not known what sparked the fighting, but, by all accounts, police officers embarked on an indiscriminate and frenzied baton-fest, bringing down men, women and children.

Demonstrators retaliated with whatever came to hand: fists, feet, broken bottles, even pulling up iron railings for weapons.

The battle reached the ears of the delegation, who rushed outside to try to calm the crowds. David Kirkwood was first out the doors and was immediately truncheoned to the ground unconscious. There then commenced a running battle between police and demonstrators, which took the fight as far back as Glasgow Green, where strikers regrouped and another battle ensued.

Exiting George Square on North Frederick Street, strikers came upon a delivery lorry filled with beer bottles. This became their artillery and the running battles continued.

The date went down in history as Black Friday, or Bloody Friday. In the immediate aftermath, as Westminster got word of events, they went . . . well, ape-shit!

London over-reacted big-time, deploying a raft of armies;

10,000 troops from England met a battalion of Seaforth Highlanders from Aberdeen – after they had been vetted for any ties with Glasgow; six tanks, at least one howitzer and an army of foot soldiers marched through the square with bayonets fixed.

Machine guns were fixed on the roofs of buildings around the square. It was the largest mobilization of military by the government against its own citizens.

A full battalion of Scottish soldiers at Maryhill barracks were locked down for fear of them siding with the demonstrators.

In the middle of all this commotion, a lone sheriff took out a copy of the Riot Act and attempted to read from it.

It was immediately snatched from his hands and torn to shreds. This is believed to have been the last time the Riot Act was read. So not all bad, then.

The over-reaction of the English parliament was fuelled by the paranoia of a government terrified of a Communist revolution by the working class. Many union members were also members of the Communist Party.

By 10 February, the strike was called off. While they failed to negotiate a 40-hour week, they had agreed a 47-hour week, reducing the working week by seven hours.

An inconvenient truce

In 1706, the publishing of the terms of the Treaty of Union caused anti-Union riots across the country.

In Glasgow, angry mobs marched on the streets towards the tollbooth on Trongate, which housed the arsenal of the somewhat gumsy Civic Guard, who were no match for the rioters. Indeed, some may even have joined the affray on the anti-Union side. And the clergy were by no means neutral.

The Reverend James Clark, minister of the Tron Kirk, preached in favour of direct action and was not averse to taking up arms. Anti-Union petitions were sent to Parliament from the Gorbals and the barony parishes, but provost John Aird and the town council refused to sign any petition.

Rioters began publicly burning copies of the Treaty, while others marched on the house of the Provost, who is said to have hidden in a secret cabinet under his bed while the armed mob rampaged around his house with murder on their minds. He later fled to Edinburgh while the mob 'rambled about for two or three days together'.

It took the deployment of a dragoon guard from Edinburgh and the imposition of an evening curfew to quell the people.

The Union of the Crowns had begun in 1603 with the accession to the throne of King James VI of Scotland and the first of England, but the two countries continued to operate as separate states. Cromwell also tried to broker stronger ties between the two countries.

While there were several abortive attempts at creating a united kingdom, it wasn't until Queen Anne, the daughter of King James II, came to the throne in 1702 that the idea took legs.

The Act of Union between England and Scotland in 1707 was hotly disputed and riots broke out across the country. In Glasgow, in particular, battles were fought on two fronts: one with muskets and swords; the other with 'pen and ink', as the journalist and author of *Robinson Crusoe* put it in his book *History of the Union of Great Britain*.

While the people of Glasgow rioted in the streets against the Union, a more eloquent battle, which became known as the Pamphlet Wars, was also fiercely contested.

Propaganda in the form of pamphlets and news-sheets ensued, with a small forest of papers being printed by proponents on both sides of the debate.

Probably the most prolific political propagandist was Daniel Defoe. He was very much pro-Union; he was later dubbed England's chief pamphleteer of the Union of 1707.

In a long and contentious war of words, Defoe – a respected polemicist and political writer of his day – was accused of being the pet propagandist of England. It was even suggested he was in the pocket of the pro-Unionist parliament in Westminster.

Letters were printed accusing Defoe of being 'an impudent scribbler', to which Defoe hit back with a scathing rebuke, calling the writer 'an insolent scribbler'. Heady stuff.

Negotiations began in earnest in 1705. Scotland signed up to a Treaty of Union and on 1 May 1707 the two parliaments merged.

Much was made of 'bribery' payments to certain influential Scots, including the Earl of Glasgow, while others argued that all monies paid were distributed correctly and were fiscally accounted for.

Indeed, our own national bard, Rabbie Burns, lamented the loss of 'oor Scottish fame, oor ancient glory' in a poem penned in 1791, concluding, 'We're bought and sold for English gold, sic a parcel of rogues in a nation.'

The tail end of the seventeenth century marked the economic nadir for Scotland, which would be compounded by English proposed legislation to levy heavy taxes on Scotland's trade of natural resources through English trade routes.

This was not an empty threat, and Scots saw it as an act of blackmail for the most part, but it did persuade influential leaders that a degree of interdependence between the two countries was already developing.

Yet, for Glasgow, the Union had its benefits: new markets opened up that English legislation had previously blocked.

The city's entrepreneurial spirit had been nurtured many years earlier, with strong business relationships already in place by the time the first cargo of tobacco landed at the port of Glasgow in 1674.

While merchants on the east coast of Scotland were better place geographically to take advantage of European markets from medieval times, the west of Scotland began to look across the Atlantic for trading opportunities.

By the time the Treaty of Union became law, trade in tobacco and other commodities, including cotton, linen, sugar and coal, was already lining a path that would create Scotland's first millionaires.

All of which looks pretty rosy – but the rest of Scotland was suffering.

Season after season of the evil triplets of agriculture – crop failure, blight and famine – were raging all across the country. Starving immigrants were flooding cities. The country was in crisis and, far from being rescued, Scotland was about to be rendered pretty much bankrupt by a silver-tongued Scottish adventurer who could spin a helluva yarn.

The Darien fiasco

William Paterson had credentials, having already traded successfully in the West Indies: he had lived on the exotic islands of the Bahamas; not least, he had successfully bid to manage the English government's national debt, which led to him co-founding the Bank of England, no less, in 1694. He had serious cred and a winning way with words.

Yet only months later, in 1695, he was to set in motion a financial and investment disaster that would bring the country to its knees and which many people believe pushed Scotland into a relationship of convenience with England, hastening the Treaty of Union in 1707.

Yet Paterson wasn't completely to blame. It seems that he fell under the charms of another smooth talker while still living in London.

Lionel Wafer was an adventurer who had sailed the South Seas. The two men got chatting, and Paterson was mesmerized by tales of great riches to be won and highly profitable trades in the Pacific and West Indies. Wafer waxed lyrical about an idyllic paradise on the Isthmus of Panama and of the friendly 'indians' who fawned over him as though he were some kind of demigod.

Darien was a large strip of land of great strategic potential, acting as a bridge between Costa Rica and Colombia, and flanked by the Caribbean Sea and the Pacific Ocean, incorporating Panama and the Gulf of Panama.

Paterson's enterprising mind grasped the potential profits to be made in setting up a trading colony on the isthmus and creating a shortcut to the Atlantic, avoiding the long and perilous voyage around Cape Horn – a route that had claimed many lives as ships perished or were lost at sea, victims of treacherous hurricanes – and reducing the risk of encountering pirate ships along the journey.

So it was a jubilant Paterson who returned to Scotland and embarked on one of the most successful marketing campaigns in history.

Seduced by the promise of riches beyond their wildest dreams, the people of Scotland – rich and poor – bought into Paterson's idealism and subscribed to the scheme, which they hoped would not only rescue their motherland from bankruptcy but also create a new step ladder of wealth for commoners and gentry alike.

The whole venture would require money – a lot of money. It needed a fleet of ships, crews, investment in goods to export to the colonies and investment in goods for the return journey home or for export further afield.

Paterson worked out that the whole campaign would need funding of almost half a million pounds – which would be a squillion in today's money.

The venture was challenged on all fronts, culminating in the threat of sanctions from the English parliament. The English were already making a lucrative trade in the Indies and were keen to maintain their monopoly.

The English East India Company was determined to quash the usurpers and many English investors in the Darien venture reluctantly withdrew their pledge of funding.

Undeterred, Paterson set up the Company of Scotland
Trading to Africa and the Indies. A funding bank was
created to manage the company's financial affairs. It became
the Bank of Scotland – and pre-dates the Royal Bank of
Scotland by 32 years.

The prospect so inspired the people of Scotland that whole
villages, burghs and towns formed syndicates and vied with
one another to raise the most funds towards the venture.
Within months, the company had reached its £400,000
purse target.

But the whole operation was pre-destined to come a gargantuan cropper.

Even before the first ships set sail in the summer of 1698,
a first financial faux pas had been made on a grand scale, as
the cargo consisted of mirrors, combs, wigs and other useless
and inappropriate luxuries. What would the colonies want
with such fripperies? The human cost was tragic. Of the
1,200 hopeful settlers, 70 died during the four-month-long
voyage.

For those who disembarked at Darien, the gossamer veil
of hope fell at their feet when they encountered a very different picture from the one they had envisaged.

Paterson later wrote of the peninsula they were to name
New Caledonia as: 'a mere morass, neither fit to be fortified
nor planted, nor indeed for men to lie upon'.

Plagued by disease and torrential rains, and the land unfit
for agriculture, the settlers were dying at a rate of up to ten a
day, according to some reports.

Add to that the lack of interest of the natives, the news
that the English had placed an embargo on any ships or

colonies trading with the Scots, and the capture of one ship by the Spanish with the imprisonment of her crew, serious malnutrition and starvation – well, could it get any sorrier?

For Paterson, too, the dream had become a living nightmare, but he had more to suffer, with the death of his wife and rumours that the Spanish were planning to attack the colony.

There was nothing else for it but to cut and run back to Scotland to face the wrath of a nation for squandering up to 75 per cent of the country's public and private funds. Only one of the returning vessels, *The Caledonian*, made it home, with only a few hundred survivors on board.

Blissfully unaware of the fate of the failed colonists, a second expedition was already under way towards the colony in 1699.

Little did they know what fate lay ahead of them. Again, lives were lost before reaching land. For those who made it, it was a rude awakening.

They tried in vain to re-establish the stricken settlement but were again to suffer the wrath of the elements, infertile ground, disease and starvation.

They were under regular attack by the Spanish and prevailed in only one pre-emptive strike on Toubacanti, but, against far superior forces, the colonists surrendered in the spring of 1700.

The triumphant Governor-General Pimiento allowed leave to those who wished to return but very few made it home.

Scotland was broken, but stumbled on towards the 1707 Treaty of Union with England. As part of the deal, England made a payment towards Scotland's debt – much of which went towards paying off some of the Company of Scotland's losses. Some funds also went towards the start-up of what was to become the Royal Bank of Scotland, which came into being in 1727.

The tobacco lords

Glaswegians are natural entrepreneurs, forward-thinkers and excellent organizers. When the golden age of tobacco trading was at its peak, the merchants of Glasgow and Edinburgh were set to clean up. They created a network of funding – including setting up their own merchant banks – as well as personal inheritance or profits from existing businesses, which acted as a syndicate and allowed free flow of funds so that the partners could offer long-term credit to suppliers and small plantation owners. Some funded their own plantations in Virginia and Chesapeake. The most successful had their own fleets of ships built.

As well as crew and cargo, shipowners were often approached to take on board passengers, some of whom were searching for new plants and flora, while others were seeking to discover exotic marine life and wildlife; yet more simply sought to capture these strange new lands on canvas, or more likely as lithographic drawings, another trendy hobby.

These were heady times. The New World beckoned. People began to talk about 'old money' versus 'new money' in the pecking order of a changing society.

Among the nouveau riche, vast amounts of money were lavished on playboy lifestyles, or invested in laying down a marker for dynasties, commissioning elaborate mansions with gardens to match, featuring waterfalls, marble statues and intricate labyrinths.

Others would invest in grand collections of rare plants and flowers, and present thousands of species in magnificent glasshouses. Some commissioned 'botanic gardens', which were later bequeathed to the public. This new trend would spawn generations of botanists, the most adventurous of whom would travel the globe seeking rare and beautiful flowers. The most ardent would go to perilous lengths to explore new lands, collecting their precious cargo of seeds to take home and propagate.

This could be a dangerous business, however, as some have grown so prolifically that landowners and farmers today treat them as weeds. Once they root, they spread in great swathes and are very difficult to tame.

One such example was the rhododendron, with its stunning flashes of shocking pink or crimson-red umbles, putting on an impressive display of colour against the deep green of their leaves.

The wonderful array of orchids that we enjoy today originates in foreign lands and exotic islands, particularly the Reunion Islands, where they are cultivated for their beauty but also for scrumptiously delicious bourbon vanilla, which chocolatiers and bakers treasure.

Chartering one's own ship for such daredevil exploits was very rare. Instead, botanist explorers would negotiate a berth on a merchant ship travelling to the Indies and the Americas and return triumphant with tales of adventure and piracy on the high seas. They held lavish masquerade balls and entertained guests at their private gentlemen's clubs. It was a time of decadence among the wealthy merchant families.

The Industrial Revolution had Scots blazing a trail of innovation, motorization, mechanization, mass production and globalization.

It was all kicking off.

The geography of Glasgow continued to shift with the times. What had at one time been the heart and lungs of Glasgow, and the foundation of the city, had by dint of growing westwards rather than outwards from the centre become what we now talk of as the East End.

Of course, there was bound to be a hierarchy among these astute businessmen and a handful of merchants became a kind of tobacco-trading aristocracy, dubbed the Virginia Dons. Money not only talked, it listened. The big money knew that, as well as investing in suppliers and plantations, it was prudent to invest in shipping and carriage to help absorb the costs of transporting goods.

One of the most successful of these businessmen was John Glassford, who amassed a huge fortune from trading in tobacco.

His family had made its fortune in textiles and so Glassford was well placed financially to speculate. Tobacco trading was a long-haul investment.

Glasgow's merchants also benefited from Scotland's long-standing relationship with France, negotiating exclusivity to export tobacco into Europe.

Glassford seized the opportunity to corner much of the burgeoning new market. He knew that the Port of Glasgow had at least two or three weeks of a head start over other British ports in crossing the Atlantic and began to amass his own fleet of vessels to ship the magic weed, as well as securing trade links with other British Colonies in the Caribbean, from where he would import sugar, rum and other exotic commodities.

Another who blazed the Chesapeake and Virginia tobacco trail was William Cunninghame (latterly of Lainshaw in Ayrshire, where he built a sizeable estate).

Again, he defies the general belief that the tobacco trade went belly up after the American War of Independence from England.

While some businesses lost fortunes in the course of the war, it is suggested that there were fewer casualties than some sources claim. By the time the war began in earnest, Glasgow ports were already shipping tens of millions of pounds in weight of tobacco and had a strong network to export across Europe.

Transatlantic trade was helped enormously by the engineering nous of the civil engineer John Golborne, who devised a way to flush out the silt layers from the Clyde using a system of jetties along the riverbanks.

This solved the problem of the shallow waters of the Clyde, which Cromwell and his agent had warned more than a century earlier would become a sticking point for the expansion of international trade and movement.

With Golborne's system, the Clyde was able to receive with open arms far larger vessels closer to the city than ever before. This was around 1770, and the town was gearing up for another boom time. Bon viveur and poet Rabbie Burns was on a mission to plant more seeds than the local farmers and was courting a post as exciseman.

Scottish engineers, inventors, innovators, artists, botanists and architects became the darlings of high society: James Watt, after whom the electric unit is named, transformed industry and travel with his development of steam power and the steam engine (c.1775); William Murdoch, who also experimented with steam locomotion, is better known for the introduction of gas lighting (1792); Lord Kelvin, after whom the Kelvin scale of absolute temperature is named (1848), developed the science of thermodynamics. He is said to have attended the University of Glasgow at the tender age of ten. James Young isolated paraffin oil from shale and coal (c.1850), making a fortune selling the oil to industry and wax for candlemaking; and John Boyd Dunlop developed inflated rubber tubes (1888), the forerunners to modern pneumatic rubber tyres.

They followed one another, blazing a chronological trail of invention and inspiration by birth and innovation as though some cosmic astral alignment was afoot to introduce each new genius of engineering over a generation.

Cunninghame was well placed to make a killing – excuse the pun – in tobacco sales. He already had extensive experience running the Virginia operations of Cochrane, Murdoch & Company, headed by Andrew Cochrane of Brighouse. He became a senior partner in the firm around 1762 and, within a decade, the firm's name had changed to William Cunninghame & Company. This was just a few years before Andrew Cochrane died in 1777.

Cunninghame certainly liked the sound of his own

name and named his flagship *The Cunninghame*.

The ship made twice-yearly Atlantic crossings to Chesapeake Bay, stocked high with silverware and furniture, among other luxury goods, to satisfy the lifestyle ambitions of America's colonial new rich. The ship's return load was mainly tobacco, with perhaps some of the rums, sugar and silks of their colonial neighbours.

When the US War of Independence from England got under way, Cunninghame bought up as much stock in tobacco as he could get. Not only did he have a reputation for using his credit terms to put the squeeze on plantation owners, making them sell to him at hugely discounted prices, but he had also amassed a huge stockpile, which he would sell on at massively inflated prices, taking advantage of the scarcity of the precious commodity as the war continued.

Aside from his grand estate of Lainshaw in Ayrshire, Cunninghame purchased land in Glasgow and built a colonnaded mansion which today houses the collections of the Gallery of Modern Art at Royal Exchange Square. The road up to his estate, he named Queen Street.

When these gentrified merchants weren't naming ships and buildings after themselves, it seems they were wont to name streets.

Alexander Speirs, associated with the Glasgow firm Speirs, Bowman & Company, which managed imports and exports from the Glasgow ports on the firm's ship, *The Bowman*, named Virginia Street in Glasgow after the state which begat the mass of his fortune, where he owned a large plantation. Speirs was also a senior partner of the Glasgow Arms Bank.

The US state of Virginia itself is believed to have been

named by Sir Walter Raleigh after the 'Virgin Queen' Elizabeth I. As an aside, it was he who introduced the royal courts to the strange new social drug, tobacco, described in one advertising booklet as 'the means of sleeping with our eyes open'.

Enterprising merchants in this cross-Atlantic trade are often spoken of as the Tobacco Lords or the Tobacco Barons. While it is a seemingly interchangeable title, I have my own unsubstantiated theory that, in their day, the big three – Glassford, Cunninghame and Speirs – were the Tobacco Lords by dint of eventually controlling the lion's share of the trade.

By the start of the American War of Independence, the trio handled more than half the trade that went through Glasgow and, as the war churned on, the syndicates they controlled managed around 80 – some say as much as 90 – per cent of exports.

These were the big guns. Glassford and Cunninghame hailed from Ayrshire, while Speirs was of Edinburgh gentry. However, there were other successful tobacco merchants in the city, with more than simply business ties to the East End.

I tend to think of these gentlemen as the Tobacco Barons: those who made an extremely profitable living from tobacco and other business interests but who would never attain the heights of the Big Three.

Merchants with ties to Tollcross, Dalbeth and Shettleston had mixed success.

Thomas Hopkirk, grandfather of the botanist and lithographer of the same name, was a wealthy Glasgow merchant who used his gains from tobacco trading and trading with the West Indies to diversify into coalmining, brewing and banking.

He was a co-founder of the Glasgow Arms Bank. His Glasgow pied-à-terre was a tenement on High Street just yards from the Cross, which was known as Hopkirk's Land; he rented the ground floor premises to an agent of the Bank of Scotland – Glasgow's first branch, operated by merchant David Dale from his shop selling delicate yarns from France.

While many merchants also sought high office in the town council and guilds, Hopkirk, unusually, had in 1752 been elected as a town councillor but was fined £20 for refusing to take up the post. Two years later, he purchased the Dalbeth Estate, now known as Dalbeth Roman Catholic cemetery, where he lived until his death in 1781. Interestingly, he had to take a court action in 1770 in defence of a £40 fine imposed on him for declining the post of Dean of Guild.

His daughter married into the wealthy Glassford family and gave birth to the possibly more celebrated Thomas Hopkirk, publisher of books and catalogues of Glasgow's flora and plants. At the Dalbeth Estate, Hopkirk junior introduced and recorded almost 4,000 plant species and their varieties, which he later donated to a public botanic garden in Sandyford Place, which he helped establish.

The Dunlop family were known for their politics. Generations of them held posts as provost, baillie, Dean of Guild and other influential offices.

The merchant John Dunlop of Carmyle also held a position on the town council. He later acted as Collector of Customs at Port Glasgow. A member of the Hodge Podge

Club, a private club for the tobacco aristocracy, he was a casualty of the War of Independence, losing his shirt as owner of a tobacco house that didn't fare well during the war. He was a prolific and well-respected poet and songwriter, successfully publishing three anthologies of his work.

John was the son of Colin and brother of James Dunlop. Colin established the family business of Dunlop & Sons and co-founded the Ship Bank. He was also at various times a Glasgow baillie, Dean of Guild and provost. Colin's father, John's grandfather, James Dunlop of Garnkirk, also took a massive hit because of the war, eventually being forced to sell the family estate of Rosebank.

The tobacco merchants were a very close-knit community. Often the offspring of one family would marry into another.

The Dunlops were extremely close with the Corbets of Tollcross. Almost all of the big wigs came together to form syndicates to exploit the American and West Indies trading markets. Dunlop & Co. was one of Corbet's business partners, along with 15 others, including Russell & Co. These syndicates dominated the golden age of the tobacco trade and offered some financial buoyancy in times of strife, but the Dunlop family's downfall was by no means an isolated case.

When merchant James Wardrop died in 1783, he left the magnificent and beautifully appointed Springbank Estate and mansion house. Whether he escaped the knowledge of the financial collapse of his sons' Virginia trading business – or perhaps because of it – he at least didn't live to witness the dissolution of his labour of love, which he had only recently completed, having bought the land only three years earlier. The brothers were bailed out by their sister, who took over the land and property. It was sold in 1806 to another successful merchant.

The McCalls of Glasgow, Scotland, and Philadelphia, USA, managed to sidestep disaster. The brothers' business straddled the Atlantic. George emigrated to the States, while Samuel remained in Glasgow. Samuel's son crossed the water and had great success as a merchant in Virginia, keeping it all in the family. When they lost their plantations in the aftermath of war, they were in a good position geographically and financially to diversify into sugar, importing the commodity from the West Indies. It may have been this triangle of trade that helped them weather the storm.

At one time, the McCalls were, predictably, in partnership with another merchant firm, trading as McCall & Smellie. This became another victim of fortune, and when the company was dissolved, the Smellies moved into coalmining.

While the American War had claimed many mercantile businesses in Glasgow and Edinburgh, it made a tidy fortune for the trustees and lawyers brought in to wind up estates.

Accountant Walter Ewing McLae seems to have had the business pretty much sewn up, as his name comes up regularly as the wind-up merchant.

He was from an extremely successful family who made vast fortunes during the tobacco bubble. They owned enormous swathes of real estate and held many powerful positions in public office.

At one point the magnificent mansions bought or built on Virginia trading were changing hands almost as fast as the exchange rate. The losers in the tobacco years were extremely astute businessmen and investors in the future. Most of them had the acumen to move on to other lucrative enterprises, and today's students of business and the economy often look back to these innovators as exemplars of successful enterprise. Like their modern-day counterparts, they understood that one cannot quantify luck, nor can it be factored into any business plan. Sometimes luck falls on the wrong side of the coin.

Glasgow's gentlemen's clubs

They say nothing succeeds like success; at the height of the tobacco bubble, it seems, nothing exceeded like success.

Glasgow streets at this time were still dirt roads and the sound of cowbells rang every day, as herds of cattle were driven through the town. There were no kerbs or pavement, or any protection from mud and puddles on rainy days for a gentleman's silver-buckled shoes of fine Spanish leather or the hems and petticoats of gentrified ladies.

The first proper pavement was a series of flagstones laid out on the Trongate in front of the town hall. This would become the Tontine Hotel in a later incarnation.

This pathway would later be extended to Argyle Street as a popular promenade for all citizens, but the first pavement was the reserve of the haughty tobacco lords – 'vulgar commoners' were barred from stepping on it.

Wealthy merchants, mimicking the garb and gait of the elite merchants of Venice and Genoa, adopted a style of dress, aloofness of countenance and a swaggering walk that set them apart from even the well-to-do traders and crafts-men of the town, whom they of course looked down upon.

They were said to be 'strutting about on the *plainstanes* like princes', each wearing a distinctive scarlet cloak, a cocked hat and carrying a gold-topped walking cane. They were a laughing stock to the commoners, who would whisper most disrespectfully outwith the earshot of their social superiors, though no one dared approach them without a bow and a doffed cap.

As bank accounts grew fat on tobacco, coal, sugar, textiles and rum, these round-bellied fops and dandies would gather together for a sup of rum or a whisky toddy at the many private gentlemen's clubs that were emerging around town.

Some were pretty staid affairs, where the elder statesmen of trade and politics would debate the issues of the day or retreat for a read of the complimentary newspapers and journals.

Others were proper dens of iniquity, where young dudes would play pranks (or *geggs*) on some gullible *geggee*. Some of these pranks, fuelled by drunken daredevil, could get wildly out of hand, such as the devastating fire set by members of the Hellfire Club at the Tron Kirk Session House, which destroyed everything bar the steeple.

On a lighter note, it wasn't unheard of for a shopkeeper to arrive in the morning at his place of work, ready for his day's trade, to be met with the sight of a bewigged, powdered and painted gentleman suspended from a club window, silk-stockinged legs dangling in the air and ordering his immediate release in a comically high-pitched and haughty tone.

The quirkily named Hodge Podge Club was one of the first of these retreats, originally founded by only nine close friends. Its numbers quickly grew, with its reputation for fun and frolics. Its fortnightly proceedings were genteel and tame. It is commemorated by the writer Samuel Hunter.

What began as a meeting of minds and a platform for literary appreciation and debate soon added gambling games of sixpenny whist to its order of events. Around nine o'clock, the maid or butler would arrive with a hot supper. One invited guest, John Moore, the physician, poet laureate and celebrated author of classic tales including *Zeluco* and *Mordaunt*, would entertain his hosts with amusing stories of his travels in Europe. He would devise witty poetry describing the peculiarities of the club's founding members and much hilarity was had by all. His particular style of stand-up comedy reached out to ridicule many of the city's superiors – Dunlop of Garnkirk, John Baird of Craigton, John Orr of Barrowfield, all victims of his incisive wit – all of whom and more became stalwart members of the club.

Mr Orr of Barrowfield would tell the story of the brave man who saved the life of another who was extremely un-popular – a so-called '*quisquis* character' – while riding out in the country. The horses had bolted and were galloping at a hammering pace, with the man being thrown about in the carriage. His saviour managed to control the wild horses and by the time Orr and his companion, Mr Baird, caught up to the halted carriage, the hero was gone.

Mr Orr enquired if the man had been rewarded for the great risk he had taken. When he was told the man was given a mere shilling for his troubles, Mr Orr started to berate the ungrateful sod for being so cheap, only to be interrupted by his friend, who said, 'Come away, sir, it is quite enough. Every man knows the value of his own life.'

The club continued for more than a century and had the tradition of electing worthy society belles to be toasted at the end of each meeting. Among them were Miss Farquhar Gray, Susan Maxwell of Monreith, and Mary Campbell of Garscube. In its day, it was compared with the prestigious London Beefsteak Club.

On High Street, My Lord Ross's Club is described by Hunter as 'a club of gallant gay Lotharios'. Named after the landlord of its regular meeting place – and not the *Debrett's* peer – the club was open to members every night of the week barring Sundays, out of respect for the rules of the Sabbath.

It was a drinking man's club and its imbibement of choice was the Jamaica rum. Its nightly revelry could be heard around the streets, with loud and raucous singing, dancing and laughter. Many of these clubs survived for generations and entertained many of the country's most revered scholars, artists, physicians and politicians.

Homes and gardens

I don't mean to keep banging on about the tobacco merchants, but they pretty much made Glasgow and, between the trades and merchant houses, guilds and charities, they left a legacy of artisanship, industry, social responsibility, commerce and architecture that few cities can rival even today.

Their entrepreneurial drive and their innate sense of

adventure sent them and their agents to far flung corners of the world. They ventured into the unknown, to tropical lands and exotic South Sea Islands; they explored new worlds and brought the New World home. They introduced us to exquisite silks, Moreno and cashmere wools, sweet rums, heady opiates, rare jewels and gemstones.

Their travel partners were often botanists and artists who embraced the dangers of the high seas and tropical rain forests: poisonous snakes, disease-carrying insects and terrifying lions, elephants, bears and gorillas – all of which were almost completely unknown in so-called civilized society. They were as important to our culture and history as the buckleswashers of Drake's and Raleigh's era. Let's face it: Sir Walter Raleigh introduced the addictive weed to the Elizabethan court in the sixteenth century, but its popularization was only initiated two centuries later when these enterprising merchants launched it onto a global marketplace. Raleigh also funded two abortive attempts to colonize in the Americas. The Darien disaster nearly brought the country to its knees – but it was the Glasgow mercantile elite who created the trade triangle and made it work.

Their contemporaries were inventors, engineering and scientific geniuses, and pioneers of modern medicine, whose innovations changed the world. It was more than seren-dipitous that the makers of the modern world, the industrial revolutionaries, should occupy the same period in history as those very men and women who would know exactly how best to exploit their genius. They looked forward. They were the future-makers.

Yes, for the most part, they were vulgarly rich, but they had exquisite taste. They were aloof, haughty, supercilious, condescending, shrewd to the point of ruthless. But they knew not only how to make money – but also how to spend it.

When they needed a crash pad in the city, they commissioned the most esteemed and talented architects, designers, masons, sculptors, carpenters and artists to build magnificent townhouses.

Their summerhouses outside the city were beautifully appointed with exquisite gardens. Many of these can still be enjoyed by visitors in the twenty-first century.

There is a wonderful book, *The Old Country Houses of the Old Glasgow Gentry*, written in 1870 by John Guthrie Smith and John Oswald Mitchell. It was updated in 1878 and, in the short time between editions, the authors lament the loss of some of the city's grand edifices.

It is thanks to advances in computer technology and, in particular, the Centre for Digital Library Research (CDLR) at Strathclyde University that we can have access to such ancient books at the click of a button, or mouse, preserving for posterity images of almost all of the buildings of note around Glasgow and beyond its boundaries. This particular little gem was recreated in digital form by Alan Dawson at the CDLR.

In the introduction, the author mourns the passing of a well-defined class system and writes of the 'memorial of the old Burgher aristocracy . . . an unquestioned social supremacy'. He also describes two fading sub-castes: the Rentallers (or tenant farmers) and 'the sons of the Manse', of whom he writes, 'Time is sadly against both these useful classes.'

While he grudgingly accepts that Glasgow needed updating and, in his words, the reshaping of the city's streetscape makes it look 'almost as new as Chicago', he concentrates on the grand city mansion houses and countryside estates and shuns the less salubrious farmhouses as not worth photographing, much less preserving their history in any book. The abandoned, couthy homesteads of freehold farmers, he decries as occupied at the time by 'labourers, probably Irish' and previously owned by generations of 'Bonnet Lairds'.

He adds, laughingly: 'If Aristocracy . . . be dying, let it die and let us dance on its grave!' But warns that social 'integration is at work in many forms' and proclaims that this newfangled 'Gospel of Equality . . . surely is a serious matter'.

But what of townhouses and tenements?

Much has been made of the new millennium trend of purchasing 'air rights' in order to protect a view from a home. One couple in Seattle recently paid around $600,000 for the house across the street from them in order to pre-empt the building of another floor, which would have spoiled their picturesque views of the waterfront.

The couple rented the property out for a time and then sold it on for $100,000 less than its market value in order that they would retain 'ownership' of the space above the roof. The new owners were prohibited from 'building up'.

As Mark Twain said: 'Buy land. They're not making any more.'

And buying air is a trend that is born of huge increases in population. If one can't build outwards, the logical alternative is to build upwards.

This need for privacy and unbroken views is nothing new, though. In old Glasgow, rich householders used similar tactics to protect their privacy.

Around 1804, Alexander 'Picture' Gordon built his townhouse on land previously owned by Andrew Buchanan, on Buchanan Street. He bought the land opposite his property so that no one could build a house overlooking his. This strip of land became known as Gordon Street. Gordon had the unusual and rather expensive hobby of collecting works of art, mainly paintings, hence his nickname.

The Gordons favoured that part of mainly rural land around Buchanan Street. An ancestor of Alexander, John Gordon of Aikenhead, had bought a house on East Buchanan Street, which became the Prince of Wales buildings. This Gordon was known as much for grand balls as for his politics. He represented the Tory party in Westminster as MP for Glasgow and the west of Scotland.

Parties and banquets were sumptuous affairs, but the mother of all parties was indisputably the so-called Peel Banquet, which John Gordon laid on for the newly installed rector of Glasgow University, Sir Robert Peel. It was a truly grandiose affair, with the likes of Gladstone et al. joining a reported 4,000 guests – that may be an exaggeration, right enough, but one cannot exaggerate the plush pavilion with rich velvet drapes that was erected in the garden of Gordon's magnificent mansion house.

Many of the opulent manor houses survive today in one

guise or another, and it's worth checking them out. Of course, some of these are open to public visitors, but others are used by commercial or municipal organizations and are only available for visitors during the annual 'Doors Open' day, when nosey parkers can get a sneaky peek at parts of the buildings that are not normally open to the public.

Feudalism

The expression 'feud land', as either a verb or a noun, comes up a lot in relation to large tracts of land and how they were split into subdivisions which, in turn, were split and sub-feud, known as subinfeudation – kind of like letting and subletting of property but with added mutual benefits.

So the king, or the Crown, laid claim to all the lands under royal jurisdiction. It was King William I, the Conqueror, who introduced the European system of 'feudalism' to England and Wales, an economic definition that is believed to have been coined by the esteemed economist John Adam.

King William was not a natural heir to the English throne. His reign was not one of royal succession or heredity; rather, it was very much a 'hostile takeover' decided by the Battle of Hastings in 1066.

He was not a welcome visitor. Neither could he straddle the Channel, ruling simultaneously over England and Normandy in France.

He had to find a way of gaining the trust and loyalty of the English lords and vassals alike.

He therefore mapped out huge swathes of land, not dissimilar to modern day counties. He then had his trusted advisors go out into the land and find the most influential leaders and members of the local gentry, and offered them prestigious titles and these parcels of land.

But power and land came at a cost. In return, a commit-ment to raise a set number of knights and foot soldiers to fight for the Norman king in times of battle was agreed. They also had to swear allegiance to the Norman king, which was a very solemn and serious undertaking.

The land could be subdivided as the lords or lairds saw fit and feud to others in exchange for a commitment to fight for the king and develop the land.

These subdivisions were entitled the lord's 'manor'; his residence, usually an elaborate and ostentatious mansion house, was the manor house. Thence the expression, 'lord of the manor'. Some even built castles to reflect their wealth and nobility.

And so the so-called feudal pyramid would have the king at the top, above nobility, then knights and serfs or farmers on the bottom rungs.

Thus, when a lord conferred land to the next tier of the pyramid, an oath would be sworn to the lord, who was seen as acting for the king; therefore, all in the pyramid were symbolically swearing allegiance to the king. In this way, King William could exercise some control over a generally hostile realm.

Lords, barons and other nobility were also required to raise and collect taxes on behalf of the Crown.

William had no way of knowing exactly how many vassals were in his defeated kingdom and, consequently, how much in taxes he could expect. To keep tabs on his potential income, though not exclusively for this reason, William the Conqueror commissioned a land and population survey on the grandest scale to monitor projected income and pre-empt any attempts by the nobility, the vassals of the king, to shave a sneaky cut off the top before declaring their taxes.

The stats from this project were kept in a massive document called the Domesday Book. This was the first example of the population census as we know it today.

A similar form of pyramidal feudalism was also introduced in Scotland by King David I, who appointed 'sheriffs' to act as administrators and collect taxes. Over time, sheriffs were given greater responsibilities and legislative powers. Presently, these sheriffs could hold their own court and hear cases on behalf of the Crown.

Now, kings like to fight – a lot. If the monarchy needed to raise an army to expand the realm by invading, capturing and subjugating foreign lands and their people, they would call upon those loyal to the current Crown to form an army. It was an expensive affair. Similarly, armies would need to be raised quickly in defence of a realm or strategically important areas of land.

In ancient times, the monarchy was the law of the land, ruling arbitrarily. When anyone wanted to take a case to be heard at court, they had to pay a fee to the Crown and had to abide by the Crown's ruling. These fees, as well as punishment for the loser, varied incredibly: people in the king's favour would pay a nominal sum, if anything, while anyone out of favour would be charged such an exorbitant fee they were usually unable to pay.

There are many documented cases of men being forced

to pledge their estate or castle and, indeed, members of their own family, until a court fee or fine was paid in full. It wasn't uncommon, an estate having been confiscated by the Crown or by one of its entitled lords, and before a hearing could be raised in court, for it to be sold off or passed on to new owners.

Quite frankly, the Crown or, on its behalf, lorded nobility could renege on agreements and impose sanctions on lesser citizens or upon their enemy without fear of retribution.

King John, in particular, would demand exorbitant sums from prisoners to buy their freedom. In one reported case, he forced a landowner to give up his castle and hand over his four sons as hostages until the court fees were paid.

This kind of draconian rulership was eventually challenged, leading to a charter of human rights that became the Magna Carta – the Great Charter.

It was King John who finally brought things to a head.

His expeditions into France to subdue the Normans and protect his governance in that part of France were abysmal. He raided the tax coffers of his English subjects too many times in his exploits abroad, which were almost invariably doomed as embarrassing failures. With every loss, King John demanded more and higher taxes, and more and more military, until his subjects had no choice but to rise against him. Eventually, he was surrounded in the meadows at Runnymede by an army of nobles and knights and challenged to adhere to a set of regulations that were to be unchallenged by the sovereignty.

The result was the drawing up of a set of rules and rights of man, which called for the rights of free men to have their cases heard in a court of their peers without prejudice, among more than 60 other clauses, including one that asserted papal supremacy over the monarchy. This would become the Magna Carta.

In reality, the ink was not dry on the document before King John rejected the whole thing; there were so many changes to the original that very little of it remained. However, the principles of equality and rights to a fair hearing, as well as having to follow a rigid protocol, sometimes called 'due process', remained the ideological imperative; it was this that inspired the drawing up of the American Constitution and the law of the land in Britain.

Why is this relevant to the formulation of the East End of Glasgow? Because it changed fundamental laws surrounding feudal agreements and gave nominal protection to gentried citizens. Those who eventually drew up the charter were noblemen, so it's not surprising they failed to include the common man.

When only the king heard cases at the royal court, pursuants would have to travel to wherever the king was residing. King Henry II introduced a permanent court at Westminster where cases could be heard, which was a welcome innovation.

In medieval times, there existed not one central court but three prongs of jurisdiction.

The Royal Court would hear cases that affected the peace of the monarchy at the Westminster court, while appointed judges would travel throughout the realm, hearing cases and dispensing judgments locally.

Issues that were of significance to the clergy were heard

by members of the ecclesia. Church leaders could rule on matters affecting the Church, such as heresy, morality and marital disputes. They had the power to banish or imprison heretics, for example, which included anyone who spoke out against the supremacy of the Church over the monarchy or parliament.

The baronial hierarchy would hear cases that affected their provincial jurisdiction, involving tenants and other members of their local community. Lords and other nobility could dispense the law on their baronial turf, and the Crown had the final say on most other local issues.

So the Magna Carta was the result of King John's general balls-ups, really. While it wasn't ideal, and was generally held in disdain, the charter was a protection against a man's superior arbitrarily confiscating his land, his home and his means of making a livelihood.

King John also managed to alienate Pope Innocent III, who not only officially ex-communicated John from the Catholic Church but also banned all masses in English chapels.

The situation was becoming acrimonious and John was eventually forced to concede supremacy to the Church, thereby surrendering England to the Pope. The Pope then granted the English lands back to John as a fief, which effectively made the king a vassal to the Bishop of Rome.

Not every one of the king's subjects was all that keen on getting down and dirty in the field of battle. So landed gentry could get out of the knight's service by paying a fee, or fief, in lieu of military service.

In most cases, a 'fee' was a parcel of land, enough to feed

a knight for a year from the harvested crop or rents – which could vary in size, according to a crop's expected yield and under-tenants – and to maintain the knight's esquires in readiness for battle, the usual obligation being to be ready to fight for up to 40 nights. The land fee had to produce enough income to raise enough horses and arms in time of war.

Often, overlords would feu a parcel of land to a knight with the condition that the knight would take his place in battle, or they would pay a 'scutage' to buy their way out of these military obligations.

A scutage was a kind of 'buy-out' from knight's service and was levied against the number of fiefs held by a lord or knight.

However, scutage was also a tax that could be levied during times of war to fund certain battles.

Just as tontines were used to raise war funds, scutage was similarly used and named for a particular battle – for example, the scutage of Toulouse.

Now, harping back to King John, the normal unit of scutage or war tax was one marc – or, in Scotland, merk – per fief, which was equal to around two-thirds of an English pound. But John increasingly levied taxes of up to three merks, whether for a battle or not.

This and other abuses by King John became the last straw for beleaguered barons, who raised their own rebel army and marched on London with demands for the protection of certain liberties. It was somewhat of a stand-off and could have got pretty ugly, with no worthwhile conclusion, but then the king was persuaded to attend a meeting of the barons and Church leaders at a meadow in Runnymede on 15 June in the year 1215. It wasn't unusual to hold this kind of outdoor meeting.

So, to finally get to the point, when a lord or baron 'feud' land to an individual, it was generally in perpetuity or, in some contracts, for 'one million and eleven months'.

The land remained the 'property' of the barony in title only. The new landholder or 'tenant' would agree to pay a feu, usually annually, and was free to develop, build or feu parcels of land out to others.

It was only as recently as 2004 that this feudal arrangement was officially abolished.

Eventually, these lands were developed into highly populated districts, or burghs.

Dennistoun

In its infancy during the late 1800s, Dennistoun was to Glasgow as Brooklyn is to New York, in that it quickly evolved as the city's suburban family district. While the trendy money partied till the wee hours in Manhattan, it was to Brooklyn that they turned when it came to bringing up baby, it being possible to get more bricks for your bucks and certainly more garden space for your kids.

Alexander Dennistoun, who laid out plans to develop the land north of the cathedral, may have had a similar vision for his proposed garden suburb. It is surmised from original feuing blueprints that he intended to present at least part of the area as an upmarket residential district, with rows of villas, cottages and terraced housing.

It appears that the master plan was then abruptly modified to include rows of tenemented housing, attracting upwardly mobile working-class couples with growing families.

This radical shift in demographic, however, seems to have come about not by design but by the wealthy merchant's untimely death, with the result that it ended up looking like the whole project was designed by committee – and everyone got their way!

This is also suggested in a report supporting an application to designate parts of Dennistoun as a protected conservation area.

Of its architectural structure, the report suggests that buildings are 'an eclectic mix of cottages and terraces . . . [with] no prevalent architectural style', giving examples as: 'imposing gothic villas side-by-side, with classically detailed villas, single-storey cottages, restrained classical terraces and some more ornate terraces . . .'

This eclectic mix of varying styles of housing, design and scale, together with the use of various building materials, according to the report, 'creates a distinctive neighbourhood entirely different in character to the surrounding modern and tenemental development'.

Another cool architectural feature is the use of red and white ashlar, a material that could be smoothed, squared and 'combed' with metal prongs and which was prevalent in the construction of ancient Greek and Cretan palaces.

It's tempting to presume that Alexander Dennistoun was the first to acquire the eponymous estates, but the area has a far more ancient history.

The unimposing 'grey mound' on which St Mungo

founded his church and, consequently, the city of Glasgow became known as the Firpark, after the firs that surrounded the sacred grove. The cemetery where the saint consecrated the burial of the holy man Fergus was later dubbed the Necropolis, City of the Dead. Its history goes back even further to the Celtic Druids, who claimed it as their place of worship and ancient religious rites.

This sacred site lay north of what we now call Alexandra Parade. By the twelfth century, at the time of Bishop Jocelyn, the place was known as the Crag (rock) and, later again, the Craigs.

In the 1400s, a watermill was erected over the holy waters of the nearby Molindinar burn, which St Mungo consecrated and used to baptize new members of his flock. This was the town mill and the street nearby became Town Mill Street.

It wasn't a straightforward case of villagers building a mill where a mill was needed. Only the bishops could give permission for such an amenity. It wasn't so much con-sidered a right as a privilege. So, when the Lord of the Barony himself, Bishop Cameron, deigned to award the citizens this valuable amenity in February 1446, the burgesses and com-munity leaders wasted no time in agreeing to the bishop's proviso that, in return for the favour, the church be gifted 2 lb (almost a kilo in weight) of wax candles yearly to light St Mungo's shrine in the cathedral.

Much of the surrounding lands that were to make up the district of Dennistoun were acquired by the Merchants House around 1650.

The wider area of the Craigs was eventually bifurcated, with Craigpark and Whitehill estates becoming part of

Easter Craigs and Golfhill taking up most of Wester Craigs. Roughly speaking, from Craigpark to Cumbernauld Road would become Easter Craigs and, again, stretching as far as the Necropolis, we find Wester Craigs.

Golfhill was acquired from Bishop James Hamiltoun of Argyll by Sir Ludovic, one of the Stewarts of Minto, who eventually sold it on to the Merchants House. It remained with the House for more than a century.

In 1756, Golfhill was purchased by Glasgow merchant John Anderson, who flip-flopped it on almost immediately to his brother, Jonathan. The elegant Golfhill House gave the land at Wester Craigs a focal point. The manor house was built by the new owner, James Dennistoun, who bought the estate on Jonathan's death in 1802. By this time, Golfhill had been in the families of three very wealthy merchants.

Work on the grand house began almost before the ink was dry on the deeds, which was only fitting for this very well-respected gentleman who would go on to act as a city magistrate and, in 1809, head up the Glasgow Bank until his retirement 20 years later. He was so well thought of that, on his retiral, he was guest of honour at a lavish banquet held in his name at the prestigious Royal Exchange building.

In fact, James was known affectionately as Lord Dennistoun. This tongue-in-cheek nickname was in reference to the confirmed rumour that he had turned down an offer of a title from the then Prime Minister, Earl Grey.

James, from all accounts, was a beloved and highly respected citizen, of whom it has been said had more charity and helped more people achieve their ambitions than anyone could imagine. He was described by his contemporaries as a 'captain of industry' and made very shrewd investments. He wasn't afraid to take a punt either, having eschewed his friends' advice and taken a calculated risk buying shares in the fledgling Glasgow Gas and Light Company, which was experimenting with coal to harness a by-product of 'inflammable air'. The main gas works was established in Townhead, just west of the cathedral and north of Alexandra Parade. On his death, his family inherited a hefty £300,000.

Dennistoun's son, Alexander, inherited the property on James's death. He went on some years later to complete the estate, buying up Whitehill and Craigpark, along with other adjoining land, the whole making up the district of Dennistoun. Craigpark became available on the death of its owner, James MacKenzie.

As with many merchants who had vast estates, MacKenzie's land purchases were not only for the view or for the privacy, or even just for showing off. In Lanark, for example, estate owners made vast fortunes exploiting natural resources on their lands, mining coal.

It took MacKenzie a number of years after his investment in 1798, in lands that he formally named Craigpark, to yield dividends. It was a serendipitous purchase as, little did he know it, in that same year a young Ayrshire man was experimenting with new road surfacing methods that would eventually create for MacKenzie a very healthy income, exploiting Craigpark's natural resource of whinstone, which he quarried to turn a quick buck supplying most of the ore that was used locally in the newly patented Tarmacadam road-surfacing.

In these pioneering times, Scotland had a proliferation of inventors, many of whose innovations are still used in some form or other today.

As with the paving with *plainstanes* at the Trongate and along Argyle Street for ladies and gentlemen to strut along promenades and piazzas without muddying their silver-buckled shoes and pretty hems and petticoats, Glasgow's dirt roads were playing havoc with wheeled carriages. Enter Ayrshireman John Loudon McAdam.

Having raked in a hefty fortune working in his uncle's business in New York, McAdam, on his return to Scotland, was unimpressed with the state of Glasgow's highways.

As a newly appointed roads trustee, he experimented with road-surfacing materials that could cope with modern traffic. He was instrumental in raising the question of road construction in parliament after writing a lengthy thesis on the subject and he was appointed Surveyor General of Roads in Great Britain in 1827. An updated version of the tar and chip is still a main surfacing material today. It was McAdam who suggested cambering the road surface to allow rainwater to be channelled along the sides of roads.

The original structure of mixing tar with small chippings of rock and slag was a gift for MacKenzie of Craigpark, with a quarry load of whin chips in his garden. Indeed, his quarry may well have provided the stone chips that were used for the road surfacing of Duke Street when it was widened just a few years later in 1831.

The two men probably never met, though the timeline of their lives would unwittingly meet, as they walked parallel paths at times through the symbiotic relationship between invention and resourcefulness: McAdam's roads and MacKenzie's quarry shared an invisible tether. Interestingly, the two died within two years of each other, in 1836 and 1838 respectively.

When Alexander Dennistoun took over Craigpark in 1850, his nearest neighbour was one John Reid, residing at the stately Whitehill House. Were it not for the sudden death of Reid, less than two years later, we might very well have been reading about Reidstoun or something similar.

For it was Reid who had the original idea to develop the area as a residential district and, in the two years that they were neighbours, Reid would surely have confided his development plans to Dennistoun. They may even have come to an agreement to work together, as the two were prolific in buying up parcels of land around Duke Street.

The Reid family's loss proved to be Alexander Dennistoun's gain. He wasted no time in contacting the trustees to purchase Whitehill House and those areas of land that were earmarked for the new development project of what was described as a 'garden suburb' within the city. All he needed to complete his property jigsaw was to go after Meadowpark to give him ownership of all Westercraigs.

Marketing of the new suburb clearly targeted the middle-class doctors, teachers, merchants and clergy. Dennistoun's advertising strategy made distinctions between an aspirational lifestyle and the tenement closes, with shared entry and back courts. He played upon the luxury of self-contained housing, free from the chattering, partying and disagreements of their neighbours, and that all-important question of whose turn it was to clean the common close. One ad in the *Glasgow Herald* newspaper describes the tenements and their lack of privacy as 'common flats by which the comfort and economy of family are so much in the power of others'.

Dennistoun created a dream: wide macadamized streets that he called 'boulevards' would replace narrow, uneven dirt tracks; there would be picturesque public gardens for picnicking and croquet; pretty fountains associated more with the open spaces of Paris or Milan. And all this could be had for a 'moderate rent and price'. It was clear there was no place in his grand scheme for rows of crowded tenements.

What happened next, after his death, partway through the development, would have had him turning in his grave.

The lucrative design and development contract would have been a feather in the cap for respected architect James Salmon, who had to compete for commissions with the likes of the Carswell brothers, who had pretty much cornered the market for commercial and industrial fabrication. Many of the factories would have seen the hand of the brothers, William and James, pioneers of using cast-iron mouldings, columns and straps in their construction. The innovative use of cast-iron in construction may well have been incubated in Glasgow.

Brothers-in-law Thomas Gildard and Robert McFarlane were carving out a good living, their star project being the Britannia Panopticon Music Hall at the Trongate, which launched the early careers of Hollywood stars Cary Grant and Stan Laurel, and remains the last existing music hall in Britain. Salmon would have had the world-renowned Alexander 'Greek' Thomson to contend with, while Charles Rennie Mackintosh would later arrive on the scene. Add to that the whole dynasty of the esteemed Adam family and it puts into perspective the intensity of competition for any major construction projects.

To win the tender for the creation of a small village within the city was no mean feat.

Alexander Dennistoun's vision of the new suburb to be called, of course, Dennistoun was of an upmarket des res community, with rows of handsome detached or terraced villas. Apparently, the locals nicknamed the area 'Villadom'.

Shortly after the foundation work began at lower Wester-craigs in 1857, the development was in the news again: cafes, taverns and private clubs were abuzz with the discovery at the building site of ancient fossils, which experts dated to as far back as the Ice Age.

Over the next four years, work got well under way; new streets were named and the suburb was taking shape according to Alexander's future vision, but building work came to an abrupt halt with the death of Alexander Dennistoun in 1874.

By this time, there were townhouses built along Onslow Drive as far as Whitehill Street's junction.

While architect James Salmon was keen to keep construction moving along the original lines, town planners went cold on the whole concept.

Times were a-changing; new city slickers had new ideas and, given that there was a gap of 16 years between Dennistoun's death and the start of construction again, contentious matters remained unresolved.

By the time Dennistoun's urbanization resumed in 1890, the trend for decent but affordable tenement housing had come to the fore and the direction of the development switched to accommodate shifting housing priorities. Besides, there was more money to be made by building up and maximizing living space.

Thus, the area of Dennistoun drew smart working-class couples with growing families – doctors, ministers, teachers. Temperance campaigner the Revd Fergus Ferguson and Forth Bridge engineer Sir William Arrol were among the founders of the emerging community.

Many of the streets – Finlay Drive, Garthland Drive, Ingleby and Onslow – were named for members of Dennistoun's extended family. Other street names – Meadowpark, Craigpark, Whitehill, Golfhill – are mere whispers, alluding to the grand houses after which they are named, memorials to a bygone era whence Glasgow's elite merchants bought and sold estates as if indulging in an exaggerated game of Jacks, hosting splendiferous masquerade balls and bloated banquets, whereupon the landed gentry ruled the roost and the hoi polloi knew their place.

While many of the original hundred or so majestic homes have disappeared, a few remain in various guises, having taken on a new mantle as museum, plush hotel or commercial premises. Others have been taken over by charitable trusts and lovingly restored to their former glory, and are open to the public. In this modern context, they welcome visitors or guests of a very different ilk.

Interestingly, many more of the municipal and commercial buildings withstood the passing of time and tide, George Square being an exemplar of Georgian and later Victorian architectural excellence.

In Dennistoun, one of the most enduring – and arguably one of the most important architecturally – is the politely named Great Eastern 'Hotel', known for generations as a hostel for homeless men.

The pioneering use of concrete in its construction and clever incorporation of wrought- and corrugated-iron broke new grounds in building design. It owes its longevity to the use of new materials and the new ways of using established construction materials to create a grand and imposing structure that can withstand the passage of time. This, coupled with its versatility of design, has allowed changing custodians to reinvent the shell over its lifespan. This is in no small part attributed to the imagination and expertise of the already well-respected Glasgow architects Charles Wilson and J. Alexander.

Its original manifestation was a cotton-spinning mill to process the cotton imports of merchant and mill owner Alexander Dennistoun. This was the beginning of the end for the cottage industry of weaving for which Glasgow weavers were known worldwide.

The mill's design was lauded for its pioneering use of corrugated iron within its structure. The internal positioning of its massive cast-iron frame between internal brick vaults and an external facing of random rubble rendered the building's shell almost fireproof.

Corrugated-iron arches supported huge concrete vaults on its upper levels and trusses of wrought iron supported a piended roof. This style of roof was also innovative and far more difficult to construct. Also known as a hipped roof, there being no gables at the sides, the gentle slope required more complex structuring of trusses and rafters. However, it made the building of the walls simpler.

This attention to detail and the embracing of new ideas typifies the Glasgow architects' outside-the-box way of thinking.

Possibly more than any other of the noble professions, architecture came to define Glasgow. It had journal writers, travellers, poets, philosophers, even royalty waxing lyrical on the beauty of the city. In the 1700s, a century earlier, polemicist and prolific writer Daniel Defoe described it as 'the cleanest, the most beautiful, the best built city in Britain', qualifying this by adding: 'London excepted' – which we should take with good grace since, only a couple of decades earlier, he had dismissed it as a quagmire of 'rabble and riots'.

By then also known as the Duke Street Cotton Mill, its second incarnation saw the building stripped back to its shell to be redesigned as a homeless men's hostel.

Ironically, the scene in 1907 would have been reminiscent of a Luddite sacking, as dozens of workers were brought in to dismantle and remove all the textile-making machinery, the power looms – everything had to go.

It's perhaps a crueller irony that many of these casual labourers may well have been the direct descendants of the handloom weavers and spinners, the penniless refugees of the Industrial Revolution.

Mass-production machinery was replaced with spartan living quarters on the upper floors – no more than basic cubicles – and communal amenities on the ground floor.

It continued to operate as such into the 1980s, accommodating up to 300 men. Various plans for upgrading the building as a modern social housing facility have been considered over the years since its closure in 2001 and today it stands forlorn, awaiting its fate, which is more likely to be demolition than reinvention.

Duke Street Prison

Another major construction project which occupied a large parcel of real estate within Dennistoun's original estate was Duke Street Prison.

Its first inmates were incarcerated in 1798. They would soon become familiar with the jangling of keys, the clanging of prison doors, the relentless outbursts of crying from fearful first-time offenders being silenced by the threats of hardier criminals, and the occasional whistling or singing of those optimistic few who had resigned themselves to the loss of their freedom.

Prison life was no picnic. And Duke Street gaol was certainly no hotel. Conditions were hard; some wardens were harder. The inmates' lot was summed up in a satirical little ditty sung to the tune of 'There Is a Happy Land'. It goes:

> There is a happy land
> Doon Duke Street Jail
> Where a' the prisoners stand
> Tied tae a nail.
> Ham an' eggs they never see
> Dirty watter fur yer tea
> There they live in misery
> God Save the Queen.

Architecturally, the prison building has failed to withstand the passing of time: all that remains of the original is part of an external wall which, it is claimed, came under fire from the pistols of sharpshooter Annie Oakley herself during an extensive three-month stop-off in Glasgow as part of a touring show led by Buffalo Bill, aka Colonel Will Cody. The troupe included real-life 'Red Indian' braves of the Sioux tribe.

The all-shootin', all-shoutin' spectacle played from November 1891 until February the following year. It was reportedly an invitational, as part of a fundraising campaign for the People's Palace Museum.

Another Native American connection with Glasgow was the so-called 'Ghost Shirt' believed to have been worn by a Sioux tribesman during the Battle of Wounded Knee.

The story goes it was sold, or left behind, by the Wild West show's Lakota interpreter, George C. Crager. It was held by Glasgow Museums for more than 100 years before being returned to its rightful place, with the Lakota tribe.

Buffalo Bill's elaborate bead-decorated gloves recently turned up in an episode of the long-standing television programme, *Antiques Roadshow*.

We may gasp in disbelief that such valuable cultural gems could be left behind after the show moved on, but in those days it was quite common to shed much of the show's memorabilia in order to reduce the transportation costs of trunks full of weighty gear that would likely not be used again.

The travelling show certainly made an impact on Glasgow. Indeed, a commemorative bronze life-size statue was erected at 'Dennistoun Village' as recently as November 2006.

Somewhere in its annals, the prison was thought to have been made-over as a 'women only' correctional institute, but it's more likely that female prisoners occupied a block within the main building – that is, until HM Prison Barlinnie was built in 1882, when male prisoners were transferred. Duke Street Prison remained open as a women's prison until 1955, when the jail was closed. It was later demolished.

During the early part of the twentieth century, women suffrage activists underwent the torture of force-feeding while incarcerated at Duke Street Prison. This would generally become a violent exchange, as suffragettes were brutally held down by female prison warders and their arms bound with a sheet in the style of a straightjacket; the fatter warders would often sit on the prisoner.

If an inmate became too ill to withstand further punishment, she would be released under the infamous 'Cat and Mouse' Act until she was well enough to return to prison for further brutal sessions.

Activists and Red Clydeside leaders Mary Barbour, Agnes Dollen and Jessie Stephen all faced Duke Street barbarism during their political careers. The activist Wendy Wood, an inimitable and some say eccentric campaigner for an independent Scotland from the 1920s, also spent time in Duke Street jail as a result of her unorthodox methods of raising awareness of the then almost unheard of Scottish Nationalist agenda.

The last woman to be hanged in Duke Street Prison – fully half a century after the previous female hanging – was Susan Newell in October 1923.

By all accounts, she was a hard woman, a husband beater and a crap mother.

Some say that the 30 year old took a 'flaky' and murdered a young paperboy in her tenement flat in Newlands Street, Coatbridge, because he insisted that she pay for her newspaper. Others maintain that she killed him in a fit of rage because he refused to hand over the coppers in his pocket.

Many tend towards the latter motive. It seems unlikely that she would murder a small boy for a newspaper – or in fact that she was wont to keep up with the latest news and woman's pages. It's more likely that she lured the boy indoors intent on relieving the young innocent of his paper-round takings.

There are many different versions of this tale, but I wouldn't rule out the contention that it was a 'red mist' murder; that the boy was the victim of a murderous rage and that this encounter was the last straw for a woman so wound up that she snapped.

It sounds a bit drastic, but then she was known to fly into fits of rage. She had already been given notice to quit by her landlady, owing to the violent outbursts and constant rows with her husband, John – himself no angel.

Little did the enterprising 13-year-old John Johnson know, when he stepped over the threshold of Newell's tenement flat, that he would not come out alive.

At her trial, Newell's defence put forward a plea of temporary insanity, but this was dismissed by the testimony of an expert witness.

This case had more than one young casualty: imagine the scene that met Newell's eight-year-old daughter from a previous marriage, when she came in from playing with her pals. Not only was she faced with the lifeless body of a boy lying on the sofa, strangulation marks on his neck betraying the murder method, but she was then sent to bed with that vision in her mind.

Newell went to sleep that night ruminating on how best to dispose of the body.

For such a dreadful deed and tragic tale, what happened the next day is darkly comical as it plays out.

At her trial, the jury heard how Newell involved her young daughter, Janet, in the crime, getting her to help bundle up the dead boy's body and carry it downstairs to the close mouth, stuff it in an old abandoned pram and sit perched on top of the wrapped-up body, while Newell started walking, pushing the pram along the old Cumbernauld Road towards Glasgow. Little Janet was effectively made an accessory after the fact and co-conspirator in the dastardly plan.

The details are all a bit hazy and it is difficult to separate fact from conjecture, but the gist of the story – which by this stage describes an incongruous cameo that wouldn't seem out of place in a Peter Greenaway dark satire – is borne out by witnesses.

Given the evidence, it was probably inevitable that the jurors would take less than 40 minutes to bring in a guilty verdict. Yet it was not unanimous. At least one juror, it seems, was disposed to believe Newell's lawyer's plea of temporary insanity. This may have somehow influenced the jury to unanimously recommend mercy for the paperboy's killer.

Insanity might have been the defence's only plausible option and it's not as daft as it may appear. After all, who but a complete lunatic would murder a small boy for pennies, perch her daughter atop the lifeless child's body, crammed into a pram that was obviously not intended for a small teenager, and march out into the street with apparently no idea where she was going to dump it?

I rest my case.

And so did the lawyers.

Two indisputable factors were the woman's undoing: the damning testimony of the murderess's own daughter and the common female pastime of windae hingin'.

Look up at any given time, on any given day, in any given street and one would witness dozens of (mainly) women in noisy and, sometimes, raucous exchange with neighbours up, down and across the street. The wide sash windows would be thrown up, so that neighbours could lean out and watch the world go by. They would have to shout above the hustle and bustle of busy streets below, so one was never really sure – without stopping in the path and cocking an ear upwards – whether these exchanges were angry or friendly, but, being Glaswegians, for the most part they would certainly have been caustically witty. Windae hingin' was a convenient way of keeping up with the latest news and gossip rather than traipsing down three or four flights of stairs to meet at the close mouth, which many also did. Besides, windae hingin' was more inclusive; more neighbours could put their tuppenceworth in. It was probably an early social form of a conference call today.

And it was this practice of social interaction that was the undoing of Newell.

Helen Elliot was a windae hinger.

It defies belief, but the story goes that The Pram, The Daughter, The Boy and His Killer were spotted by lorry driver Thomas Dickson. Seeing the woman struggling with a heavy load, he offered to give them a lift. He was heading towards Duke Street, so could drop them off there – and Newell accepted the offer! Insanity: thy name is Newell, me thinks.

According to witnesses, while the pram was being unloaded, the bundle came loose, revealing the top of John's head, while his little foot and ankle were sticking out. Whatever the driver had on his mind, amazingly he didn't notice.

But the sorry sight wasn't missed by Mrs Helen Elliot, who was looking out of her window. As Newell secured her bundle and went on her way, the eyewitness called to her sister and the two went running down the stairs and out the close in hot, and none too stealthy, pursuit.

They passed a man in the street and sent him off to find a 'polis', while they continued chase.

At least one account tells us that they saw her dump the body up a close at 650 Duke Street – said to be the longest street in Britain – only to be caught trying to escape over a back court wall, running straight into the hands of a waiting policeman.

I doubt that this was her plan. In fact, her 'plan' seemed to be evolving on the hoof. Why would she decide to turn out her bundle at a specific close on Duke Street?

I reckon that discretion was not in the arsenal of our amateur sleuths and, coupled with the stooge and the singular Keystone cop, Newell soon realized she had to make a quick retreat. She abandoned the pram and, presumably, her daughter – whom she had primed to accuse her stepfather of the killing.

Although the previous version of events describes her arrest by a bobby, it was two men who apprehended Newell and foiled her escape before calling for police, naming them as Robert Foote and James Campbell.

Other details are also inconsistent in reports: was it a barrow or handcart instead of a pram? Was the witness out shopping instead of at her tenement flat window?

Newell claimed that her husband was the killer and that he had forced her and her daughter to go along with him, but her story was dismissed, as her husband had an airtight alibi, having been among the chief mourners at his brother's funeral when the murder took place.

There were rumours at the time that her husband's alibi was a little too 'airtight', with numerous members of his family insisting he was with them at a funeral when the crime took place.

The judge threw out the accusation, however, and Newell's husband left the witness stand a free man, without even a sideways glance to his wife – might that have betrayed a guilty conscience?

Prosecutor Lord Kinross took great pains to pursue the couple for the boy's murder. His argument didn't win the day.

Newell was sentenced to death and, ironically, was brought back to Duke Street to its prison, where she was hanged on 10 October 1923. The details of the hanging itself make for harrowing reading, the hangman having attempted suicide only months later.

Personally, I wouldn't be so quick to dismiss John Newell. There is a growing school of thought that the man may have killed the boy in a drunken rage after a violent row with his wife. Men are as capable of 'red mist' syndrome as women, or perhaps more so.

Was it he who was the dominant one, the wife beater, the child beater? I'm loath to repeat the details of the torture the young boy would have endured, and respectfully apologize to all those who suffered the loss of John Johnson.

While those capable of the torture of a child include women as well as men, the females are fewer in number. Would a woman strangle a child so violently as to snap his windpipe? Does it require brute strength or merely technique? Can it be done by accident?

It is unimaginable to envisage what heartache John's family would have endured on hearing the extent of the vicious attack on their beloved boy. Medical evidence showed John had been beaten so badly about the head that part of his skull was smashed in. There was also evidence that the boy's killer or killers had inflicted extensive burns while he was still alive. Was it an act of lunacy in an attempt to prevent the body from being identified?

Susan Newell was said to have been the calmest person in the room when she was hanged. People reported that she seemed to have accepted her fate at the trial.

Her husband was so easily dismissed from the witness box that it might have been obvious to Susan Newell that she would hang for the vile crime, whether she committed it or not. They say she showed little or no emotion during her trial. Was this indicative of no remorse, or was it merely that she had accepted her fate even before the jury retired to consider its verdict?

Did she do it?

Only she would know.

And, of course, her husband.

Peter Manuel – Serial Killer

One of the last men to be hanged in Scotland was serial killer Peter Manuel, dubbed the 'Beast of Birkenshaw'. His reign of terror over the people of the East End and as far as Uddingston lasted less than two years – the height of his murderous campaign between June 1956 and May 1958 – but it left the families of his victims with scars that would never be healed.

On his arrest, his killing spree was halted, but the people of Glasgow and Lanarkshire still slept uneasy. He had successfully defended himself against earlier crimes. No one would breathe easy until they knew for sure that he was dead. Shortly after eight o'clock on the morning of 11 July 1958, the soft breeze in the air outside Barlinnie Jail and further abroad seemed almost to carry the collective sigh of relief of the local populace, as news of Manuel's execution was released.

Few people who had encountered the killer in his lifetime were surprised at his arrest. The warning signs had been there throughout his short life.

From a very young age, in his hometown of Manhattan, New York, he was in and out of the corrective system for petty crime, theft, housebreaking and violence. His parents had moved to the States with dreams of a better life, but his father's ill health forced them to return home to Motherwell in 1932. The family moved again, this time to Coventry, whence Manuel's criminal streak was unleashed.

Stealing from a church collection box was the least of his crimes. Shoplifting and housebreaking ensued, and even a youth house of correction couldn't contain him. He escaped and went on a thieving rampage. Then the house attacks became more violent; he seemed to be completely unperturbed that there might be people in the houses he broke into. He started carrying an axe, traumatizing one victim and later bashing in a woman's head while she lay sleeping.

Though the authorities, teachers and child psychologists were well aware of his violent and unruly behaviour, giving details in numerous reports, they seemed at a loss as to what to do with the boy. He admitted to his crimes but would give no explanation as to his motives. The head of one reform school concluded in a report that no amount of punishment would diminish Manuel's lust for blood.

He is reported to have attacked and attempted to rape the wife of a member of the school staff, leaving her to wander around the neighbourhood, beaten and dazed.

A number of geographical relocations to various borstal-style reform schools proved ineffective and the single-minded boy continued to grow into a dangerous young man whose violent urges would only increase.

Released from a borstal in England in 1946, at the age of 18, he headed to his family's home in Birkenshaw, Lanarkshire. While on bail awaiting trial for housebreaking, he attacked three women, one of whom he raped.

He was tried and sentenced to eight years in prison. In Peterhead Prison, after another violent outburst, he was labelled an 'aggressive psychopath' by the prison psychiatrist, who concluded that the man was beyond help.

On his release, seven years later, he again went home to his family in Birkenshaw.

This was a period of new beginnings. Many East Enders were seduced by the promise of modern housing in East Kilbride and Manuel landed a job laying gas pipes for the new town. But it wasn't long before his crimes escalated to extreme violence and rape. A pattern was emerging which would later reveal that Manuel was sexually dysfunctional and this fed his lust for extreme violence. It was conjectured that he could not reach orgasm without terrorizing and bludgeoning his victims.

His first murder victim was a 17-year-old girl, found badly beaten in a small woodland near a golf course in East Kilbride. Despite his later confession to her murder, he was not convicted, as the judge ruled that there wasn't enough evidence to link Manuel to the crime.

His next victims were a woman and her sister, Mrs Marion Watt and Mrs Margaret Brown, as well as Mrs Watt's 16-year-old daughter, Vivienne. In a cruel irony, Marion had invited her sister to stay with her while her husband was away from home.

It is impossible to imagine the extent of the pain that Mr Watt endured on learning that all three women were severely beaten before their death.

How much worse when police seemed determined that he was their murderer. He spent more than two months on remand in Barlinnie before police finally had to admit that they didn't have a case to pursue.

Early in January 1958, Manuel struck again. Police were beginning to notice similarities in the killings and linked them to Manuel. This time the bodies of Peter Smart, his wife Doris and their 11-year-old son were found dead, shot in the head at close range.

A week earlier, on 29 December 1957, 17-year-old Isabelle Cooke from Mount Vernon was reported missing. Manuel's crimes were escalating in brutality and the time between killings was getting shorter.

His callousness knew no bounds. When he was later arrested and confessed to killing Isabelle, he led police to the spot where he had buried her. When he came to a stop in a field, he was asked if this was the place, to which he casually replied: 'I'm standing on her now.'

Three days before Isabelle went missing, he had broken into the home of a church minister in Mount Vernon.

The police were under pressure to find the killer. Suspecting Manuel, they stepped up surveillance.

He was finally caught paying for goods with crisp new banknotes that he had stolen from the Smart family's home.

Manuel confessed to eight murders but, in a packed court, he sacked his defence lawyer and chose to represent himself; he then denied all charges against him and retracted his confessions. He had previously successfully defended himself on an assault charge.

The trial lasted 16 days. The jury of nine men and six women found him guilty of all charges except the killing of Anne Kneilands, after instruction from Lord Cameron, the High Court judge hearing the case. This despite leading police to where he had disposed of two guns and the iron bar that had been used to kill Ms Kneilands. Manuel had been suspected of killing her two years before his hanging, but was released with an airtight alibi from his father.

After Manuel's execution by hanging in Barlinnie Prison on 11 July 1958, the 32 year old was posthumously pronounced guilty of the murder of a taxi driver, Sidney Dunn, during a visit to Newcastle for a job interview.

The case of Oscar Slater

One of the most celebrated, nay disgraceful, cases of miscarriage of justice involved the murder of a wealthy spinster, Miss Marion Gilchrist. At her death in 1908, Miss Gilchrist had accumulated a collection of jewellery that, today, would be worth the equivalent of hundreds of thousands of pounds.

Not only was the case a mystery of Sherlock Holmes proportions, it attracted the attentions of author and sleuth Sir Arthur Conan Doyle himself.

The murder was pinned on a ne'er-do-well character of ill-repute who, after a concerted campaign by Conan Doyle and other respected citizens, escaped the hangman's noose only to spend almost two decades in Peterhead Prison for a crime he didn't commit.

Oscar Slater – only one of a number of aliases he used – was a victim of circumstances in a case that relied on mere coincidences rather than actual evidence.

There's no doubt whatsoever that Slater was an unsavoury character at best and this may have had a role in the ensuing 'frame-up' that led to his conviction.

Marion Gilchrist was beaten to death in her flat in Glasgow, which she shared with her maid and companion.

It is believed that her killer would have at least been acquainted with his victim, being familiar enough to know that her maidservant would be out dealing with errands as was her habitual routine.

For such a dodgy character to attract the support of many of Britain's finest, not least the Scottish Secretary Lord Pentland, is curious in itself.

Slater was born Oscar Leschziner of a Jewish family in Germany and only came to Britain initially to escape being called up for compulsory military service. He first settled in London under another alias surname, Anderson.

He was attracted to the murky underbelly of city life. Working as a bookie, he wasn't long in finding his niche as a pimp and a fence for stolen goods.

He was a hoodlum, a gangster, and he was tried for assault and acquitted on two occasions while living in London.

He spent some time in Edinburgh before moving to Glasgow, where he lost no time in befriending the thieves, housebreakers and gangsters of the city's mean streets.

He told people he was a gymnastics instructor, a dentist, a trader in precious gemstones – anything that suited his purpose at the time. Yet he was known to the police from London to Edinburgh as a petty criminal at best.

Marion Gilchrist was unlikely to be an acquaintance of his. Yet it was he to whom detectives turned when the old lady, who was in her eighties, was bludgeoned in her home. None of her expensive jewellery was taken bar a diamond brooch; her flat was ransacked.

Circumstantial and anecdotal evidence was given undue credence: he boarded the ill-fated *Lusitania* from Liverpool to New York with a female companion only days after the killing. This was interpreted as 'fleeing from justice'. He had tried to sell a pawn ticket for an expensive brooch sometime before the murder. This was found to have taken place weeks before the attack on Miss Gilchrist.

And one neighbour told the police that she had heard a man at Miss Gilchrist's home demanding to see a Mr Anderson, one of Slater's pseudonyms.

Police demanded he should be extradited from the States, but Slater chose to return of his own accord. Was this the action of a guilty man?

Everything from witness statements to a dodgy identity parade was prejudiced and designed to point to Slater's guilt. Much was made in court of his sleazy connections and previous form.

He was destined to swing for the murder, yet a campaign and petition signed by around 20,000 people, including some very lofty citizens, influenced the Secretary of State for Scotland, Lord Pentland, to commute his sentence from hanging to life imprisonment.

The first book that sought to discredit his conviction was written by William Rough a year after Slater's conviction. It was this book, *Trial of Oscar Slater*, that convinced big-hitters such as Ramsay MacDonald and Sir Edward Marshall Hall that the case should be looked at again. Conan Doyle published his work, *The Case of Oscar Slater*, openly appealing for Slater to be pardoned. In commuting the sentence,

Lord Pentland had issued only a conditional pardon to allow Slater to serve his time.

Two years later, in 1914, the learned Liberal politician and the then Secretary of State for Scotland, Thomas McKinnon Wood, opened a private inquiry into the case.

Another casualty of the case was the diligent detective John Thomson Trench. He was kicked out of the police force and later fitted up on bogus charges for which he was later acquitted. Not for trying to pervert the course of justice or for withholding valuable evidence, but for disclosing valuable information that was withheld from the trial to ensure a conviction.

It was clear that the real murderer had friends in high places, too, who were prepared to tamper with evidence and even see a man hang for a murder he didn't commit.

The private inquiry found the conviction was sound and that should've been the last of it. Yet another book by journalist William Park, published in 1927, entitled *The Truth About Oscar Slater*, finally persuaded the authorities that Slater's conviction was unsafe.

It had taken almost 20 years, but in 1928, following a recent Act of Parliament, Slater's conviction was quashed.

The Scottish Court of Criminal Appeal, which had recently been introduced, was not accessible to Slater because it would only reconsider cases from the date of the Act.

Park's argument was so compelling that it persuaded the Solicitor General for Scotland, Alexander Munro MacRobert, to approach the then Secretary of State for Scotland, Sir John

Gilmour, to reconsider the case. This could only be done by extending the jurisdiction of the Act to before 1926.

Lord Craigie Mason Aitchison spoke for a reported 13 hours on Slater's behalf, pointing out, for example, that witnesses had been coerced into naming Slater by police and authorities had withheld valuable information from the trial, along with other flaws, but still the High Court judge ruled all this out.

Even given all that, the court would not admit wrongdoing on the part of the investigators. Slater's conviction was quashed on a technicality: the judge had misdirected the jury.

Detective Trench was convinced that Miss Gilchrist had been killed by a family member, possibly one Dr Charteris, whom he believed had ransacked the flat looking for a valuable document and had taken the brooch to make it appear as a burglary. Trench died in 1919 and never lived to see his name cleared.

Until very recently, there had been at least three key documents which were withheld from public scrutiny. In the early 1990s, investigative writer Thomas Toughill gained access to previously undisclosed papers, which he asserted proved conclusively that Oscar Slater was fitted up to protect people in high office.

In his book, *Oscar Slater: The Mystery Solved*, Toughill asserts once and for all that Miss Gilchrist was murdered by her nephew, Wingate Birrell, and that the family used their influence to protect him.

It is understood that Birrell was involved in a secret love affair with Miss Gilchrist's maid, Helen Lambie. This would have made her easy prey to be persuaded or threatened into lying to the police.

He tells how the future prime minister, Sir Ramsay MacDonald, sought to intervene to set the record straight by providing evidence that would exonerate detective Trench and prove police had lied during the private inquiry.

All of this was hushed up, and Slater and Trench hung out to dry – or to die, in Slater's case.

Slater was released on 8 November 1927 and paid £6,000 in compensation, but he was not pardoned. No one was prosecuted for the murder. Toughill, in an article in the *Herald* newspaper in 1994, called for Slater's pardon and the posthumous reinstatement of detective Trench to the honour roll of the police force.

The settling of Marion Gilchrist's estate was messy. She was a woman of property and great wealth, and owned land in the East End of Glasgow. Barras Queen Maggie McIver had sought for years to acquire the land to complete her own business empire, Barrowland Market and Ballroom.

Mine's a lager

Duke Street in Dennistoun was said to be the longest street in Britain. It could, therefore, accommodate far larger enterprises and allow companies to expand. As well as the Duke Street Prison and the Wills & Co. cigarette factory, another sprawling operation was the Tennent Brewery.

Tennent's lager is a global brand; in fact, in some parts of the world it is considered a fancy imported brew. Founded at Drygate Bridge in 1740 by brothers Hugh and Robert Tennent, it has continued a tradition of brewing at that same site, conveniently close to the Molindinar burn, which reaches back to the middle 1500s.

The Tennent brewery was probably the first exponent of commercial 'real ale' in Glasgow since the Reformation. Indeed, J&R Tennent's hallmark proudly proclaims: 'Wellpark Brewery Established 1556'.

By the end of the 1600s, the Enlightenment movement in Europe had heralded the demise of some religious establishments in Glasgow. The Dominican Blackfriars and the Franciscan Greyfriars – named for the colour of their livery – as well as many other monasteries, were traditional brewers of ale as far back as the twelfth century. Glasgow Cathedral had probably been brewing beer since its founding days in 1136, using holy water from the Molindinar burn.

The Tennent family moved into brewing as a natural progression from the family businesses of maltings and ale houses, including the White Hart Inn and, it is believed, the Saracen Head bar. There are still several Tennent's bars operating in the city, while the golden brew is served in millions of bars around the world.

The brewery name appears in the first business directory in 1783 and continues to operate on the Wellpark site today.

The business has been in the same family for generations. Hugh's sons entered the business in 1769, by which time J&R Tennent had grown to become the largest exporter of bottled beer in the world.

But the ubiquitous golden lager that the company is known for today on draught and in cans is not what made the firm its fortune in the early years. Rather it was the

A family gather at the magnificent fountain at Cathedral Square with Provand's Lordship in the background, 1893.

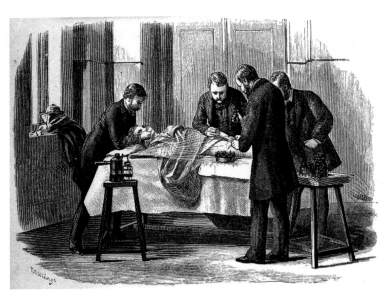

This etching depicts Joseph Lister demonstrating his pioneering carbolic spray at the Glasgow Royal Infirmary on Castle Street, where he perfected his life-saving innovation. In 1861, the year that Lister took up his post as a surgeon at this hospital, a new surgical block was opened in his name, comprising eight wards. Each ward had 16 beds, a nurse's room and a new operating theatre. Ward 24 was particularly identified with Lister's pioneering work in reducing infection rates.

Back court at 46 Saltmarket, 1868. Men and boys take a break from towing their barrow around the streets to pick up old 'rags and bones' and sell them.

Children washing in a tub on Glasgow Green while the linen is laid out to bleach and dry in the sun after a session at the steamie, c. 1900.

Above: Rummaging at the Barras on London Road, c. 1916.

Left: Women, kids and laundry hang out at the Old Vennel, off High Street, c. 1904.

Above: Glasgow Corporation Tramways tailoring workshop, c. 1900, making the uniforms for transport workers.

Below: The large Jewish community, mainly living and working in the Gorbals, are served by women workers at a factory making traditional Jewish caps, known as the kippah or yarmulke, c. 1910.

Above: No.2 Committee Room at Glasgow's Juvenile Delinquency Board at Green Street Industrial School; a board official presents a mother and her three children to the committee, 1886.

Below: Children learn to write at Dennistoun public school on Meadowpark Street, c. 1916.

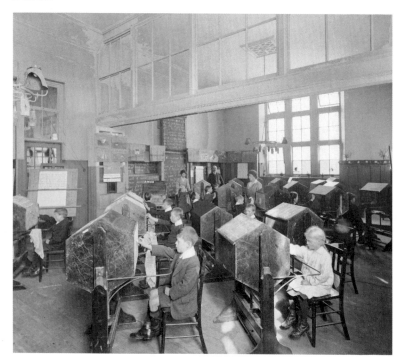

Dubbed the Battle of George Square or Bloody Friday, many remember the storming of the square on 1 January 1919, as the day Prime Minister Winston Churchill waged war on unionized workers, women and children calling for a 40-hour week. Delegation leaders David Kirkwood and Manny Shinwell went on to become MPs in Westminster after the 1922 election. Jimmy Maxton joined them as MP for Bridgeton and John Wheatley became MP for Shettleston.

A woman nurses her baby while warming a bottle of baby milk on the range in a slum tenement, **above left**, in stark contrast to the demure and clearly well-to-do mother and baby posed picture, **above right**, believed to have been taken in 106 Maitland Street, Cowcaddens; both pictures c. 1910.

Workers pose for a snapshot at R. White's ice-making factory on Laird Street, Bridgeton, c. 1935.

Conductresses show off their new uniforms as war breaks out in 1939.

Cissie Smith, of Tollcross, with the fashionable Betty Grable 'up-do' that was all the rage in wartime Britain, 1939.

Relaxing in the sun at Glasgow Green, c. 1955.

Above: Kids queue up for the Saturday matinee at the Odeon Cinema in Shettleston, 1955.

Below: The Modern Homes Exhibition at Glasgow's Kelvin Hall brought people in their droves to see what the best-dressed homes were wearing, October 1956.

stouts and ales that were the drink of preference in the eighteenth century.

The second generation of brewers expanded the business, acquiring a rival brewery from William McLehose that became the Wellpark Brewery, as we know it today. The brothers were astute businessmen and maintained a healthy bank balance into the nineteenth century. They died within a year of each other, Robert in 1826 and Hugh in 1827, at which time the third generation, Robert's elder son Hugh, took up the reins until he retired in 1855.

It was he who over the following three decades steered the expansion of the firm, building up a massive export portfolio which would elevate Tennent's as the world's largest exporter of bottled beers.

However, they faced growing competition from German lagers whose 'gas tight' casks were superior to Scottish wax-lined hogsheads and kept their oxygen content, giving the impression of a lighter, fresher taste.

In a bizarre coincidence, Hugh and his son Charles died less than ten years later, again within months of each other. While the fifth generation, another Hugh and Archibald, inherited the business, they turned it over to trustees, who ran the company on their behalf.

As with many of the city's employers, they had a deep-rooted sense of social responsibility and were fondly remembered by the workers as model employers, not least having built houses for the brewery labourers in 1811.

This philanthropic attitude continued over generations, with the company offering educational talks and social events by some well-known artistes and comedy shows, which no doubt launched the careers of some well-kent favourites of the stage.

They organized walking trips in the country to promote well-being and personal development of their workers, many of whom may never have been out of the city confines, let alone had a chance to witness wildlife at rest and play.

The company was run under the governance of trustees for two decades, before being handed over to Hugh Tennent in 1884.

It was he who moved the business on, introducing the first Tennent's lager only a year later. He stormed ahead with new plans for expansion that included the construction of a new German-style lager brewery at Wellpark, which was denounced at the time by the press as 'a madman's dream'.

Then the bickering started between the Glaswegian and German workers. Known for their diligence and strong work ethic, as well as Saxon arrogance, the Germans complained that Scots workers were 'licentious, slothful, prejudiced and jealous', while the Scots advised the Germans to 'get a sense of humour'. The inevitable language barrier added to strained industrial relations and compounded construction difficulties, leading to delays in the final commissioning of the new lager brewery, which eventually commenced production late in 1891.

With more than 10,000 bottles of lager reportedly leaving the brewery on hot summer days, Tennent's provided free ice to the pouring trade during the summer months. Specially designed ice compartments in the lager crates allowed the firm to supply ice-cold beer to the buffets and bars at Glasgow's second International Exhibition in 1901. That same year King Edward VII took over the throne after Queen Victoria's death.

Hugh was astute enough to employ German head brewers – the first, Jacob Klinger, being poached by Edinburgh rivals John Jeffrey.

The Scottish–German alliance prevailed at Wellpark right up to the start of the First World War.

The company won a raft of prestigious awards for its products, including the lofty accolade 'the Highest Possible and Only Award of Merit', no less. Hugh's lager won the firm top prize at the prestigious Chicago World Fair in 1893.

Hugh's was the hand behind exciting innovations – draught lager, 1924; cans, 1935; kegs, 1963 – between 1891, when the new brewery was completed, and 1963, when the business was taken over by the London firm Charrington United Breweries. The new owners merged a few years after acquiring Tennent's to become Tennent Caledonian Breweries.

The familiar sight of Tennent's award-winning Clydesdale horses and delivery carts continued throughout the years, through the 1940s and the Second World War.

But Glasgow's cobbled streets proved difficult terrain for the stout beasts. The firm commissioned custom-designed rubber 'galoshes' devised by Black Boab, the brewery blacksmith, but they weren't ideal.

While whisky distilleries employed cackling geese as security at their premises, Tennent's employed former Barlinnie warders as Wellpark's security.

By the year that Celtic won the European Cup, 1967, most of the characterful old buildings with romantic sounding names, such as the Bruce, the Wallace, the Victoria, the Ruby and the Tanjore (where the beers were loaded for export to Tangiers), had been demolished and replaced with fancy new premises and equipment. The Ruby was so called because old brewing experts espoused that stout was at its quality peak when a candle viewed through a bottle of beer showed a ruby hue. The Ruby survived in its new guise as Tennent's museum, the St Mungo Heritage Centre. The distinctive big red 'T' trademark so strongly associated with the products dates back to the 1860s at the height of the Victorian era.

Tennent's has built its reputation in today's market for its consistency of flavour, which is no mean feat considering many beers, real ales and stout – not least the Irish stout Guinness – were known to not travel well. Yes, beers can get travel sickness.

But it must surely be the sultry beauties whose pictures adorned the cans that many drinkers hold dear in their memories.

From the mid-1960s, Tennent's girls have appeared in various campaigns, from Housewives' Choice to Bathing Beauties. Tennent's models became mini-celebrities, with their own fan base: remember the series 'Anne on Vacation', 1966–9?

Many of the models were beauty pageant winners. Remember Miss STV? Miss Scotland? The beauty contest was elevated from Butlin's lovely legs and popular holiday beachside line-ups to become a sophisticated network of pageants culminating in Miss World contests, televised around the world. The majority of these were the brainchild of Mecca dancehall and bingo house boss Eric Morley. Tennent's Lovelies campaigns ran well into the 1980s, when feminism found its voice and campaigners were fighting for equal rights in all areas, from the kitchen to the Cabinet in Westminster. And their voices, agonizingly slowly, began to be heard.

Every tiny concession for equal rights that led to legislation was hard fought and took years, decades, generations to bear fruit.

And that marked the end of Tennent's Lovelies and other marketing campaigns that perpetuated the objectification of women. No longer could a man sit on a stool at his favourite bar ogling sex kittens on beer cans and ordering that second packet of KP nuts to reveal another tantalizing inch of naked breasts on the dispenser pack hanging up near the gantry.

Apropos of nothing much, did you know that Tennent's Wellpark Brewery stands partly on grounds that used to be No. 4 Ark Lane? So Tennent's can claim as their son William Miller, who gave the world 'Wee Willie Winkie', first printed in the cult anthology *Whistle-Binkie: A Collection of Songs for the Social Circle*, because he lived for a time at No. 4 Ark Lane, which was demolished to make way for the construction of the brewery.

Tennent's erected a plaque to commemorate their famous son, but it was destroyed over time by vandals. A replacement plaque was commissioned in 2009 from the sculptor Graciela Ainsworth.

Where there's a Wills . . .

There were three cigarette factories in Dennistoun, but by far the largest and most productive was W. D. & H. O. Wills on Alexandra Parade. A huge, imposing building, with 425,000 square feet of floor space, it employed at one time 3,500 workers producing 260 million cigarettes per week.

With Glasgow's mercantile wealth having been built to a large degree on tobacco trading, it would naturally follow, presumably, that the tobacco barons would create a cigarette manufacturing empire. However, the most successful was not born of Glasgow but set down its roots in Bristol in 1786, which became the name of their first cigarette brand, followed by Three Castles and Gold Flake. The W. D. and H. O. of the company name refers to William Day and Henry Overton, who took over the running of the business in 1826. They introduced the more familiar brands of Woodbine and Embassy, the brand most associated with the firm's Glasgow operation since the 1940s.

It was Wills's own engineers who designed the building on Alexandra Parade, which opened at the end of the Second World War.

Wills was understandably proud of its reputation as a benevolent employer, being one of the first firms to introduce canteens for workers, paid holiday leave, a company gym and free medical care. Yet the class and sub-class system couldn't be shaken off, as many former workers recall having to enter the building by different doors according to what position they held in the factory.

One woman who worked in the typing pool remembers: 'We had to enter by the side door, while the managers entered from the front, but production line workers went in through another entrance, and you daren't break this rule.'

Other rules were made for breaking, and pilfering was considered a perk of the job.

A former Whitehill schoolboy recalls: 'I passed Wills every day on my way to school. I remember the "three nuns" clock tower on the corner of Hanson Street and Alexander Parade. It was a handsome landmark. Such a shame when they knocked it down. I wonder if anyone managed to preserve it.

'The bowling green on Hanson Street belonged to the Wills factory. I remember it was bordered with crab apple trees and we used to climb over the palings and shinny up the trees. We were aye gettin' chased. We were always amazed at how the wee old silver-haired bowlers could be so fast, but they weren't as fierce as the Alsatians and Doberman dogs that used to guard the scrap yard. We really took our life in our hands trying to steal stuff that we would sell on to another scrappie.

'Even as a wean at Golfhill primary, I remember the smells from the cigar factory coming in through the windows in summer. Depending on how the wind blew, we either had the smell of the brewery or the cigarette factory.

'Back then, you used to get cigarette cards, like coupons, that you could save up and redeem for gifts. They had a catalogue that you could pick from. We used to hang about outside the factory and pick up discarded cigarette cards from the street or in the bins. There was always a bin attached to a street lamp at the bus stop. I had a Kensitas Club album. It was a musical compilation, but we didn't have a gramophone, so we used to take it over to our mate's house. His dad had what my mum used to call "a good job" and a company car – a Humber Hawk, I think it was – and they had "a boat hoos"; that's how people said it, but it wasn't a *boathouse*, it was a *bought* house. They were the three factors that made up the well-to-do. They didn't rent. They were homeowners. They always had "stuff" before anyone else: a Bendix mixer for baking; a stand-up Hoover; a washing machine with a mangle attached. I was fascinated by it and would sit in the kitchen and watch my friend's ma folding up a newly washed flannel sheet and pull it through the mangle rollers. It had a turning handle, so there was a bit of a knack to the procedure. So she didn't have to take her stuff in a pram to the steamie, which is probably a shame because the women in the steamie were always laughing and telling stories.'

When the Glasgow arm of the operation closed in 1992, production was moved back to Bristol.

From humble beginnings

Modern-day notables with Dennistoun connections include multi-award-winning author Campbell Armstrong; Lisbon Lion Stevie Chalmers, who scored the winning goal in the 1967 European Cup final for Celtic FC; singer and song-writer Lonnie Donegan – 'My Old Man's A Dustman' – who was raised in Duke Street and became known as the King of Skiffle; renowned comic actor Rikki Fulton, who attended Whitehill Secondary school and fought in the navy during the Second World War, almost losing his life when his ship, *Ibis*, sank under enemy fire on the Mediterranean; and another Whitehill Secondary pupil, Alasdair Gray, author of *Lanark*, a prolific and award-winning writer, artist and stained-glass artist.

World snooker champion John Higgins – the Wizard of Wishaw – honed his skills at Craigpark snooker club, as did Alan McManus. Turning professional in 1992, Higgins became the first teenager to win three ranking tournaments in one season.

Art dealer Tom Honeyman gave up a career as a general practitioner with a surgery in Dennistoun to move to London. When he returned home, London's loss was Glasgow's gain, as it was he who negotiated the acquisition of Salvador Dali's *Christ of Saint John of the Cross* (or simply known as *The Crucifixion*) for the city. He played a key role in acquiring the Burrell Collection of 8,000 works of art and was a founder of the Citizens Theatre.

Actors Jimmy Logan, Ford Keirnan, Dorothy Paul and John Kazek are Dennistoun stalwarts, as are 'Ultimo' bra designer Michelle Mone and iconic designer Charles Rennie Mackintosh, who lived in Firpark Terrace.

There are so many worthies that hail from this suburb, I don't want to end up just listing names, but I can't resist dropping a few more and would recommend further reading on all of the aforementioned, as their stories are well worth the telling.

My favourite Dennistoun Darling has to be poet William Miller, who, from his home in Ark Lane, penned the enduring nursery rhyme 'Wee Willie Winkie'. And we owe the rainproof Mackintosh coat to inventor Charles Mackintosh, who worked out of his factory at Wellpark.

But my Blue Riband goes to Essex boy Joseph Lister, who,

although not from the East End, introduced revolutionary sterilization techniques to modern medicine while practising at the Glasgow Royal Infirmary. He developed antiseptic and anti-bacterial products and practices such as using swabs soaked in carbolic acid and instructing medical and auxiliary staff to wash with early forms of disinfectant between visits to patients. This completely transformed the expectant outcomes of medical procedures – remember the pink block of carbolic soap in every school and hospital washroom? This was not an entirely new concept, as we are all well aware of the importance the Lady with the Lamp, Florence Nightingale, placed on cleanliness. Even today, hospitals are fighting against bacterial infection using modern versions of carbolic.

The cleansing and anti-bacterial qualities of carbolic were so commonly known that youngsters caught swearing or badmouthing would be told to 'go and wash your mouth out with carbolic'. This was usually just a rhetorical chastisement accompanied by a gasp and a look of shock to demonstrate intolerance of verbal disrespect. However, some zealots would take this admonishment to barbaric and humiliating extremes, forcing children to keep the soap in their mouth and even swallow it, often leading to choking, vomiting and diarrhoea.

On a brighter note . . .
Shouty singer Lulu hails from Dennistoun and, in an exclusive interview, confided she liked the acoustics of the close landing for belting out songs as a young tot.

She told me: 'I've got a very selective memory, so I might

be making things up, but I remember my mother used to go to the Barras and buy "cuts" of material and have pencil skirts made for herself and little sticky out skirts for me. She would buy vintage dresses and fur coats and things like that. My mum had lots of friends who had stalls there. She used to go to one barrow that sold old singles, 45s and 78s.

'My parents used to go dancing at Barrowland. They called it the Dahncin'.

'I lived up a close and we didn't even have a bath. There was a tiny scullery and you would have a sink bath in front of the fire or, when you got bigger, you went to the steamie in Bluevale Street off the Gallowgate, where we could go once a week for a big bath, and shut the door and have a bath in privacy.

'We shared the toilet between the neighbours. You had to go out and down the stairs to it, and there might have been a neighbour in, so you'd go back up to the house and listen for them coming out. That's how we were brought up and you never thought anything of it.

'We had a coal fire and they would come round the streets and deliver your coal. You could hear them shouting "Cooooaaal!!" all the way up the street. My father used to say I had a voice like the coalman. My parents took me to Rothesay [home of child singer Lena Zavaroni] – I was about five and I won a wee competition.

'I used to love singing up the close and all the aunties and uncles would get drunk on a Friday night and everyone would come up and do their "turn", as they called it, after the pub.

'I probably got my big break at the Barrowlands. There

was a competition run by the *Daily Express* for bands. I was in one of the bands, the Gleneagles. We had been working at the Lindela and we did gigs around the US army bases. We became Lulu and the Luvvers. There was this influx of American and black R&B music to Glasgow through the ships and the American army bases. Imports were very prized and Glasgow loved the early soul music.

'The Barrowlands didn't really give local acts a turn. We were never big enough for that. It was a big thing to be playing at the Barrowlands. It would have been quite nervewracking. It's not like I became a big name and then did the Barrowlands.

'I think the big band was there on the night, too. Billy McGregor and, I think it was, the Gaybirds. We just played in between their sets, if I remember. I was a "something" winner. I don't remember what category it was, but I didn't win the top thing. But I got to go to London to audition for EMI.

'When EMI turned me down, I got a chance to audition for Decca. I was just 13 or 14. I left Glasgow for London permanently when I was only 15. Then I got to join a band called the Ball Rocks. Alex Harvey was a big influence and that's when I first heard "Shout".

'I heard him after he'd come back from Germany around the same time as the Beatles. He came back emaciated and I now know that he was on all kinds of drugs.

'There was great excitement that he was returning to Glasgow, but my dad didn't let me out after 9.30 p.m., though my mother managed to finagle that I could get out. I so wanted to see him – and he sang "Shout". I'll never forget when I first heard him singing that. Alex and I became great friends, and with his brother Lesley, till they both died.'

Camlachie

The village of Camlachie can be traced back to at least the late 1200s. Its existence is first noted in 1300 in the Chartulary of Glasgow – a medieval register of lands and buildings of note, among other documents. A chartulary can also document important events and public notices. This practice of keeping such records may have been introduced by William the Conqueror, since an early version itemizing properties and events was extant in Normandy from the 1000s. King William I liked to count things. It was he who introduced the population census, which became the Domesday Book, when he took the English throne in 1066.

In a recurring pattern of land ordinance, Camlachie is bifurcated by a burn to comprise Easter and Wester Camlachie.

The ubiquitous signature of wealth and commercial success, the mansion house, was built in 1720 by the third John Walkinshaw. His father and grandfather were hugely successful merchants. The first John bought both sides of Camlachie and the burn, which at that time ran rich with trout. He also purchased the estate of Barrowfield. This Walkinshaw was a generous benefactor, having donated some 100 merks to the Merchants House to help the needy. He was thrice married and, when he wed his third wife, Janet, he began to think about his legacy.

He bought Wester Camlachie lands from the Wilkie family to provide for, as he put it, 'the aires and bairns' in 1669 for 3,500 merks. A Scottish merk was equal to about two-thirds of an English pound.

Janet was the daughter of another wealthy merchant, the Laird of Easter Craigs, which became Dennistoun.

Yet the riches she longed for – a brood of children – were denied her and this marriage produced no babies. So, on his death it was the eldest son of his second marriage who inherited the estates of Camlachie and Barrowfield.

John the third was an explorer and self-styled 'adventurer' who travelled the world and presumably had no inclination to settle down. He finally did marry, but the lands of Camlachie had to wait for the third generation of John Walkinshaws before the mansion house was built. It was not as ostentatious as many of the grand residences and town-houses, but a dainty two-storey house with a pretty parterre at the front.

John the third inherited a grand estate and, in 1703, he married into a staunchly committed pro-Jacobite family, being of the Jacobite persuasion himself.

It was he who co-founded the nearby village of Calton around 1706. Camlachie and Calton were to become re-nowned around the world for the unequalled skills of their weavers.

But during the first Jacobite uprising, in 1715, Walkinshaw was captured at Sheriffmuir and imprisoned at Stirling Castle until his release in 1717. There is the lovely story that he escaped by changing clothes with his wife on a pre-arranged visit and escape bid. That her husband would leave his wife to face the wrath of his jailers sounds anything but chivalrous, but it seems Mrs Walkinshaw was quite a feisty lady and would have persuaded her husband to submit to the cunning plan.

His incarceration and Jacobite sympathies had a costly outcome. Much of his lands were confiscated and it was a further three years before Camlachie mansion was built.

John and Catherine had a daughter, Clementina, whose claim to fame was that she had become Bonnie Prince Charlie's lover while in Glasgow during the '45 rebellion and she bore him a daughter who became the Duchess of Albany, immortalized in the Burns poem 'Bonnie Lass o' Albany'. Before that, though, the estate had changed hands, and thus began another dynasty of three generations.

John Orr had bought the lands for £10,000, with a view to raking in some of the huge wealth that coalmining was yielding. While Lanarkshire was the hub of mining, there were many mines scattered throughout the East End, including Camlachie. However, with the burns regularly flooding and poor logistics, compared with other areas, mining in Camlachie would contribute to the downfall of a number of optimistic investors.

The Camlachie mansion was in the title of Lady Barrowfield until John Orr made her an offer of £500 for the house and a parcel of land. The deal included the right to mine for coal.

By 1788, John Orr's grandson had finally sold the two estates of Easter Camlachie and Barrowfield, but new co-owner James Dunlop of Garnkirk was destined for a massive financial meltdown from his investments in tobacco plantations, which he lost during the American War of Independence.

While the two dynasties of Walkinshaw and Orr dominate the history of Wester Camlachie, perhaps its most colourful character was a tenant, one Major General James Wolfe. The much-celebrated Wolfe has been described as Britain's greatest general, although team Horatio Nelson might put up a staunch argument for that accolade. Wolfe fought successfully in several wars around the world but is perhaps best known for his role in the taking of Quebec during the so-called Seven Years War (or the French and Indian War) of 1756–63. His battle nous and influential connections earned him a fast track to Major General at a very young age. Born in 1727, the son of an army general, he signed up to his father's regiment, First Regiment Marines, in 1741. He was noted for his pioneering military training reforms, both strategically and practically, introducing more efficient loading, firing and bayonet techniques, which were eventually published with the title General Wolfe's Instructions to Young Officers. He died at the Battle of Quebec in 1759 after successfully overcoming the French army under the Marquis de Montcalm, who also met his fate at that battle, dying of his wounds the morning after. It was a crucial victory that represented a key turning point in the war. Despite many losses, it demonstrated that the British had the will and military power to overcome the French. That led to the taking of Montreal and sealed Britain's supremacy over Canada and North America. The war culminated in the signing of the Treaty of Paris and the divvying-up of French territories in Canada and America 'east of the Mississippi River', not including New Orleans.

The Battle of Quebec was the young Major General Wolfe's finest and final hour, but he was no stranger to the battlefields, taking part in numerous combats, including the War of the Austrian Succession and, in Flanders, the Battle of Lauffeld and the seizing of Bergen-op-Zoom. Probably the best-known painting of him is *The Death of General Wolfe*, which is famous worldwide.

In Scotland, Wolfe served under General Henry Hawley in the campaign to crush the Jacobite rebels, fighting in the Battles of Falkirk and Culloden. And he was very popular with the Royal Highland Fusiliers under his command in North America.

In 1749, ten years before his heroic victory in Canada, Wolfe was quartered at the Camlachie Mansion, which he dubbed in one of his many letters 'the queer old house in Camlachie'. Before it was demolished, the building was added to on both sides, which further diminished its status as a manor house.

Although he was a popular man, he may not have been so well-liked by the women of Glasgow whom he described as 'coarse, cold and cunning' and unduly interested in the 'circumstances' (financial) of eligible men.

He, on the other hand, was remembered by locals as a dashing young sergeant-type, riding through the village on a striking grey charger.

The house was later rented to a wool manufacturer at a rate of £16, 13 shillings and fourpence per year, with a 'grassum' of £20 every two decades for the period of 'one million of twelve months after Whitsunday, 1753'.

The business didn't really take off, though, and the house saw a succession of tenants over the coming years, including a stint as a public house, before finally being condemned to meet the wrecking ball in 1932.

A house that was built on a small plot of land, named Little Hill, in Easter Camlachie across the burn, was destined for a longer life and a less drastic retirement.

The key figure in these parts was James Corbet. His main estate was at Tollcross, but he seems to have followed the advice of writer and philosopher Mark Twain: 'Buy land. They're not making any more.' Corbet was a wealthy landowner and it was he who owned the eastern twin of Camlachie from the turn of the eighteenth century.

Corbet leased the land to a Robert Dreghorn and granted him licence to mine for coal there. Dreghorn bought the land outright in 1731 and passed it on to his son, who wasted no time in selling Easter Camlachie to James Buchanan in 1750.

The parcel of land at Little Hill must have been quite a special little gem, as Corbet feud it out rather than selling it outright. Buying that part of Camlachie and Little Hill would have been a logical move for Corbet, as it was in such close proximity to his Tollcross manor.

It was eventually sold on to Robert McNair, who ran a grocery on King Street with his wife. They built up their property portfolio from humble beginnings. The story goes that Robert started out by selling a basket of over-ripe fruit – he surely had the gift of the gab, then, and may have been one of the first street traders, emulated in later years by market barkers whose oratory skills made them renowned hawkers of the Barras market many generations later. The McNairs were colourful characters who didn't always do business by the book, which got them into trouble more than once.

The most-talked-about episode was when Robert was called to account by the exciseman. In court, the judge (or Advocate) tried to sway the jury to find in favour of the court, going so far as to offer them a guinea per juror and a hot supper, at which point McNair, with the court's permission, stood to talk. He offered two guineas per head 'and as much wine as you can drink', if they would let him off.

Needless to say, the story goes, McNair got let off.

It was he who built an elegant house on Little Hill and named it 'Jeanfield' in honour of his loving wife.

Future owners of the property were printer John Mennons, who ran a weekly publication called *The Glasgow Advertiser*, which would eventually evolve into a daily newspaper, the *Glasgow Herald*, under George Outram & Co.

The land at Little Hill became known as Jeanfield after the house name.

For Camlachie, 1846 was a significant year: first, it was officially taken in as a district of Glasgow, as opposed to being a neighbouring village; then, in the same year, the Eastern Cemetery Joint Stock Company began laying out the Jeanfield land as a burial ground, reflecting the growing communities of the East End, there already being a fairly new gravesite in the nearby Gorbals.

A well-kent poet, satirist and polemicist, Bridgeton man Alexander Rodger, dubbed 'Radical Poet', is remembered in a monument at Jeanfield.

Born in 1784, in Midlothian, he was probably destined to work in agriculture and continue his father's farm, but times were tough and the farm was becoming a liability. When the Rodgers moved to Edinburgh, Rodger's mother was in poor health and his father was working long hours in his new role of innkeeper.

Rodger senior farmed the boy out to boarding school since he was very young. It may be argued that his father wasn't much good at anything really. He eventually gave up the pub as a bad job and repaired to Hamburg to seek work, dropping the kid off with relatives in the East End on the way.

Rodger was naturally creative. Before he was sent to Glasgow, he had served a year as apprentice to a silversmith.

In Glasgow, he was living in the hub of world-class weaving communities, so he took to the art like a natural.

He later married and lived in Bridgeton with his wife and augmented his income as a music tutor.

But it was his poetry and songwriting that prevailed throughout his life.

Like his father, Rodger's working life was sporadic and varied. He was inspector of textiles for printing and dyeing at the Barrowfield Printworks. Later, he ran a pawnshop for a friend.

In the East End, he was immersed in an area that is almost defined by its proletarian politics, protests, lobbying and strikes in the constant struggle for equality and justice.

It would be no surprise then that Rodger became involved in campaigns for political and social reform.

Having spent time working as a 'sub' at the seditious

weekly paper, *The Spirit of the Union*, he was in the sights of lawkeepers intent on stamping down rebel or revolutionary activism. He was arrested and imprisoned as a 'suspect citizen' for a short time, managing to avoid the fate of the paper's editor, who was seized and packed off to Australia.

Rodger maintained connections with the print media – he contributed to the *Glasgow Chronicle* and worked on *The Reformer's Gazette* as well – until he died. He also contributed to the anthology of contemporary verse, *Whistle-Binkie*.

His poems and songs were wickedly satirical and often ridiculed politicians or gentrified society and events.

But that didn't stop him being invited to perform his witty social commentary at very prestigious banquets.

He is described by some sources as a 'minor' poet. Yet, besides other grand events, he shared the spotlight with Lord George Byron at a sumptuous banquet in honour of King George IV, who visited Edinburgh in 1822. His popularity owed a lot to his cleverly humorous writings, which was probably why he could get away with some politically risky pennings. That, and his writing style and delivery being mostly in characterful vernacular Scots.

If you are unacquainted with Rodger's work, you may want to seek him out. Some of his work was simply warmly whimsical. Of note are the songs 'Robin Tamson's Smiddy' and 'Behave Yourself Before Folk'.

He was guest of honour at a banquet hosted by the Regius Professor of Astronomy at Glasgow University; he was in the company of some of the most influential and diversely political worthies. At the dinner, he was presented with a silver box filled with (presumably gold) sovereigns.

Now, I tell the story of the cemetery with the usual caveat that information differs widely depending on the source.

The Little Hill of Camlachie lay close to John Corbet's manor at Tollcross and has been claimed by nearly every district in the East End. It has been named Little Hill of Tollcross and Jeanfield of Camlachie; Parkhead historians have claimed it and, due to its immediate proximity to Celtic football club in Bridgeton, no doubt the good people of 'Brigton' know it as their own.

Also, Jeanfield cemetery and the house it was named after is often referred to as Janefield. Indeed, while there is a Janefield Street that runs along the front of the cemetery, there is no Jeanfield Street, other than in Perth. So something has got lost in translation somewhere along the way.

Indeed, even within some texts, both Janefield and Jeanfield are quoted!

Thankfully, the powers that be have solved the problem while not resolving the anomaly. The cemetery – one of four burial sites that are unattached to any religious institution – was renamed Glasgow Eastern Necropolis. So, there you have it.

The site had a section of the ground laid out for members of the Jewish community in around 1855 and Jeanfield is also the final resting place for men who died in the two World Wars.

Other citizens of note residing at Jeanfied include the activist Duncan Livingstone, and footballer and goalkeeper Alexander Cruickshanks, who died on the pitch in a tragic accident in the summer of 1932.

He had stepped onto the field as goalkeeper for

Strathclyde FC in a match against Rutherglen Glencairn at Barrowfield Park. When the whistle blew to herald the start of the game, the popular and respected footballer could never have imagined that he wouldn't live to hear the final whistle blow; that this would be his last match. During the game, he had a clash with an opposing player.

One month before the tragedy, the same necropolis that would lay Cruickshanks to rest was the subject of an overnight raid during which at least 50 gravestones were pulled out and overturned or smashed. Many huge and heavy monuments were dragged or carried away from the graves before being violated.

Grave-wrecking is not a modern act of extreme violation. In 1932, the incident so shocked the people of Glasgow that the aftershock drew throngs of onlookers, while the families of the defiled graves struggled to take in the news. The public, either curious or paying respects to the dead, hampered police investigations, tramping over forensic material and contaminating potential evidence that might have helped catch the mindless marauders.

Investigators despaired at the destruction of footprints. They ruled out that it may have been an act of mischief by wild youths or gangs by dint of the sheer brute strength that would have been employed to pull out, carry and smash the hard stone and granite slabs, as well as the kinds of weapons that would be needed to break through the giant stones.

Does my Butt . . . ?

Now then, the Battle of the Butts doesn't refer to the rivalry between fans of the singers Beyonce, Mariah and J.Lo – although that would be some shoot-out.

I've already mentioned the battle that went on between the Earls of Arran and Lennox on Glasgow Muir in 1544. It is remembered as the Battle of the Butts. The name of the small hill has, as with most ancient places, gone through a handful of name changes or corruptions.

Enter John Walkinshaw of Camlachie again – he had several landholdings that he eventually lost after his imprisonment in Stirling for favouring the Jacobite agenda.

Glasgow Muir became Gallowmuir, Blackfaulds, Borrowfield and Barrowfield. This parcel of land had undergone various incarnations since the war years of the sixteenth century and would eventually evolve into what we now know as Bridgeton.

In one incarnation, the area was used for military training and as a barracks. Historically, when an army marched on the town, they were billeted at local homes, but residents were not always too keen to put the army up.

In calmer times, Blackfaulds served local burgesses as a cattle-grazing common.

By the turn of the eighteenth century, John Walkinshaw had acquired Blackfaulds, which he added to his growing land portfolio, bringing it in as part of his Barrowfield estate.

It is believed he built his Barrowfield mansion on the ruined grounds of a previous manor house. There's a chance that the original house dated back to medieval times after a sundial was found on the grounds inscribed with the digits '1311', which popular theory claims was the year that the first ancient manor house or castle was erected.

When his land was forfeited for being on the wrong side of the Jacobite uprisings, his wife, 'Lady Barrowfield', was allowed to continue in residence and to benefit from the profits of coalmining on the estate – despite the legendary clothes-swapping ruse that is said to have been her husband's get-out-of-gaol-free card.

In 1705, before the first uprising, he began to feu out land with a view to developing a small village community, but the uptake of feus was a trickle rather than a flood.

The estate was eventually bought in 1734 by businessman John Orr, who fared better than Walkinshaw in developing the land. He had already bought the Camlachie estates from the Magistrates of Glasgow and later acquired the estate of Stobcross.

He had studied Divinity at the University of Glasgow, returning in later years to serve as Rector. He bequeathed the princely sum of £500 to be used to stock the university's library.

Barrowfield House was demolished in 1844 to accommodate the expansion of the district of Bridgeton, which got its name from an old three-arch bridge completed in 1896 to replace an older five-arch bridge, known sometimes as Rutherglen Bridge or Shawfield Bridge.

Bridges are great! They connect places and people. They quite literally bridge communities. New York's population grew as each new bridge connecting its islands to its heart was constructed. Business exploded on hitherto islands of

Manhattan, Brooklyn and Queens. In Glasgow, the erection of bridges over land or river had a similar effect. Tentacles reaching out to offer mutual opportunities. With the new bridge came the new name of Bridgeton.

Thence, Blackfaulds for all intents and purposes became the village of Calton, cradled by Bridgeton, with thousands of cottage industries, not least the weavers and potters of the village.

The famed covered meeting place, a bandstand known as the Bridgeton Umbrella, built in 1875, was recently restored to its former glory and is a little gem of architecture, hosting small events and mini-markets where modern-day artisans can ply their wares, just as in bygone years; the new state-of-the-art Bridgeton Olympian library and theatre is a significant jewel in Bridgeton's crown.

While it was created as an exemplar of modernity, the library was part of a major upgrading programme that included the top-to-toe refurbishment of what had been the Olympia Theatre of Varieties. Predictably situated on the corner of a street named for John Orr, it was state of the art in its day, with an impressive two-tier gallery and an auditorium designed to reflect the opulent French Renaissance period. The theatre's marble balustrades and elaborate plasterwork added to the sense of occasion, of theatre and drama.

What's more, it had a sliding roof that blew away the acrid pipe and cigar smoke of its patrons and breathed fresh air into the place – an early form of air conditioning. This was heady stuff in 1911, when the building was opened. It caused quite a stir, attracting throngs from the opening night onwards. It was a far cry from other local theatres, music halls, dance halls, cinemas and fleapits.

The current library – which is a showcase of contemporary research and social events – is a treasure trove for visitors, with books, films and other media preserving the magnificent building's place in history.

Just across the road from this building is the abandoned premises of what used to be my place of work. Both myself and James Doherty (who wrote the foreword) worked as journalists on the now defunct East End *Independent* newspaper. Together with journalist Tracey Miller – who has since crossed over to the dark side of the PR sector – and our fabulous multi-award-winning editor Eileen MacAuley – who scooped the scandal of blatant sectarian discrimination in the Monklands Council – we raked in awards and award nominations in news, features and newspaper design.

Yet, it was when I was researching the local area for a Millennium Special edition that I discovered the newspaper premises had originally been the constituency office of the celebrated Independent Labour Party leader, the great Jimmy Maxton, whose biography was written by politician Gordon Brown while at university. Brown rose to walk the hallowed halls of Westminster as MP for Dunfermline East, later appointed Chancellor of the Exchequer under Prime Minister Tony Blair following the 1997 General Election. Eventually, he took over from Blair as Labour leader and Prime Minister.

James (Jimmy) Maxton

Hailed as one of the most charismatic and politically astute men in British politics, Maxton's skills as a persuasive and inspiring orator were equalled only by his sense of right; social justice, a fair pay for a day's work; equality; decent affordable housing and access to healthcare were among the social issues that got him so fired up as an undergraduate at Glasgow University.

His compassion and sincerity were a seductive draw to like-minded socialist 'radicals'.

Born in Barrhead in Glasgow in 1885, his parents were teachers and encouraged curiosity, open-mindedness and social equality in their children. It was as a teacher of evening classes at Pollock Academy that Maxton met and bonded with Red MacLean. If one was the spark, the other was the blue touch paper.

Maxton would later describe MacLean as his greatest political influence.

Maxton's career choice as a teacher led him towards like-minded people who stoked the spitting fire of political righteousness. It also served as a fount of understanding of the plight of the poverty-stricken slum dwellers. He could see which children were turning up barefoot or which were wearing hand-me-down shoes to school but playing barefoot in the streets to keep their only pair 'good'. Others only wore shoes to mass on Sundays.

He recognized the symptoms of social poverty: scurvy, rickets, tuberculosis.

His heart went out to these children, many of whom

displayed the 'bandy legs' or 'bow legs' caused by a severe lack of essential nutrients. Malnutrition was the blight of the poor in the East End. Rickets was caused by a deficiency of vitamin D, calcium and other nutrients relating to malnutrition.

Maxton taught skinny boys and girls whose little legs just weren't strong enough to carry their slight bodies. He met and related to families who had to decide who could get the tram to school and who had to walk.

Most walked – with a jeely piece (jam sandwich) to sustain them until home time.

Maxton got more and more involved with socialist politics.

Born into a conservative middle class and, at university, a member of the Unionist (Conservative) Association, it is testament to his parents' influence that he soon lost interest in the Unionist agenda.

Maxton was an influencer and chose to use this power to further the cause of the common man, woman and child rather than to fill the coffers of a fat cat bourgeoisie.

Despite being athletic during his student days – a respectable half-miler and member of the university 1st Lanarkshire rifle volunteers – he was beset with illness from a young age. That didn't stop him speaking out on the Glasgow Green 'soap box' and at other gatherings, sometimes three a day.

It was his 'seditious' views against parliament and his vocal opposition in both World Wars that got him noticed outside of Glasgow.

He was a vociferous conscientious objector and refused to accept even a place on the army medical corps in the First World War. He, along with other Red Clydesiders, was also involved in the mini-victory of reducing the working week to open up more jobs, especially for those returning from the war in 1918. Maxton spent time in Calton jail in Edinburgh, and Duke Street Prison for his views. David Kirkwood was among a number of the Clydeside heroes who were deported for their politics – only to Edinburgh, right enough – which merely served as another platform for the furthering of the cause and recruitment of new members.

Times were a-changing and the rich and powerful were beginning to feel the gravy train carpet tugging at their well-oiled heels.

But what can you do when the powers that be in London are holding the purse strings and pulling the puppet strings?

Answer: *Steam in wi' the heid doon!*

You have to be in the game to win it.

Maxton, who by 1904 was a committed Independent Labour Party member, became a driving force in the organization, eventually taking the chair of the party in Scotland.

He stood for Parliament in 1918 as a Labour candidate without success. At the general election of 1922, Maxton, who won his seat for Bridgeton, and his elected *comrades* boarded the train at Glasgow Central Station bound for Westiminster.

They were hoisted high on the shoulders of a sea of bunneted followers drunk with optimism for a brighter and fairer future. A bit like crowd-surfing at a gig but without the bouncers.

Maxton wasn't shy of dispensing some Glaswegian punch during debates in Parliament and fellow party members were getting chary about some of the quite militant rhetoric ejaculating into the room during debates. Not only was this upsetting the fruitful applecart; it was quite literally spoiling their party.

They were 'nice' Labour and the Reds were, well, a bit too brightly hued.

There quickly developed a widening divide between Right and Left Labour.

It wasn't helped when Maxton called Tory MP Sir Frederick Banbury a 'murdurur' after backing a governmental decision to withdraw free milk for school pupils. For that, he had his parliamentary privileges forfeited for a short time.

And there was no love lost between him and Ramsay MacDonald. They crossed swords many times in the House.

As MacDonald's mental and physical health declined, his already rambling speeches became almost incoherent. He finally agreed to step down as Prime Minister, conceding to Stanley Baldwin, in June 1935. His swansong speech dragged on so much and was so unintelligible that Maxton blurted out, 'Siddown, man, you're a bloody tragedy.'

Maxton was held in such high esteem and with such affection that the standing joke among his constituents was that he brought in so many votes at elections that they had to be weighed rather than counted.

He continued to represent his constituency until his death in 1946.

Race Riots

Newspapers reported incidents of a crowd of black and Asian sailors running for their lives, being chased down by frenzied dockers at the Broomielaw in January 1919. Shots were fired, windows smashed, people were stabbed.

This dreadful and sullied battle came within a week of the so-called 'race riots' that took place in seaports across the UK against black, Asian and Chinese sailors, dockworkers and seafarers.

Blood was spilled at the docks in what turned into a violent attack on foreign seamen and dockers working as scab labour, undercutting union agreed rates of pay and usurping jobs from their white British custodians.

It was one of the most horrific incidences of workers battling workers.

The press were having a field day, reporting all kinds of atrocities. A far cry from today's politically correct editing, newspapers often used terms such as 'coolies' to describe Asians who were persecuted.

In historic texts the Glasgow race riots are often overshadowed by the more noble Battle of George Square later that same month. That is until a controversial book by Dr Jacqueline Jenkinson was published in 2009.

Attempting to lift the thick bloody mantle of racism on the docks, Jenkinson describes what transpired during that battle. Some people, understandably, would rather that the details of that day were erased from the records; her no-holds-barred account of the Glasgow sailors' and firemen's actions shocked the nation.

Jenkinson, in many people's eyes, tarnished the memory of the Red Clydesiders, whom she wrote about with regard to apparent rabble-rousing rhetoric used to inflame good men to carry out gangland-style running battles down James Watt Street.

Her accusations catapulted the family of the celebrated Manny Shinwell into a fervent and furious denial of assertions made about their beloved father – who soon after the race riots had faced down a hostile army tank in George Square.

Calton

By 1817, the area of Calton had acquired burgh status, which is a testament of respect to the small industries therein; it is often quoted as the very first centre of industry in Glasgow.

Calton's motto is 'By industry we prosper'.

It having been adopted as a burgh, with its own bridewell (small gaol), burgh council and post office, demonstrates that this community was held in respect by the powers that be.

Pretty much every craft guild bore a mantle of secrecy surrounding the tricks of their trade and the Calton weavers were no different. Each new member of the guild would swear an oath that promised: 'I will eat my shuttle ere I reveal the secrets of the craft.' Mind you, not very practical if you want to pass trade secrets down the ancestral lineage. The shuttle was a part of the weaver's armoury, as much as the knight his sword, a sliding thread-holder for passing the yarns of the weft under the threads of the warp.

Indeed, the weavers would later release their arsenal of bricks, stones, bottles and whatever else they could find to ward off the troops who were called in to storm a throng of hundreds of the disgruntled craftsmen. The story of the strikers, mentioned earlier in the book, is often referred to as the Calton Weavers' Massacre. The six weavers who died in the bloody battle – three were shot and died instantly, and another three died of their wounds – became known as the Calton Martyrs. A memorial garden commemorates the bravery of the weavers, who some say were the first modern trade-union activists.

The weavers' legacy is manifest in the Templeton Building on Glasgow Green, which housed the famous carpet factory.

Templeton's

As well as spinning and weaving fine silk shawls and garments, the artisans of Calton became a worldwide phenomenon when they made a revolutionary advance in curtain and carpet weaving which drew the attentions of the rich and famous.

The First Lady of the US, Mrs Abraham Lincoln, was so enamoured of the fine, soft chenille that she commissioned a Templeton carpet for the presidential house.

A Templeton chenille carpet was also commissioned for the christening of the royal infant who would be named Edward VII.

Merchant draper James Templeton moved from weaving silk shawls in his factory in Paisley to set up what would become one of the world's most renowned carpet makers of its time. At the peak of its popularity, it was declared the world's largest carpet manufacturer. But it was an encounter with an Irish artisan weaver, William Quigley, that inspired Templeton to create the bespoke picture carpets that were soon sought after as status symbols by the high and mighty.

Quigley and Templeton pushed the boundaries in experimenting with new techniques and styles. Chenille was already being used for producing exquisite fine curtains, panels and elaborate pelmets and other soft furnishings. Ever open to new ideas, Quigley discovered that steaming and pressing the chenille could transform the fabric into a fine, silky-smooth weave.

The fine fabric was not suitable as carpeting on its own, but binding it with a strong, durable backing made it perfect for flooring. The savvy pair knew they had something special and, to protect their latest production process, they secured the new technique with a patent in 1839.

The Calton-based business took off exponentially, with orders rolling in from around the globe. By 1959, the business was so successful it sprawled out in all directions, with factories taking over premises on Crownpoint Road, Kerr Street, Brookside Street and Fordneuk Street. Calton was expanding, too, and would soon be engulfed by the industry and development of Bridgeton. Nevertheless, the small community retained its former name within the boundaries of Bridgeton. At its height, Templeton's empire made him a potent and influential figure. Chenille Axminster was the first word in floor-dressing.

Yet, the company's success was tainted by two disastrous events.

It was Christmas Day at the workhouse in 1856. Templeton had installed the must-have gas lighting that was introduced in Bridgeton around the 1840s, but the factory and its weavers would become a casualty of progress that fateful day.

One of the weavers was using his gas burner when tragedy struck. A fire in a fabric factory could only go one way, and the whole building was completely destroyed.

Templeton went on to buy McPhail's cotton mill on William Street, which, predictably, was renamed Templeton Street.

In November 1889, tragedy struck in spades. During the construction of a new build, which became an architectural and design icon, fashioned on the style of the Doge's Palace in Venice, its elaborate facade came crashing down, taking the lives of 29 women weavers working in sheds (workshops) very close by.

A carved stone at Templeton Gate commemorates those who died and also tells the story of the fire in 1856. The stone was erected as late as 2005, when a period of repair and reconstruction allowed planners to take advantage of the opportunity to embed a memorial within the construction.

Following the disaster, the building was reconstructed. Its facade, which can be seen in all its glory from Glasgow Green and the People's Palace, stands proud – almost regal – as a tribute to the craftsmanship of construction and masonry expertise so prevalent in the East End's golden years.

The garish red and white brickwork and elaborate design of the showy facade wall, fronting a utilitarian factory behind it, was an architectural example of the saying: 'Aye, she's aw fur coat an' nae knickers.'

Templeton was not as ostentatious as some successful businessmen. Behind the fancy wall is a plain and functional factory, with no special character, which residents in the vicinity objected to.

The Doge's Palace feature wall would have been the product of a lengthy and strongly contested compromise agreement after lobbying from disgruntled residents worried about a huge carpet factory on their doorstep, spoiling their outlook.

Business was so good that Templeton's first foreman, John Lyle, took a chance on himself and started his own factory. His company flourished and these two firms commanded the higher ground of the industry sector for generations.

Jobs for the boys . . . and land . . . and titles . . .

It became crystal clear very early in my research that the Glasgow gentry had pretty much everything sewn up, from property to business to banking to politics . . . it just went on and on.

While bishops of old bestowed land gifts and titles on people – and, remember, the title of bishop brought its own rich gains – they could still appoint members of the elite to powerful positions such as Provost, another important and influential post.

From the mid-1600s, Merchants House was acquiring land right, left and centre, and selling it on to its gentrified friends and family. If grand estates weren't sold on, they were inherited by their offspring, who sold them on to their mates.

The deeds of title of any random estate read like a baronial fat-cat version of the modern game of Twister. Lists of heirs to these mini-empires read like the 'begating' chapter in the Bible (Genesis, Chapter V onwards): this man married that woman who was cousin to the next owner, over and over.

Many documents listing property owners over generations reveal a game of musical chairs, with all the same families, their names the same, differing only in their position on the list and their chronology.

I can't help thinking of analogies – which, of course, are never a good fit – but, if the estates of the *'plainstane'* walkers of the tobacco generation were a box of chocolates, they would indeed be Quality Street chocolates.

But the texts that got my socialist gland throbbing were those that used wording such as: 'Walkinshaw sold Bridgeton to his son-in-law.'

Whether in good times or hard, the Glasgow gentry, for the most part, looked after one another and left the poor to look after themselves.

I say 'for the most part' because that's not entirely true; many of the East End aristocracy contributed to charities, bequeathed money or property to charitable associations, and forked out for the building of institutions, almshouses, hospitals and schools for the poor.

The thing is, they were a mere drop in the ocean for the poor families who didn't have the choice to move to a cleaner, healthier part of the city.

As smaller businesses expanded or outgrew their premises, bigger, noisier and smellier operations stamped their immense corporate footprint on the East End: the truly beautiful districts that so enamoured Daniel Defoe were stamped out like a butterfly under a mine worker's dirty boot.

Dalmarnock

As Bridgeton grew in industry, it began to encroach on the picturesque village of Dalmarnock. It became a popular area for industrial expansion, not least for the proximity to water that it and other districts enjoyed. Industrialists moved in on the pretty district, leaving the place gasping for breath – like many other districts in the East End – under the mantle of one enormous dirty hanky.

The dominant dynasties in Dalmarnock in the 1700s were the Grays and the Waddrops.

Dalmarnock House, variously called Springbank and Springfield, was a lovely detached manor house on Springfield Road.

While the '*big hoose*' in all these communities was the landowner's symbol of success and of dynasty, it often took a third generation heir to finally build this jewel in the family crown – that is, unless the last heir in the family line had liquidized the assets soon after inheriting the estate.

The Grays of Carntyne were heavily into coalmining, mainly in that part of the city. They, of course, had accumulated an extensive landholding portfolio before purchasing Dalmarnock.

They had held the Dalmarnock land over generations and the last in the line, John Gray, inherited the estate from his brother, James, in 1778. It was a big piece of real estate – maybe not as big as some, but stretching to around 160 acres.

The last Gray of Dalmarnock held onto his inheritance for six years before selling the lot to his son-in-law, Thomas Buchanan of Ardoch.

It was Buchanan who finally furnished the land with a detached mansion for posterity.

It went from a coalmining family to a money magnate and later sales were kept within the providence of members of the banking fraternity.

John Buchanan and his son, also John, were associated with the prestigious Ship Bank.

John senior was also, at various times, a Lieutenant of Dunbartonshire and Parliamentary MP, Justice of the Peace and school governor, but he is best remembered within the family as the man who raped and pillaged their Dalmarnock estate. Against all wishes and warnings, he stormed ahead, quarrying the estate's natural resources of stone and slate.

Perhaps when it became no longer practical to quarry the land, he decided to maximize its selling potential.

He embellished Dalmarnock House, commissioning a new front facade and expanding it on both sides, so now it had an east and west wing, and looked ever more impressive. It certainly bumped up the value of the property and made it more attractive to purchase as a large family estate.

The refurbishment was grand and, on its completion, the house went up for sale.

Who did he sell it to? He sold the whole estate to a banking associate, Archibald Grahame, of the upper-class Thistle Bank.

Grahame also owned the Barrowfield estate, that of the

ill-fated Jacobite sympathizer Walkinshaw. Grahame went on a spending spree, buying other estates in the area.

It didn't take long for Bridgeton to encroach further into the Dalmarnock estate.

And soon that pretty landscape became a centre of industry.

While the demise of greenbelt is to be mourned, we have to remember that all these heavy industries incubated geniuses of engineering that put Glasgow on the world map.

Cottons and Dyeing

Glasgow was famed for its cottons and dyeing processes, and it was in Dalmarnock that Pierre Jacques Papillon first introduced to Scotland the secret process used in the making of the first colourfast fabrics in 1785.

Turkey Red dye was revolutionary, complicated and expensive – and the world couldn't get enough of it. It originated from the Middle East and reached Scotland through trade routes to Europe.

Papillon was living in Glasgow and chose Dalmarnock as his headquarters. In those times, 'Turkey' was a catch-all term used to describe the Middle East in general, not that specific country. And Turkey Red was not simply a dye: it described the whole very complex dyeing process.

This process was big news because it promised bright orange-red colours that could be bonded to cotton and retain their fastness of colour. Before this innovation, colours would fade and bleed over time and frequent washing.

Papillon worked with George Charles Macintosh, who had introduced waterproof fabrics in around 1823.

Sir William Arrol

On Dunn Street, Sir William Arrol founded his engineering empire in 1872. Dalmarnock Iron Works' expertise in structural engineering is seen in some of the world's most iconic bridges, including London's Tower Bridge and the Forth Road and Forth Rail bridges in Scotland.

The Caledonian Rail Bridge across the Clyde was completed in 1878 and the firm's successes continued for generations, as recently as 1966 and the building of the Severn Bridge, then in 1981, the Humber Bridge.

The company finally closed its doors in 1986.

Its contribution to Clyde shipbuilding is commemorated in the giant cranes that were commissioned for three of the main shipbuilders. A tourist draw in themselves, they were some of the largest cranes built at that time.

The cranes have made it possible to immediately identify the Clyde skyscape since the 1920s.

Despite Dalmarnock earning the nickname 'Glasgow's chimney pot' as a result of the black smoke drifting up from its factories, we all have a lot to thank these pioneers for. Scottish inventors were the most prolific innovators, I'd say, of any country in the world, per capita, per annum.

Latter-day Dalmarnock worthies include the indie rock band Glasvegas, Celtic and Liverpool football hero Kenny Dalglish and jazz trombonist George Chisholm.

Rivals in Paradise

The year 1888 is marked by a series of important firsts. The Independent Labour Party was formed, leading to Scotland's first Labour MPs in Westminster. Glasgow held an International Exhibition, attended by Queen Victoria. Celtic Football Club was created. And Renton Football Club won the Scottish Cup – and claimed the accolade of winners of the football World Cup by presumption, having gone on to beat West Bromwich Albion, the English Cup winners.

When Neil McCallum donned the green-and-white tunic and stepped onto Celtic Park for the club's first-ever game, he would surely have known that he, along with his teammates, was making history. And it must have been on his mind that he might very well score the first goal of the game.

Then again, perhaps not.

Football was in its infancy. And Celtic were not the multi-million-pound global brand that they became. The club has blossomed from very humble beginnings.

Humble, but ambitious none the less.

The East End football club was the brainchild of a Marist Brother, Walfrid – birthname Andrew Kerins.

In the early 1800s, there was little love shown to the Irish immigrants by the poor and unemployed East Enders. The Glaswegians resented Irish families vying for housing and undercutting the Scots for a day's labour.

Brother Walfrid's aim was to bring the two communities together, to forge common bonds through the shared Celtic roots of Scots and Irish, both Gaelic brethren.

He also wanted to do something to alleviate the poverty that so defined the East End of the city.

His choice of club name was not a fanciful one. It was designed to recognize the Gaelic or Celtic roots of both communities. Although it's not clear why the people have chosen to pronounce it 'Seltic'.

Walfrid also had ambitions to use funds raised at the turnstile towards helping the poorest in the area. He set up the charity the Poor Children's Dinner Table to at least put food in the bellies of poor children.

The first proper game was a 'friendly' against Rangers on 28 May 1888. Celtic won 5–2. And so began a rivalry that has continued over generations.

Interestingly, many of the first team were poached from Hibernian, an Edinburgh club which was mainly made up of Irish immigrants who were seduced by cash incentives by sponsor John Glass, but the signing of James Kelly, who had played for the 'World Cup Winners' Renton, was a very shrewd move. He captained the cup-winning team to their Scottish League Cup victories in 1893, 1894 and 1896.

Kelly's prowess and popularity with the team and its fans was summed up in a four-word slogan: 'No Kelly, No Keltic!' coined by teammate and later manager Willie Maley.

Maley was appointed as the club's first manager when he retired as a player in 1897, the year the club went commercial, becoming a limited company.

Celtic's first strip was a simple white shirt with green collar, black shorts and green socks. Vertical stripes of green and white on the team shirt were designed in the following year. It was in 1903 that the now familiar green and white horizontal 'hoops' became the trademark strip.

Celtic's original ground was near Janefield Street cemetery, and it is this that is said to have inspired the nickname 'Paradise'.

When the site owners hiked up the annual rent for the grounds by a hefty £50 to £450 per annum, Celtic's management started looking for a new home. They found it not far away on the site of an abandoned brickworks and moved there in 1892.

Celtic's early years were the club's first golden era; they saw the team winning the Scottish League Championship in six consecutive years from 1905 to 1910. During this halcyon time, Celtic were the first club to win the coveted 'double', winning the Scottish League Championship and the Scottish Cup in 1907 and, again, in 1908.

To any Celtic fans, the names of Alec McNair, Jimmy Quinn, 'Sunny' Jim Young, Alec Bennett, Jimmy McMenemy and goalie Davie Adams are said with pride; Celtic could almost do no wrong.

And they certainly lifted the spirit of fans during the war years, between 1915 and 1918, winning the Scottish Cup in four consecutive years and clocking up a whopping record run of 62 games unbeaten.

Despite this success, the club suffered, with low takings at games and the loss of players to trench warfare.

Peter Johnstone signed up with the 6th Battalion of the Seaforth Highlanders, who were under orders to take and hold a chemical factory during the Battle of Arras. Johnstone was one of forty-three who died during that battle. He was one of Maley's Darlings, who won the league in six consecutive years. He is named as one of the fallen soldiers on the war memorial in Arras.

Patrick Slaven lost his life fighting with the Royal Scots to take the village of Serre.

The 1st and 7th Argyll and Sutherland Highlanders were under orders to take the village of Fontaine Notre Dame. Despite coming under heavy fire from the enemy, they achieved their goal, but there were many casualties, with 128 soldiers wounded. Archie McMillan, who had debuted for Celtic against Rangers in 1913, was among the nine who died that day.

Former full-back Donnie McLeod had notched up 155 games for Celtic before leaving the club in 1908. He was a gunner with the Royal Field Artillery. He fought in Belgium and died during fighting at Passchendaele.

Another full-back, Robert Craig, was with Celtic for three seasons, leaving in 1909. He died defending the town of Messen.

Not enough is known about how these men died, but it is clear that they were very much at the business end of close-up warfare and they will be remembered on both sides of the Channel for the role they played during the First World War.

One former player who donned the green-and-white jersey only once for Celtic returned from the war a hero.

William Angus was born in Armadale exactly three months before the inaugural match on 28 February 1888. While his natural route to work, leaving school aged 14, was to go down the mines, Angus showed he had football talent and managed to attract the attention of Celtic scouts. While he only played one game for the club in the first team, it was enough to win him a place with Wishaw Thistle in 1914. His people skills also shone and he was made team captain before long.

His football career was cut short with the start of the First World War, when, as a member of the local Territorials of the Highland Light Infantry, he was sent off to the Front almost immediately.

His battalion was incorporated into the 8th Royal Scots, where he served as lance corporal.

In the trenches near Givenchy-lès-la-Bassée, the Royal Scots were coming under heavy fire. Amid a barrage of bombing and shellfire, Angus spotted the body of an officer lying wounded just yards from the enemy line.

Without a second thought, Angus was up and out of his trench, running towards the slumped body of the officer. The air was thick with gun smoke; grenades had blown craters and scattered mud on the ground. Bullets rained down on him, as both sides exchanged fire, but Angus carried on running right through the line of fire.

He could probably have made out the faces of enemy soldiers with rifles aimed straight at him as he lifted the officer's body and made his way back to his trench.

He was seriously wounded and taken to a military hospital, where he was told he had sustained forty wounds in all during that one encounter.

For his gallantry, he received the Victoria Cross, the highest military award for valour in the face of the enemy, receiving the award on his return to Britain, when he was invited to Buckingham Palace to receive his medal from King George V.

He returned to Scotland to a hero's welcome.

In peacetime, the football club lost one of its own in a tragic incident on the pitch at Ibrox Stadium, home of Celtic's greatest rivals, Rangers FC.

The talented prospect John Thomson was signed at the age of 17. He played his first match in goals against Dundee and the world was introduced to a new rising star of the beautiful game. Thomson helped his team to victory in the 1927 Scottish Cup final, beating East Fife 3–1, and again in 1931 against Motherwell with a respectable 3–1 scoreline.

The fans loved him, the press raved about him, and rival teams knew they had to bring their 'A' game to every match he played in goal.

He didn't have the typical physique of a top goalie, being short and skinny with small hands, but that didn't stop him from helping to bring home the silverware, as they say. Neither did it deter the then Celtic chair Desmond White from hailing the diminutive sportsman the best 'keeper he had ever seen.

The tragedy began shortly into the second half. He and a Rangers striker went for the ball. Seconds later, Thomson was on the ground. His head had collided violently with the striker's knee, which proved to be a fatal clash.

Thomson's skull was fractured and the blow had ruptured an artery in the goalkeeper's temple. The injury was beyond the scope of St Andrew's Ambulance medics, who did their best for the boy. He succumbed to his injury and was pronounced dead at 9.25 p.m., 5 September 1931.

Rangers striker Sam English would have anticipated a glittering career with Rangers. He had already been capped twice for his home country, Ireland. He helped his team cruise to a 3–0 win over Kilmarnock in the 1932 Scottish Cup and played an exemplary role towards Rangers winning the Scottish League Championship.

In his short time with the Ibrox club, he had scored a record-setting 44 goals for the team, securing his place in the Rangers Hall of Fame in 2009. In the same year, silversmith Cara Murphy was commissioned to create a silver bowl filled with 44 silver balls in recognition of his prolific goalscoring prowess during his first season at the club.

It is a fitting tribute to a talented player, and a tragedy that he is too often remembered only as the player involved in the collision that cut short a promising career and ended with the death of John Thomson.

Tracking success

Some of the country's best known sportsmen and women hail from the East End, not least in athletics, and many of our track-and-field stars would have worn with pride the distinctive blue-and-gold vest of the Shettleston Harriers.

For more than a century, the Shettleston club has dominated the record books in track and field, with great names such as Allan Scally, Nat Muir, Graham Everett (primed to become Scotland's first four-minute-miler), David Morrison, Norman Morrison and Al Blamire.

Possibly the club's most famous son has to be Olympic runner and Commonwealth champion Lachie Stewart.

Having taken up the sport 'because I got fed up going to the pictures', Stewart's achievements have earned him star billing in the world's sporting chronicles, but more importantly to him, in the hearts of the people. His fans have charted his success with pride.

The quiet, unimposing character has inspired countless athletes to go for gold in the world arena, including his own son Glen, who clocked up numerous championship successes himself.

Described in the Scottish Amateur Athletes Association centenary publication as 'one of the most successful Scottish distance runners since the War', Stewart chalked up no fewer than 16 SAAA titles between 1966 and 1973 at different distances, including twice winning the Scottish Cross Country Championship.

His versatility at distances ranging from 5,000 metres to 10-mile runs on various running surfaces was legendary.

One of his most memorable runs has to be during the ninth Commonwealth Games, held in Edinburgh, against a big-name line-up that included world record holder Ron Clarke, defending champion Naftali Tenu, UK record holder Dick Taylor, Canadian Jerome Drayton, Australian steeplechase superstar Kerry O'Brien and many more.

To a crowd whose excitement reached nothing short of fever pitch, Stewart's tactics on the back straight paid off, as he bided his time behind leaders Clarke, Taylor and O'Brien.

Confident of a storming sprint finish, Stewart ripped past the leader to take the tape to the delight of the home crowd. His finishing time of 28 minutes and 11.8 seconds shattered the Games record and the Scottish all-comers, national and native records.

Recalling one of his favourite moments, Stewart told me: 'I ran in the AAA championships in the Shettleston vest and took the silver for the club.'

It was a significant gesture, the message having not been lost on the event organizers and the selection committee of Team Scotland.

Only two weeks earlier, Stewart had put in a stormer, running the 5,000 metres at the Scottish Championships.

He had applied to run at the newly opened flagship stadium Crystal Palace at the three As in London in the 10,000 metres – his favourite and most successful distance – but the organizers made the controversial decision not to select him for the Scottish team on what was believed by many to have been a flimsy pretext.

'I decided to run on my own account for the club anyway,' Stewart recalled, 'and I travelled down on my own steam and stayed in the same hotel as the rest of the boys. They were all really supportive and, when it came to handing out the Scottish team colours, the team manager went to hand me a Scotland vest.'

But the Shettleston club's favourite sporting son shunned the offer and chose to run in the blue and gold of the East End club. He put in a stellar performance, coming a close second to David Bedford's record-breaking performance on the day.

Ironically, the same race was an Olympic selection race and Stewart qualified for the Olympic team on his finishing time.

Had he bowed down to non-selection and stayed at home, he would have lost out on his bid for Olympic gold.

'Knowing your opponents is the key to beating them,' said Stewart. 'It sounds obvious, but it's often not given true priority. I always studied the strengths and weaknesses of other runners. I learned how they liked to run, how they built up to a finish. Then, the trick is to not let them run the way they want.'

Sound wisdom that was to play a major role in the much-heralded mile race in Vancouver in 1954 at the Empire Games.

Both John Landy and Roger Bannister had crushed the four-minute mile earlier in the year. This would be the first time since running a sub-four-minute mile that Roger Bannister would meet fellow sub-four runner John Landy.

Both men knew that neither would let the other run their own race. Bannister was a kicker with a killer finish. Landy preferred to run fast and even, and stay out front. Having qualified in different heats, this was their first encounter of the Games.

Landy knew he couldn't win in a sprint. He had to pull Bannister out of his game zone by forcing him to tackle the race at high speed from the start and, hopefully, tire him out, robbing Bannister of his finishing kick.

Bannister knew if Landy's game plan played out, Landy would win the tactical race.

And Bannister was racing more than one man. The two New Zealand runners, Halberg and Baillie, were on Team Landy, keeping pace with him as long as they could.

When Landy upped the ante to take the lead, Bannister

had been holding back, but had to move up to second place, or risk losing sight of Landy, who was working up a 12-yard lead. Bannister could see himself losing to the Australian. It took everything Bannister had to focus on keeping up pace with his rival.

He later said he had tried to imagine himself attached to Landy by some invisible cord. It seemed he had no more self-talk in his arsenal to gee himself on. Instead, he said later in an interview: 'As we entered the last bend, I tried to convince myself that [Landy] was tiring.'

Closing in on the final straight, Landy allowed himself to believe Bannister was broken.

It was an infinitesimal gesture, the tiniest twitch that told Bannister this was his race to win.

Landy looked over his left shoulder, just as Bannister threw himself past on the right.

In that split second, Bannister wrote in the book *First Four Minutes*: 'I flung myself past Landy. As I did so, I saw him glance inwards over his opposite shoulder. This tiny act of his held great significance and gave me confidence.'

Both men had put everything they had into those few minutes, Bannister collapsing as he crossed the line in three minutes and 58.9 seconds. Landy was four fifths of a second behind him.

The melee that followed was almost comical. So many officials, journalists and press photographers swarmed onto the track, congratulating both men on their epic race, that other runners had to fight through the crowd to finish their race. Kiwi runner Murray Halberg, who had to shove his way through to a fifth-place finish, described the scene as 'a seething clutter of mixed-up officialdom'.

It must have been one of the most exciting encounters in athletic history to date – but what on earth has that got to do with the history of Glasgow's East End? Yep, ah hear ya.

With all the excitement concentrating on the Mile, it seemed almost all the officials had left their posts at the marathon, which was going on at the same time.

These Games were famous and infamous in equal measure.

The Miracle Milers were the draw of the Games, for sure, but the lack of officials on the marathon course – presumably because they had left their posts so that they could say they were there during the clash of the sub-four Titans – would surely have had an adverse effect on the long-distance runners.

There was a barrage of complaints from marathon runners, from the length of the course and the timing of the race (at a blistering high noon) to a lack of officials. The prevailing description was 'a shambles'.

The hot favourite to win the race, Londoner Jim Peters, claimed he was robbed of first place, which went to Shettleston Harrier hero Joe McGhee.

McGhee, who rarely spoke to the press, reportedly said after the race that he was unaware of what was going on in the stadium and was delighted to know he was going to finish second. What transpired was a shock to everyone involved in the controversial race.

Jim Peters' star had most definitely been in its ascendancy at the Vancouver Games. The 1950s were his golden years, during which decade he repeatedly broke world records: he broke the world record for the marathon four times.

And when he became the first man in the world to crack the 2 hours and 20 minutes barrier for marathon runners, his feat was likened to the sub-four-minute mile in the sprint world.

There's no doubting this man could pull out some sexy numbers from his running bag and he was hotly tipped to skate the marathon in Canada in 1954.

When he entered the stadium for the final lap of the marathon, he was fully 17 minutes in front of Joe McGhee.

But this was the swansong race for Peters, although not even he knew that at the time. A combination of exhaustion and heat exposure made a bad situation even worse. The audience in the stadium watched in horror as Peters repeatedly collapsed as he fought his way, foot by foot and inch by inch, to the tape. Around the world most would have heard of his plight by radio and some would have had their eyes on their television set as the seconds passed. The tortured athlete is said to have struggled on for 15 minutes before, mercifully, being stopped by a physio, then stretchered off the track to hospital unconscious.

He is later quoted as saying: 'I was lucky not to have died that day.'

It is understandable that so much time elapsed before people ran to help him. He was a mental three miles in front of the next runner and many athletes would rather pass out than be helped over the line – an act of kindness that would disqualify a runner from finishing the race.

In an agonizing twist, Peters, in his state of mental and physical meltdown, would have believed he had crossed the line and, therefore, won the race. The line he crossed was the marker for another event; the one he was aiming for was farther round the track.

It would be difficult not to be bitter after such a cock-up, and he clearly blamed the organizers for miscalculating the route so that it was longer than the standard course. Had he known he was so far ahead of the rest of the runners, he would surely have eased off to a healthier pace, but he pushed himself dangerously hard.

While he presided over the Road Runners Club the next year, Peters retired from competition and pursued a career as an optician.

In another interesting connection with the sub-four king, the recently qualified doctor Bannister stayed on in Vancouver after the Games to help look after him. Peters was entered into the Sports Hall of Fame in Vancouver, where his kit is on display beside a medal he received from Prince Philip, the Duke of Edinburgh, inscribed with the words: 'To a most gallant marathon runner'.

But Peters was not the only casualty of the marathon race that year.

Peters believed that fellow runner Stan Cox was his competition, thinking it was he who was coming behind, not McGhee.

Cox, suffering from the heat, too, collapsed after running headlong into a telegraph pole. You couldn't make it up – and it's not funny. No, really, it's not.

People have already calculated every permutation, concluding that Peters had, in fact, completed the statutory mileage for a marathon. Had he known how far ahead he was, he would have had time to not only slake his thirst at the last refreshment stop, but have a shower and rub down as well, before cruising to victory.

Now, all this takes the shine off the gold medal that went to McGhee for being the first to cross the line that fateful day. But he ran his own race – he would've been crazy to keep pace with Peters. He managed to avoid running into static obstacles, albeit he faltered slightly, tripping on a pavement kerb. He stopped to drink water to avoid dehydration. And he was among only a half-dozen runners to finish the race, which started with 16 competitors.

So it's not necessarily fair to shout, 'They was robbed!' McGhee was a dominant force in cross-country and distance running. Marathon running isn't just a matter of putting one foot in front of the other. And Shettleston Harriers are rightly proud of their gold medal winner.

The revered Shettleston club took its first steps towards athletic stardom in 1904, 110 years before Glasgow was to host the Commonwealth Games in 2014.

It was primarily a running club but diversified into other track-and-field sports in the 1920s.

The club's first officers at its inception were Bob Nicol and Donald McColl of the West of Scotland Harriers. Their historic first meeting with the Howieson brothers and the club's inaugural meeting in Houston's Tearoom in Shettleston led to McColl being elected the club's first president, Nicol as secretary and John Howieson as treasurer. Howieson was later to become president of the National Cross Country Union in Scotland.

The club took the National Cross Country title for the first time in 1920.

Marathon man Dunky Wright was Commonwealth and Empire Games champion and was a driving force in the organization for almost 50 years.

Jimmy Flockart ran his way to the Scottish Cross Country title on four occasions in the 1930s.

Boxing heroes

Scrapping, streetfighting and gang warfare are nothing new to the East End: 'razor gangs' had terrorized the city since the turn of the twentieth century.

The rise of territorial battles among the hard men of Glasgow was first described in a fictional book published in 1935 – at the height of the razor gangs' reign of terror. While the novel's full title was *No Mean City: A Story of the Glasgow Slums*, it is generally known simply as *No Mean City*.

An unlikely collaboration between a jobless Gorbals man, Alexander McArthur, and the journalist H. Kingsley Long, the novel's genesis was a series of 'conversations' sent to book publisher Neville Spearman Ltd by McArthur. Later Corgi editions were published by Transworld Publishers.

Spearman recognized that this story would be ground-breaking as an insight into the gang culture that was so associated with this part of the city.

McArthur was certainly no author, but the publisher was keen to develop the story and called in Long to take the raw material and work it into shape.

The book has been listed as one of the Top 100 Books of All Time and tells the story of Johnnie Stark, whose childhood was blighted by a violent and bullying father. The stark no-frills narrative and blunt characterization added to the raw and brutal energy of the book, which remains the definitive guide to life in Glasgow slums at the height of the Great Depression of the 1930s.

Glasgow gang culture first insinuated itself into the fabric of the city in the late 1800s. Although largely territorial, violent rivalry was stoked by religious sectarianism. Sectarianism developed mainly between Irish and Scottish Catholics and Protestants, and was exacerbated by rivalry between fans of Glasgow's two main football teams, Celtic and Rangers.

Yet this religious divide and the accompanying violence were not solely a consequence of poverty in the Glasgow slums. There have been battles royal – sometimes literally – since the times of the medieval bishopric.

When the Protestants enjoyed monarchical favour, they razed whole cities almost to the ground. Likewise Catholic bishops were involved in all-out battles with Protestant clergy. Whole castles were occupied and later destroyed. When it came to brutal conflict, the Bridgeton Billy Boys, Calton Entry and the Beehive Boys had nothing on those medieval 'men of peace'.

However, there is a queer anomaly that intertwines such violence with harmony.

Around the last quarter of the nineteenth century, youth leaders got the notion that the very violence that is exerted in the mean streets can be harnessed in a controlled environment and steer kids off the street corners.

Boxing – or rather streetfighting or bare-knuckle fighting

– has been the medium of choice for settling differences for generations, particularly among the Gypsy and Romany communities.

Those who excelled would be invited to underground fight fests, with the promise of good money if they were still standing after getting ten bells of shit kicked out of them.

The really successful fighters were paid more for what they considered a mere workout, as many challengers were no match for these bruisers and entered the 'ring' out of sheer financial desperation.

This was illegal, of course. Fighting continued its uneasy relationship with the dark underbelly of urban society.

Gradually, boys were coaxed off the streets, given a punch bag to pummel out their fears and frustrations, and then a sparring partner to teach them how to harness their fury.

Yet boxing in the high Victorian years was somewhat ennobled as a gentleman's sport, with the ratifying of rules of fair play and mutual respect underwritten in the boxing code, the Marquis of Queensberry Rules.

In Glasgow, it wasn't so posh, but the rules of the professional and organized amateur pugilists were the boxing world standard.

Entrepreneurial fight promoters and their talent scouts would do the rounds of local boxing clubs in search of new blood.

Boxing 'booths' began to appear at fairgrounds on Glasgow Green, where keen young hopefuls could book time with boxing coaches. They would learn valuable tips and techniques whilst the coaches kept an eye open for a spark of potential talent.

Gorbals and nearby Hutcheston developed as a rich source of would-be could-be's and one of the most renowned training gyms was LMS Rovers.

One of the club's greatest sons was Gorbals youth Benny Lynch. Born in April 1913, he was spotted by bookie Sammy Wilson.

Fairground boxing booths also hosted fights and Lynch saw off all-comers on the circuit. He had turned professional at the age of 18. Boxing and betting are easy bedfellows and Wilson proved a valuable friend and mentor.

Sammy took Lynch under his wing. This was no exploitative relationship. Wilson invested heavily in Lynch and built a new boxing gym, the New Polytechnic, at 49 Clyde Place.

Wilson became both manager and trainer to the young fighter, and their partnership led to the Scottish flyweight title in 1934, three years after taking the pro card. The fight went the full 15 rounds and the win over fellow flyweight Jim Campbell was by decision.

Less than a year later, he was touching gloves with the already world flyweight champion, Jackie Brown.

The result was a draw over 12 rounds, which set the wheels in motion for a return match for the title less than six months later. This time, a tartan army of adoring fans joined the massive 10,000-strong crowd in a pilgrimage to Manchester to cheer their hero on.

So strong was the will and wish to be free of the shackles of poverty and unemployment that, for the most part, anyone who had the talent, business nous or sheer good luck to escape the smoggy town and breathe clean air elsewhere was hero worshipped. It was a promise of hope. And sporting losses were heartbreaking for all.

In Manchester, the defending world champ saw more canvas than stars around his head, hitting the deck at least eight times over two rounds. And Brown was no pushover; he was just unlucky to have been on the circuit at the same time as the wee Gorbals dynamo.

Hailed throughout boxing history as possibly Scotland's greatest fighter, Lynch shunned the call of the genteel West End and continued to live in his East End home. It wasn't long before he succumbed to the ubiquitous demon drink, which he never overcame. In his short career, which ended at the young age of 25, he had clocked up some respectable stats. He died of alcohol-related pneumonia on 6 August 1946.

But it's not the booze that Lynch is remembered for. And it wasn't the hard drinking lifestyle that inspired so many young East Enders to lace the gloves with dreams of boxing glory.

Lynch's successes over a short career inspired fellow fly-weight Charlie Kerr, whose most cherished victory was in 1947 at Kirkaldy ice rink against American-born Japanese boxer Tsuneshi Maruo, who had beaten every British fighter he'd met – until Kerr. It was one helluva fight and Kerr emerged the victor. But the titanic clash took it out of him and pretty much heralded the beginning of the end of Kerr's boxing career in the ring. Yet he went on to mentor many fighters and founded Kelvin Amateur Boxing Club.

Some years ago, I met some architecture and town plan-ning students from New York who, as part of their studies, wanted to come over to Glasgow to see the 1960s 'new town' of 'Gorbells'. They wanted to study the new build and sky-scraper disaster for themselves.

OK, maybe they had it half right, but over the years I've been faced with similar misinformed overseas visitors who have had the same impression, believing the Gorbals to be a new community along the lines of Drumchapel or Easter-house. Mind you, two American visitors who stunned me silent were a pair who were astonished that the '60s band Marmalade weren't still topping the charts, only 30 years after 'Ob-La-Di Ob-La-Da'. Their visit in 1988 coincided with a series of international public concerts featuring legendary band Simple Minds to mark Mandela's 70th birthday. On his eventual release from prison, he made special mention and thanks to the people of Glasgow for their support and for giving him at least the Freedom of Glasgow while he was still in jail. He made a special visit to Glasgow to personally thank his Glaswegian supporters, who campaigned relentlessly for the release of Mandela.

So everyone was talking about the Free Nelson Mandela concerts.

Our overseas friends were bemused. They had never heard of 'these guys' and asked, 'Are they a new band?'

I kid you not.

Anyway, the Gorbals is far from a 'new town'.

The wooden bridge on Fishergate (Stockwell Street) appears in official documents as far back as the late 1200s, or 1285, according to some sources.

Later documents place a 'leper hospital' on the Gorbals land as far back as 1350.

The Elphinstone dynasty was the big guns in this part of the East End. George Elphinstone, the last of the lineage, built the stately Baronial Hall on the main thoroughfare. A particular point of interest is the square turreted tower. The Elphinstones also built their own private chapel nearby, with the traditional circular tower.

The estates that were acquired from the Magistrates Council of Glasgow or by Merchants House inevitably made their way out of the clutches of the bishopric and often ended up within the quite substantial portfolios of wealthy individuals.

The 1650s saw a frenzy of property acquisition in Glasgow and the rest of Scotland. Catholic bishops were forced to hand over their assets to the town's secular leaders, who embarked on a carve-up of the city and outlying countryside of gargantuan proportions.

Key changes in town governance and the formal adoption of the Protestant faith by the Parliament of Scotland saw a veritable trolley dash by civic bodies, gobbling up huge estates and selling them on to those and such as those.

These lands were feud into smaller parcels and farmlands, which allowed cottage industries to flourish and brought rents and taxes to the king's feudal vassals.

The Gorbals, to some extent, managed to avoid the fate of its industrial neighbouring districts.

It became a focal point for the Victorian City Improvement Trust in the 1870s.

Main Street was razed and relocated to what was to become Gorbals Street. It was a bustling thoroughfare with small-scale businesses and had a real sense of community that would be harder to fuse in areas where chimneys spewed out acrid smoke and poisonous chemicals, coating the handsome tenement buildings erected to accommodate local workers.

By the 1930s, almost 100,000 residents called the Gorbals home.

My mother, Cissie Smith, remembers her elder sisters saving up for months so that they could order a fitted dress or coat from these artisans in the Gorbals. There were Irish and Lithuanian immigrants working mostly in the factories, but the Jewish quarter was where Glasgow's middle class would travel to their favourite dressmakers, cobblers, hair-stylists, furriers and jewellers. Cissie was born and brought up in Tollcross and remembers tagging along with her sisters to the artisan village. It was an exciting treat, not something that happened every week, but she still recalls the fine stitching at close quarters, a minimum 22 stitches to the inch; the dazzling gemstones in elegant or elaborate designs.

Even what she called the 'costume jewellery' glinted in the low light.

And, of course, the revolutionary innovation of Bakelite. Bakelite was a '30s phenomenon and very soon the world and its granny had something – if not almost everything – made from this safe and versatile plastic. Nowadays, it's very collectable among the 'retro' elite. I remember we had a Bush radio encased in the stuff. Like the televisions of later years, we had to wait for the 'valves' to heat up before we could tune in to stations that included the Home Service, Forces and World Service channels.

Of course, there were areas that kids were told not to

go near. Derelict factories infested with rats. A worry to parents, but a brilliant place for the barefoot rat-catchers who could set up elaborate traps and ambushes to whack the unsuspecting little blighters.

Hooray for Hollywood

From Valentino to Tarantino, Greta Garbo to Marilyn Monroe, the heady heights of Hollywood heart-throb heroism have fuelled the imaginations of movie-goers for generations.

Over the past 100 years, men, women and children have gasped at the plight of silent movie queens such as Mary Pickford and Lillian Gish, whose stunning performance as the tormented heroine and star of *The Wind* made her one of the most evocative of the serious silent movie stars; sashayed with Astaire and Rogers; and swooned over Cary Grant, James Dean and Rock Hudson. The great 1920s screen idol Rudolph Valentino won the hearts of millions, especially with his Latin lover roles or as the mysterious Middle Eastern bohemian in *The Sheik*.

When it came to trends, be it hairdos or handbags, it was to Hollywood that women looked, fashioning themselves on glamorous starlets from the languid Lana Turner, whose wavy fringe seductively covered one eye, to the doe-eyed goddess of '50s style, diva Joan Collins.

Hollywood was a place where a shoeshine boy could become a celebrated hoofer and shopgirls got 'spotted' and tested for starring roles alongside the man of their dreams; the romance and intrigue, action and suspense, fun and frolics of tinsel town held a fascination which, at least for a while, could make us all forget our troubles and live the life that movies are made of – only in Hollywood could a B-movie actor become president of the United States, as Ronald Reagan proved.

Not even the most optimistic cinematic pioneers of the 1890s would have thought the quirky new fad, using Edison's Kinetoscope and, later, the Panopticon projector to create moving pictures, most famously and grandiosely marketed as Cinematographé Pathé-Lumière and Nickelodeon, would grow to become a multi-billion-pound industry, where millions have been made or lost before the girl behind the box office's sliding glass window sells her first ticket on opening night.

Possibly the first and biggest of the Hollywood block-busters came near the end of the 1930s, with the 1939 runaway hit screening of Margaret Mitchell's American Civil War epic, billed at the time as 'the most magnificent picture ever'. The enduring and enthralling *Gone With the Wind* starred heart-throb Clark Gable as the rakish blockade runner Rhett Butler and the relative newcomer Vivien Leigh. She was discovered by, and later married, the elder statesman of stage and screen Laurence Olivier – theirs was a marriage with as much fire and intrigue as any movie script.

'My most memorable moment,' said Cissie Smith, of Tollcross, 'was when I was working for extra cash at night as an usherette in the cinema on Wellshot Road. It was there that I saw on the Pathé news before the film came on that Britain was at war.

'I remember it clearly. It was a "Road to . . ." movie that was on, with Bob Hope, Bing Crosby and Dorothy

Lamour. *Gone With the Wind* would have been on in the town. I was just 18 and I distinctly remember opening the big door to the cinema and looking out at the sky and into the streets, with people making their way to the dancin' or to the pictures, or walking through Tollcross Park. And I remember thinking: "I'm 18 years old and my whole life is in front of me and we're in the middle of a damn world war." All the young men, it seemed, were going to war. I remember every family, near enough, or every street had a spinster, a woman who never married. When I asked my ma about why there were so many women who never got married, she explained to me that it was all about the First World War.

'So many, many men went off to war. Too many never came back. Even their bodies weren't returned. They were buried, if at all, in a foreign land, where they had been sent to kill other guys their age.

'Many bore the emotional scars of war, as well as the physical. My ma told me that many women had lost their fiancés at war. When the men returned, women who were of marriageable age were outshone by all the younger girls, with their shiny bobs and flapper skirts. There was just a whole subset of spinsters whose dreams of marriage and family were never realized; they were victims of bad timing.

'But when I was growing up, and throughout the war, we watched the pictures more for the styles than the stories. We would take in every detail of hairstyles: Norma Shearer was a big star. And Betty Grable – she was known as the girl with the million-dollar legs because she was the first to have her legs insured for what was a whopping sum.

'Anyway, we went right home after the film and copied the styles. In those days, America was the land of dreams and we watched for all the styles of the clothes and lengths of the skirts and the hats and who was wearing what. And every now and again, someone in the street would get movie magazines sent over from relatives in the States.

'Well, they went all around the streets and the work and we'd read who was marrying who, who had fell oot wi' who. The film stars were the royalty of Hollywood. And everyone talked about what picture they were going to see or what one they had seen ten times over.'

Then came the musicals in 'glorious Technicolor', which sent many a glittering couple into the spotlight, with the most famous being perhaps Fred Astaire and Ginger Rogers, Gene Kelly and Cyd Charisse, and Judy Garland and Mickey Rooney.

Films such as *An American in Paris*, *Singin' in the Rain*, *On the Town* and *Meet Me in St Louis* all shone in the '40s and '50s, as did the squeaky clean image and trill vocals of Doris Day in everything from *Calamity Jane* to *The Pajama Game*, where she starred alongside East End boy Archibald Leach, aka Cary Grant.

Westerns, of course, incubated their own genre of rootin' tootin' shootin' gun-totin' box office draws, with John Wayne and Henry Fonda usually wearing the uniform, while the likes of Eli Wallach, Lee Van Cleef and Jack Elam took on the roles of tobacco-spittin', shoot-'em-in-the-back double-crossin' varmints.

Bill Torrance from Dalmarnock never missed a Saturday morning matinee.

'My favourites were Hopalong Cassidy, Dan Dare, the Lone Ranger and Tex Ritter,' Bill recalls. 'Later, of course, it would be Raquel Welch and Brigitte Bardot. And we would meet our girlfriends there and sit in the back row. And if we were skint, we would arrange to meet the girlfriend inside. It was the highlight of the week.'

Irene Gilchrist, of Baillieston, remembers her movie-going years as family affairs. She said: 'My fondest memories of the movies were when we used to go with my mum. It was very much a family event and my mum used to take along a bag of apples and oranges and pass them along the row to us. The chomping and slurping must have been just as annoying as sweetie wrappers and drink straws in later years.

'I remember we went to see *South Pacific* – the films used to be on for months in those days. Before the film began, a big organ, which was sunk into the pit, used to play songs from the film score.'

Going to the flicks on a Saturday night was also a chance for romancing, as Irene recalls: 'When the lights went on at interval time, all at once all the blokes would get up and start swaggering around the hall, eyeing up "the talent" and, after the film, they would chat the girls up. Some of the more brazen ones wouldn't wait for the end and would find their way to the back rows for a smooch in the dark. One movie house went one step further and used to have little boxes, booths, with curtains for privacy. Of course, I was too young for any of that.'

The picture houses played a mentoring role, too, as busy mums could pack off their brood on a Saturday afternoon in the care of an elder sibling, while Mum took the week's washing to the steamie.

And in winter it was cheaper to send the kids to a warm picture house than to put another bag of coal on the fire, according to some accounts.

Growing up in an area where there were at one time thirty cinemas, much maternal sanity was saved by dint of the Saturday matinee.

Angela Austin recalls: 'There were five of us and I think the only peace my mum had was when we all trudged off to the pictures on a Saturday afternoon.'

Among the first of the public movie houses to hit the East End was Pringle's Picture Palace, opened by Ralph Pringle in 1907. This later became the Queen's Theatre on Watson Street, where many a belly laugh was to be had on a regular Saturday night variety spectacle.

In contrast to its plain exterior, the three-tiered auditorium was lavishly ornate, with Corinthian columns and Moorish domes over the side boxes. It was leased in 1914 by Bernard Frutin but was never a great picture house success. In 1934, it reverted back to a fun music hall, its original *raison d'être*. It met its demise in a fire in 1952.

'I remember Queen's Playhouse when I was just a wee girl,' says Cissie Smith. 'We would be in awe of the glamorous showgirls who used to open the show, with their feathers and beautiful dresses, and the music – it was just spectacular to a wee girl.

'And it was a whole family night out; everyone got all dressed up to go to the Queen's or one of the other theatres.

There was literally one on every corner. I remember this act – it was a real slapstick affair – this big bloke with massive big troosers and huge braces. And he'd pull them right out and they'd spring back and send him flying. We laughed and laughed. It was just great. Of course, nowadays that would be too tame for kids. It's all action films now. Mind you, when you see some of the films out these days, good old-fashioned slapstick wins with the kids every time.

'The lavish artificial waterfall on stage was the big attraction and everyone would sing, "By the waterfall, I'm calling yoo-oo-oo-oo . . ." Oh, whit a night! You would just get carried away with it all and then we would all pour out into the streets. You never felt in any danger. Everybody knew one another.'

A small gas-lit sign by a close mouth at 112 Stirling Street was the only indication of the presence of the St James's picture house, a 450-seat Nickelodeon that opened only three years after the Pringle. It ran two shows nightly and soldiered on until 1947, when its lease ran out.

Albert Ernest Pickard: London, Paris, Moscow, Bannockburn (1874–1964)

When A. E. Pickard, a Bradford-born entrepreneur, moved to Glasgow in 1904, he very quickly carved out a niche as one of the city's adopted sons and one of her most colourful characters. Or perhaps that should read that he adopted Glasgow, almost brick by brick.

He began buying up property in his new home town like it was going out of fashion. At one time, it is believed, he had a bigger portfolio of buildings than Glasgow City Council, or 'the Corporation', as it was then. Despite this, he wasn't a very good caretaker and had a reputation for allowing buildings to fall into disrepair.

Pickard would often boast: if one were to throw a stone in any street in Glasgow, it would bounce off one of his buildings. Apparently, on hearing this, a city dignitary remarked that the said building would probably fall to the ground in a pile of rubble.

And it seemed he had as many cars as he did houses, which he treated in much the same way, by abandoning them to the elements outside his mansion house when they no longer worked. Flashy American limos and shiny Rolls-Royces were his favourites.

Pickard's business card declared: A.E. Pickard: London, Paris, Moscow and Bannockburn. He sometimes introduced himself as A.E. Pickard Unlimited, and once stood for parliament as Independent Millionaire for Maryhill.

One of Pickard's first major purchases was the old Britannia Theatre, which he renamed the Panopticon. It was already in use as a popular music hall and cinema, but Pickard managed to eke out extra revenue by laying on mini-carnivals, wax model displays, 'bearded lady'-style freak shows, even a small zoo.

He was feisty, loud, arrogant and irreverent, nurturing his reputation as a 'zany eccentric'. Some historians describe him as a business genius; others, a quirky entrepreneur. Either way, he knew how to make money, becoming one of Glasgow's elite millionaires.

The music hall became the early stomping ground for

Hollywood stars Jack Buchanan, Stan Laurel and Cary Grant.

Pickard had a thing about being higher up than others – possibly the manifestation of his lofty self-image. In the theatre, he would sit perched upon a tall ladder from which vantage point he would silence rowdy audience members with a well-aimed screw nail. He also had no time for ham acts: he had a long pole made, with a huge hook on the end, with which to eject the offending entertainer.

And he carried on negotiations in much the same manner. On at least one occasion, he greeted a business associate perched upon a desk atop a table in the middle of the street outside one of his many cinemas, decked out in a theatrical cloak and top hat.

He infuriated creditors by paying large sums of cash in bags of penny pieces.

He made much of his fortune from a chain of cinemas and answered criticism in his usual style. When competitors suggested that a proposed picture house on the outskirts of town would become a 'white elephant', he decided to name it the White Elephant cinema.

Outside another of his picture houses, he erected a big placard offering 'a fur coat and dinner' for ninepence, while inside Pickard and the cinema manager were selling rabbits at ninepence apiece.

With Pickard, audiences were guaranteed entertainment from the outside in. On one picture house, he had erected a replica of the Forth Rail Bridge across the full length of the roof; on another of his theatres a mini rail track had a train running to and fro on the rooftop outside.

Crowds gathered at one of many grand openings to see a theatrically clad Pickard take a runny from across the street with a battering ram to open the doors.

His eccentricities extended to the design of his buildings: one cinema had the audience descend two flights of stairs to the floor below and then up another flight of stairs to spill out into the auditorium from beneath the stage.

His irreverence was legendary. He held no one in high esteem and was even ejected from the stand by judge Lord Wheatley during a courtroom dispute over property.

As cranky and eccentric as he was, he was also a generous benefactor. And his charitable donations came with a 'no publicity' proviso, insofar as he insisted on anonymity.

Pickard lived a full and eventful life. Even in death at the age of 90, he went out with a bang – around Hallow'een in a house fire. His ashes were scattered in the Garden of Remembrance at Janefield Cemetery in the East End.

Saturday night at the movies

In 1911, A. E. Pickard's Casino Cinema was hailed as the first 'proper' cinema, having been purpose-designed by architect George Boswell with two entrances: one for the stalls, one for the balcony.

Films included *The Priestess of Carthage*, *On a Tramp Steamer* and *The Hands*. Live acts included Healey and Mealey, H. C. Vickers and comedian Charles Champney. Pickard later sold the Casino to a larger entertainments firm. In a magnanimous gesture of appreciation and good will, the directors of the new company held a dinner in

Pickard's honour – only to find that the wily Pickard had already bought a prime cinematic site right across the road from their new acquisition. Naturally, Pickard was challenged on this somewhat underhand move and he had his response at the ready. He unabashedly proclaimed: 'How sensible it is that the ground which could have been used by the opposition now belongs to a friend of the Casino rather than an enemy.' It was a shrewd purchase. Pickard soon after negotiated the sale of the vacant site to the casino's new owners.

The Casino had a short-lived renaissance as a bingo house from 1965 until 1968, when it closed for good. Its long-term rival, the Carlton, had closed its doors two years earlier to make way for the first phase of Glasgow's inner ring road.

The Carlton had opened in the year of the great General Strike – 1926 – and could comfortably seat 1,600 bums. Designed by Duff & Cairns, it sat on the corner of Castle Street and Alexandra Parade.

Green's Whitevale Theatre, a favourite wartime dance hall, began life in 1910, when Richard Singleton created the Star Palace, a big hall capable of holding more than 1,000 dancers upstairs in the old Bridgeton town hall.

Cinemas that had begun life in another guise had more of a struggle to survive their makeover than the custom-built movie houses owned by large conglomerates showing snazzy new spectaculars such as *Gone With the Wind*.

These large purpose-built cinemas began to appear in the late '20s and early '30s, heralding the demise of the older local 'fleapits' that had usually evolved from a previous life as a theatre or music hall.

Green's Whitevale theatre, the Paragon and the Nickelodeon-style Electric Theatre at Bridgeton Cross were closed by 1932. Two that survived into the '50s were London Road Picture Palace, formerly the Bon Accord Engine Works, and the King's Picture Theatre, which was converted from an old army drill hall.

The King's had many claims to fame, not least hosting famous stars, including slapstick royalty Laurel & Hardy and the inimitable Edward G. Robinson.

Many regulars to the cinema remember buskers and impersonators, such as Charlie Chaplin lookalikes, who would entertain the queues waiting to get in.

The Royale – or the Dan Doyle, as it was affectionately known – was a favourite for its penny matinees. This is remembered as one of the cinemas that really did let kids in for the price of two 'jeely jaurs'.

Now, I like that idea but, according to social historian Eddy Cavin, the jeely jaur thing is apocryphal. Retired now, Eddy worked for many years with the City Council's culture and sports arm, Glasgow Life, and has given many lectures and talks, particularly at the Mitchell Library, on life in bygone days. An after-dinner speaker, too, he is well respected for his attention to detail and investigative skills. He told me: 'It's a lovely idea, like women using cold tea to stain their legs and an eyebrow pencil to draw a line down the back of their legs to create the illusion of seamed silk stockings. But I'm afraid there really is no evidence of jeely jaurs being used as currency by young cinema-goers.'

Fleapits, as some crummy theatres were known, gave

movie houses a bad name. They really were small, dark dens that were a natural habitat for the little critters.

And their reputation would have given credence to an imaginative advertising campaign for the newly built Black Cat picture house that opened on Bridgeton Cross in 1921. Posters, no doubt inspired by its eccentric owner A. E. Pickard, proclaimed that the high-backed seats were 'especially made to a revolutionary design to keep the bugs away'.

In the 1960s, Andy Stewart's *The White Heather Club* show was filmed by the BBC at the Black Cat. Many families enjoyed free picture shows courtesy of the Blochairn Foundry that sponsored the Scotia, while the district's grandest and most imposing cinema facade belongs to the Olympia, again in Bridgeton, advertised as 'a clean and comfortable family resort'.

Horror movies, which later earned an 'H' rating, starring the likes of Lon Chaney and Christopher Lee, became tests of stamina and a great opportunity for the blokes to show off their nerves of steel to their girlfriends, as one Dalmarnock man put it: 'No one in the audience made a sound. In Brigton, if you screamed, you were either a *fearty* or a *safty*.'

The first talking picture to hit the East End was, of course, Al Jolson's *The Singing Fool* in 1928 and it is believed that the Dalmarnock picture house that first played the movie earned the nickname 'the Geggie' (the mouth) from this claim to fame.

Cinemas themselves have served many social purposes, from gangland meeting points to havens for the homeless. One usher remembers: 'We got a lot of drunks and they just fell asleep in the warmth of the stalls. Sometimes they would lie full length in the aisles – and pee. We always knew who to throw out because there would be a wee rivulet trickling down from them, which we could see in the reflection from the screen.'

And many a romance was struck up at the movies, inspiring songs such as the Drifters favourite 'Saturday Night at the Movies'.

The East End was notorious between the two world wars, particularly as a stamping ground for gangs such as the Briggait Boys and the Calton Entry – more notably the Billy Boys from the Calton and their counterparts, the Norman Cooks, from Norman Street in Bridgeton.

Sometimes violence would spill over into the cinemas, particularly the Arcadia, which was bought over by the ABC, and when fighting broke out in the stalls, to a chorus of stamping, clapping and shouts of 'Fight! Fight! Fight!', almost the whole audience would get stuck in.

A real art deco eye-catcher was the Orient on the corner of Gallowgate, with its 2,500-seater auditorium. It showed all the latest big-name movies, such as the 'epic' *The Prisoner of Zenda*. This new emporium of entertainment was to cast another shot over the bow of smaller houses.

In Dennistoun, the Parade and Pringle's Palladium were the favourite haunts of picture-goers, while the older audience preferred the Dennistoun picture house, with its more lofty offerings, including *The Ten Commandments*.

The Rex's striking interior attracted Riddrie audiences away from the less salubrious theatres in the '30s, but it was no match for the later Riddrie cinema, with its imposing art deco exterior and faience-clad frontage, not to mention its revolving door, which became such a diversion for the punters that it was eventually replaced after it broke down through overuse.

Parkhead picture houses included the three Ps, the Parkhead Picture Palace, as it was known, and the Granada, while in Shettleston, Scott's Electric Theatre evolved from the old wireworks; the Premier on Shettleston Road was a converted back court, while stars of the *Half Past Eight Show* would entertain at the State, also on Shettleston Road.

Possibly the biggest name to come out of the East End and hit the high life of tinsel town stardom was Stan Laurel, whose father ran the Metropole music hall. Stan wasn't encouraged by his father and so actually got his first big break at a rival theatre, the Panopticon on Trongate, which has recently undergone a radical revamp, bringing it back to its former glory. It is certainly worth a visit.

And East Enders in the '30s will remember the Tollcross boy who moved with his family to the States and became a 'big Hollywood star'.

'He was my mother's cousin's boy,' recalls Cissie Smith. 'Eddie Quillan. He was in loads of Hollywood pictures, playing mainly supporting roles, such as a gangster's henchman or the guy that gets shot at the start of the film. Sometimes he got a few lines to say and we all thought he'd made the big time. We used to imagine him at the fancy showbiz parties, hobnobbing with Clark Gable and Carole Lombard, Ava Gardner and Errol Flynn.

'That's what the pictures were all about – dreams coming true, local kids making good and, oh, the glamour. And the way that you could see people on the big screen, just ordinary people, who had made it big and you could think "that could be me".'

Eddie was the son of East Ender Joseph Quillan, born 1884. It was Joseph who left Glasgow in the early 1920s to pursue the Hollywood dream. As an actor and writer, he has credits for *Hoboken to Hollywood* (1926), *A Little Bit of Everything* (1928) and *Noisy Neighbors* (1929). He died in Los Angeles in 1952 and his son Eddie picked up the baton and carved out a respectable living as a jobbing actor in more than 100 TV movies and television shows, including *The Lucy Show*, *Perry Mason*, *The Man from U.N.C.L.E.*, *The Big Valley*, *The Virginian* and *The Doris Day Show*.

As a young vaudeville performer, he and his siblings were treading the boards as children in the music hall act The Rising Generation, managed by their father.

Cissie has fond memories of the 1930s before the restrictions and rations of the war. And she has her own connection with Hollywood romance.

'I remember one day my friend Rena Rankine and I were in town. We used to go into town on a Saturday and look around the shops and then end up in the Peacock tearooms.

'Then we would meet up with friends and pal each other back on the tram. I had just got my hair done and we were looking around the shops when these two handsome American boys started flirting with us. We just giggled and walked on, but it seems they had taken a shine to us in the tearoom and followed us, trying to catch our attention.

'They were really charming and we eventually agreed to go for a coffee with them, then we showed them around the city. Because I was only 15 and these boys were 17 or 18, we didn't tell anyone we had made a date with them to go to the dancing. They were great dancers and showed us all the latest dance steps from America.

'When they had to go back home, Jeff insisted on giving me his address so that I could write to him. He took my address, but I'd forgotten that we hadn't given them our real names. I don't know why, but we used to do that, make up fancy Hollywood named like Eleanora or something.

'So when the postman came asking if there was a Cassandra de l'Amour or whatever I'd called myself, I was too embarrassed to say it was me. And I had a lot of older brothers who certainly wouldn't have let me go on a date with a boy at that age. So all Jeff's letters and parcels were returned to sender, as they say.

'Anyway, a number of years later, after the war, we were at the Tollcross cinema watching a war hero movie, can't remember which one, when the star comes running through the trenches and the camera closes in on this handsome film star and who was it but Jeff – Jeff Chandler – the boy who we met outside the tearooms that day. My kids often say to me how different things might have been if I'd only owned up to being the mystery girl all those letters were sent to. But, to tell you the truth, I wasn't smitten with him anyway.'

A river runs through it

East End history is peppered with colourful characters and unsung heroes who breathe life into every aspect of living in the area and who have contributed to the personality of its communities. One such character is Clyde riverman George Parsonage.

Blues legend Billie Holiday sang 'Southern trees bear strange fruit', lyrics influenced by her harrowing experiences as a touring singer in America's deep south where lynch mob mentality left black men, women and even children hanging from trees.

Since its inaugural meeting at the Tontine Hotel at Trongate on 6 August 1790, the Humane Society's officers have been hauling strange fish from the Clyde river for generations.

Parsonage is the last in a line of men who fished human bodies from the River Clyde – dead or alive.

It was a highly controversial vocation in its formative years because, until only recently, committing or attempting suicide was against the law in many countries, with grim consequences, whatever the outcome.

As well as being an illegal act, it was held in the eyes of the Church to be a sin. So, again, regardless of success or failure, those attempting suicide bore the punishment of 'ex-communication' (banishment from the Church) for the rest of their lives or indeed, if successful, posthumously. Not as bad, though, as in France, where the dead body may have been dragged through the streets face down and then publicly hanged or chucked onto a rubbish dump.

Anyone who saved or helped a person who was drowning was tarred with the same brush of shame and may have been punished as an accessory after the fact.

In England and Wales, the families of people attempting

or committing 'self-murder' had to suffer the pain of losing a loved one, the shame of being denied a daylight funeral, and also financial hardship, as the dead person's estate was transferred to the Crown as a punishment, which in too many cases made paupers of those left behind.

While suicide has never been illegal in Scotland, it was at best socially unacceptable and the families of people who chose to take their own life were ostracized as social pariahs. Glasgow was a supremely religious community and no one's god would tolerate being usurped as the giver and taker of life.

The first elected president of the Humane Society was Dean of Guild Gilbert Hamilton. The first secretary, the eminent physician and lecturer Robert Cleghorn.

According to some sources, the society was founded with a posthumous donation of £200 bequeathed from the estate of James Coulter, a wealthy Glasgow Merchant, to help found a Humane Society in Glasgow.

However, in a book entitled *Deeds instituting Bursaries, Scholarships and other funds in the College and University of Glasgow*, printed for the historical literary publisher the Maitland Club in 1850, there is a record of charitable bequests by Coulter that offers greater detail. The Maitland Club is named for the Scottish poet, Sir Richard Maitland Lord Lethington.

It identifies 'the Coulter Prizes' as awards in his name, including £500 to build a girls' school to be named Peadie's School; £400 for the erection of a 'bridewell' – a small correction centre for minor or petty criminals (this would be the Main Street jail in Calton and would be reincarnated as a Borstal school for boys); £1,200 to start a pension fund for 'worthy and deserving persons in indigent circumstances'; a £300 'Mortification' to go to Glasgow Royal Infirmary; a £200 prize fund to encourage 'invention or improvement in machinery beneficial to trade'; £200 to Glasgow University to fund an annual prize 'towards increasing a spirit of emulation among students . . . [and] for the encouragement of composition and elocution'; and £500 in conjunction with Coulter's brother towards the creation of a Humane Society in Glasgow.

This greater sum, and the inclusion of Coulter's brother in the request, suggests to me that Coulter did indeed bequeath £200, but his brother was to add a further £300 to the pot.

Coulter died in 1787. The Deed of Settlement was dated for November 1787 but not recorded in the Books of Session until September of the next year.

And the Glasgow Humane Society was born two years later in 1790.

Similar societies were being set up in capital cities across Europe – not, of course, to be mistaken for some modern day humane societies, which are more concerned with animal welfare and pet rescue – a noble cause none the less.

The object of the Glasgow society was 'to recover those who are apparently dead, from having been sometime under water, from being exposed to intense cold, or to other causes capable of suspending life without destroying it'.

The river in these times was inaccessible in some parts, so rescue apparatus was kept at locations near to the river, such as the Wash House at Glasgow Green.

People who helped or ran for help were paid a nominal sum or were awarded a medal for their trouble.

Drownings were not uncommon – in 1815, for example, the annual remuneration amounted to almost £50.

Rescue, it seems, was a family affair: three generations of Geddes men have borne the mantle of river keeper since 1859, all with the first name George. Sadly, for their efforts, the river took George Geddes III, who, on 11 November 1928, drowned during a rescue attempt that went fatally wrong. In the same year, Ben Parsonage joined the society and worked alongside George Geddes II.

Since 1932, it has been the sole remit of Ben Parsonage and his son George, albeit with the help of assistants.

Grim statistics, meticulously kept, go as far back as the beginnings of the society.

Parsonage alone has rescued more than 1,500 and retrieved countless dead bodies, which have found themselves in the river's cold, grim clutches by accident, misadventure, murder or suicide.

His home was the first to be built on Glasgow Green in 1937, when his parents moved from Bridgeton.

I had interviewed Parsonage some years previously as a journalist at *The East End Independent* newspaper. In 1958, as a young boy of 14, he had accompanied his father, Ben, to a rescue for the first time.

Since then, the Clyde has been his master and his mistress, and he takes every opportunity to praise his wife and children for their unfaltering support and tolerance.

He told me: 'It's a vocation that we are born into.' He added with a charming smile and a twinkle in his eye: 'As

I was just saying to the Queen when I was last down in London, "You'll know all about that."' This was in reference to his being awarded an MBE, one of many medals and awards he has received over his tenure as chief officer of the Humane Society. In 2006, he was awarded an honorary doctorate by Strathclyde University and an honorary degree by the Caledonian University. Along with the society's Antony Coia, he was awarded the Queen's Diamond Jubilee Service Medal in 2012.

For all the officers and helpers who save countless lives on the Clyde, it's not about medals or awards. Parsonage told me: 'It's not a matter of choice. For five generations, my family has been fishing people, animals and shopping trolleys out of the Clyde. Glasgow's Humane Society is probably the last fully active society of the many that came into existence across Europe.'

Now, Parsonage has his own take on the sorry act of suicide. He says: 'I don't believe in the word suicide. It really is a cry for help. No one wants to die. No matter how much a person thinks life is not worth living at that time, the moment they hit that water, they shout for help. And too often river deaths are put down to suicide totally erroneously.'

The vocation is not for the faint-hearted, either. Saving souls from drowning is a risky business at any time on the Clyde, a task made even more dangerous on one occasion by thugs who dropped a huge stone slab from a bridge, which landed on his head as he was racing down the river to rescue a drowning man.

He came close to death again in another rescue bid, as he

battled the worst of Scotland's weather while abseiling down the quayside to the lifeboat.

He was once also virtually imprisoned in his rowing boat by a pitbull terrier that had been tossed into the river by its owner for coming second in an illegal dogfight.

And, on at least one occasion, he has been threatened with arrest while attempting to get closer to a drowning woman, this being the price we pay for inappropriate health and safety laws.

Being on call 24/7 is tough on anyone, and family life suffers too.

Parsonage has on more than one occasion run to the rescue, pulling his overalls up over his pyjamas. More than once he has brought in the New Year in the back of an ambulance, giving someone artificial resuscitation.

'Don't get me wrong,' he told me. 'It's a privilege to do the job and there is nothing in the world like it. I do get very involved, though. One time, I was dragging a man up the quay ladder at the same time as giving him resuscitation. When the paramedic told me he hadn't made it, I went home and couldn't speak.

'The house was deadly silent. No one spoke for hours. I was gutted. Then it was reported on the late news that night that the man had survived. The feeling of elation is indescribable.'

George is not a religious man, but he knows the customs and culture of every faith, from Roman Catholicism to Hindu, Shinto and Buddhism.

He explained: 'These things may mean nothing to someone who has been dredged out of the water, but it means a great deal to the family. And we must always respect that.'

By day, in working life, Parsonage was a high school art teacher and any spare time he had he spent creating metal sculptures from discarded debris that he dredged out of the river. His art sells for between £50 and £1,000, with proceeds going to charity.

And his talents don't stop at art.

As a champion rower and sculler, he has won countless sporting trophies over the years and nurtured promising talent to success as well.

World champion sculler Peter Hainey would take every opportunity to acknowledge Parsonage's role in developing his talents. Parsonage himself is a record breaker in the sport, clocking up a storming nine wins in a row at the height of his sporting career.

His charity work led him to row the full length of Loch Ness in two and a half hours, knocking a full two hours off the previous record.

It's a great shame that the waters of the Clyde give up only debris and dead bodies where they once ran clean and rich with salmon, trout and other marine life.

The Industrial Revolution most certainly contributed to the contamination.

Parsonage recalls his young days, living on the Clyde: 'I've seen many changes in my time with the society. I remember the river would be a different colour every week, according to what colour dye they were producing in the dye works. At other times, the water would be white with froth from Whites chemical works. And I have seen oil floating on the water four feet deep. Now the Clyde has been cleaned up a bit and my problems are more likely to be of the feathered variety. It is nice to see swans, mink, seals, geese and porpoises on the water, but they do bring their own problems. And shopping trolleys! At one part of the river we collected more than 400 of the damn things. Another time, we nudged more than 8,000 barrels into the side.'

The Humane Society plays a different role these day, after regulations regarding health and safety were introduced and lifesaving on the river became the remit of the Fire Brigade and, later, the police.

My interview with one of the world's last rivermen came to an abrupt end when the phone rang. The river was in flood and he was needed. Within seconds, he was in his car and racing to the rescue.

Parsonage is a powerful man, but there's more to a successful rescue than muscle alone. Strength, speed and gentleness are the golden trinity of a successful mission.

'The body begins to rise with gentleness, an uncanny lightness,' he wrote in an unpublished essay on what he calls the ancient art of grappling, 'and the rope user has to be very quick and gentle in raising the body to the surface. It is like lifting a balloon. If you stop lifting, the balloon will float off and away, so with a body.'

River rescue is now the remit of Scotland's police force, but Parsonage continues to play a key role in river safety training and as an expert advisor.

In March 2014, journalist Peter Ross met with the river's

elder statesman as the 70 year old, still sporting his signature shock of white hair, reflected on his role as a modern day saviour.

In an interview for *The Scotsman* newspaper, he told Ross: 'Rescue is a privilege, isn't it? It's not everybody in this world who gets the chance to help someone.

'Every time I hear sirens, or see blue lights downriver, or see the helicopter hovering over the river, my heart misses a beat and the adrenalin starts running.

'God gave me the ability to be a good rower. I used to win an awful lot of races. But I didn't realize until later on in life that the greatest races I was winning were when I was rowing to get someone out the water. That ability, that boat-manship, is there for a purpose. Maybe I'm reading things into it that aren't there. But it's nice to think that way.

'The river can be a wonderful friend, but a cruel, cruel master. You're fighting against it, and thinking all the time of what it can do to you. You've got to give it the greatest respect.'

It is a tradition in the Parsonage family to see in the new year on the Clyde. Parsonage and his father would drift downriver in one of their boats and listen to the bells in the Trongate steeple; then, on the stroke of midnight, Ben would sound his klaxon. It is something Parsonage continues at Hogmanay with his eldest son, also Ben. 'Once, all the ships on the river would reply,' he says. 'But now, sometimes, there isn't a single answer coming back.'

The Barras

The Barras – or Barrowland, to give it its Sunday name – is as much a part of the city's heritage as Kelvingrove Museum, the Necropolis, Saturday football and jeely pieces for tea, with a history of which the stalwarts of the area are justifiably proud.

The literally 'rags to riches' story of its founder, Maggie McIver, is as close to fairy tale material as the earthy and characterful citizens of Glasgow's East End may want to get.

Trading in second-hand goods is by no means a product of modern-day recessionary trends or the increasingly high unemployment figures, albeit these may influence its continuing popularity today.

In that other historic slump of the late '20s and early '30s, the years of the Great Depression, which prompted the national strike of 1926 and numerous rent strikes, Glasgow saw the emergence of what was destined to become at one point the biggest free-trade market in Europe.

It was the formalization of a street trading practice that originated in Victorian times around that part of the city, which was home to the majority of the city's poor, homeless and unemployed, much as it is today.

Yet, there is – as there was then – a band of entrepreneurial characters and pockets of hope and optimism amongst the community from which great things have grown.

As far back as the early 1800s, peddlers of used goods and hand-me-downs were already turning over a roaring trade and documentary evidence confirms that by the middle of the nineteenth century as much as £1,000 per week was regularly changing hands. This is corroborated in a work by Robert Reid, whom I believe to have been writing in his capacity as editor of the *Glasgow Herald*, in 1849: 'It will hardly be believed that sometimes £1,000-a-week changes hands in the old clothes trade, but we are assured of this on authority, which we deem highly trustworthy.'

As if in recognition of this, and possibly to cash in on an untapped rental revenue, the then Glasgow Corporation erected a covered market on Greendyke Street in 1875. However, many of the street hawkers shunned this formalized state of affairs, preferring to continue the tradition of pushing a barrow or driving their horse and cart around the streets to sell their wares – 'a gauin' fit's aye gettin'' is an age-old Glasgow phrase, meaning people who keep on the move are likely to pick up more opportunities, information or gossip than if they stayed in one place.

When they weren't selling from the barrow, the hawkers would often be seen trudging the streets, collecting bundles of clothes and bric-a-brac from middle-class Victorian households in the posh parts of town.

Once home, they would wash and repair anything saleable, ready for display at the weekend on their barrows, where goods were bought, sold or exchanged.

This system of bartering and street hawking served many social purposes. It gave the poor and unemployed a chance to earn a respectable living rather than resorting to begging or stealing, and it also allowed the many people who just couldn't afford the price of a spanking new pair of boots or a tailored suit from the upmarket and fashionable new department stores that were emerging around that time to clothe themselves.

Nothing was wasted. Any old clothes that were no longer serviceable or reparable went to the flock factories, where the rags were cleaned and used to fill mattresses and furniture instead of the usual horsehair.

Another source for the hawkers was the dockyards, where they would meet the boats coming in and barter their goods.

From the docks, enormous quantities of clothes found their way from Glasgow to Ireland and Eastern Europe on the return boat journey – an enterprising export trade.

It was during these times that the future Barras Queen Maggie McIver was introduced as a young girl to a way of life that was to shape her destiny and affect the lives of thousands of people for generations to come.

Maggie McIver: 'Work hard an' keep the heid.'

Margaret Russell, as she was known, was born in Galston, Ayrshire, the daughter of Mr and Mrs Russell. When she was just a young girl, her father, a policeman, transferred to the City of Glasgow Police Force and the family settled in Bridgeton.

Maggie's mother taught her the secrets of her craft as a French polisher and furniture restorer, skills that were to come to the fore in later years when she ran her second-hand furniture store in the Gallowgate, but her first introduction to street trading was when, as a teenager, she was asked to mind, or look after, a barrow for an older woman from nearby Parkhead.

She took to the task like a duck to water. When the barrow-owner returned, she found the young girl laughing and joking with the punters, having sold the barrowload of produce as fast as she could talk.

No one was aware at the time that this single event was to seal this young girl's fate as the future Barras Queen.

As she grew up, Maggie readily embraced the entre-preneurial spirit of the area, eventually owning her own barrow, selling the incongruous combination of fruit and fish. It was during her regular visits to the Scotch Fruit Bazaar that the burgeoning businesswoman was introduced to her future husband and, in 1898, Margaret Russell married James McIver.

Together, they put their savings into a small fruit shop in Bridgeton, later moving to Marshall Lane in the Gallowgate.

The Glasgow Corporation had erected an enclosed market to harness all the roving hawkers, but many chose to continue going around the streets selling their wares in a two-wheeled push-barrow or horse and cart.

This gave rise to other ancillary trades for the like of Mr Campbell, who built and repaired the barrows, and Nelson's Yard, who dealt, among other things, in cart horses, for sale or rent.

Those who didn't own their own barrow would hire one for the day, as Maggie did in the early years.

After the First World War, the Corporation Clothes Market, as it was known, had to be demolished and the hawkers who used the place found themselves without permanent stands. This gave Maggie an idea. She and her husband began to rent out barrows themselves. As time went by, they bought a plot of disused land at the Gallowgate on which to store their increasing stock of barrows. At one point, there were more than 300 barrows for rent, and the couple started to accumulate more and more land. Maggie was also astute enough to take advantage of post-war austerity and, later, the Great Depression, to buy up shops and other fading business premises.

Eventually, she had so many barrows on her property that she publicized the place as a permanent outdoor market with static stalls.

The market expanded rapidly. Anything and everything was readily available, from fruit, veg and fish to clothes, bric-a-brac – or swag, as they called it – and furniture. The market's reputation as a one-stop shopping centre spread beyond the city boundaries and, by the mid-1920s, the site was so well-established that Mrs McIver decided to cover the area over to protect traders and their wares from the rain and encourage punters to linger longer.

The decision was no doubt prompted by the continuing onslaught of torrential rain over six consecutive Saturdays.

As Maggie herself put it to an *Evening Times* journalist in an interview in 1954: 'Jist think of it. The poor craturs are oot aw week long, hawking fur the stuff. When they get it hame, they take it tae the steamie, wash the stuff oot and get it ready for the public. They hing it oot on the barra, doon comes the rain and it looks like the washin' hingin' oot again.'

So, the roof went up in 1926 over what had now become known simply as the Barras.

The business went from strength to strength. With the unfailing support of her husband, she continued to govern her numerous business commitments, as well as managing an ever-expanding brood of young McIvers.

Then one night in 1930 fate dealt the family a bitter blow. James McIver fell victim to a final and fatal attack of malaria, which he contracted on his tour of duty during the First World War.

Left alone to raise nine children, Maggie soldiered on determinedly.

In the 1930s, it was difficult enough being a 'single parent' in or out of work, let alone building a successful commercial concern while established firms all around her were falling under the pressure of a devastating financial depression.

For Maggie, there was nothing else for it but to roll up her sleeves and get on with it. 'Work hard an' keep the heid' was her mantra.

In 1931, sides were added to the construction, creating a totally enclosed marketplace, the official opening presided over by Labour MP, the great Jimmy Maxton. On Christmas Eve 1934 was the grand opening of Maggie's next venture, destined to become a beloved institution among market bargain hunters and rock-gig-goers around the world – the Barrowland Ballroom.

'Ur ye dancin'?'

Dancing was the order of the day at Barrowland in its heyday as a ballroom proper. The common vernacular, 'Ur ye dancin'?', was the normal introduction for chaps who wanted to ask a lady to dance. And there was a certain protocol to the procedure.

In those days, the band would play two of any given set: two waltzes, with a short gap before two foxtrots, and so on throughout the night. So when a lady was asked to dance, it was expected that she would be in that same gentleman's company for both dances. It was not good form to leave the floor after the first of a set of two numbers. So, the quality of the gentleman's dancing was paramount; no lady wanted to subject her toes to being stepped on more than once, if she could help it.

Similarly, if a lady turned a gentleman down when asked to dance, it was expected that she would 'sit out' the next two dances. She could not favour another suitor until the set was complete.

Dancing was such a crucial part of evening entertainment that 'good dancers' were at a premium and women would pay threepence to book a dance with one of the chosen few who would gather in a corner of the hall and peruse the dance floor for equally 'good' dance partners. The visual was somewhat reminiscent of the opening scene of the movie *Sweet Charity*, starring American actress Shirley MacLaine, featuring the song 'Big Spender'.

Eddy Cavin, in his capacity with Glasgow Life, the arm of the City Council that promotes art, sport and cultural activities in Glasgow, would give talks at the Mitchell Library about old Glasgow, sometimes including personal anecdotes.

He tells me: 'There was a lot of status surrounding being a good dancer, that's for sure. My mother told me about paying for a dance. She had gone to the Barrowland with her big sister and they were like chalk and cheese. My mum was a shy girl, but Ellen was big and brash and brassy. So my mum couldn't understand why all these boys kept coming over to dance with her instead of her sister. Ellen explained that she had paid for some dances for her; her sister would point to one dancer and say, "He's dancin' with you in three dances time." So I know that definitely did happen. They would also take their "dancing shoes" in their handbag and keep their curlers in their hair till the last minute, keeping them in place with a headscarf until they reached the dancehall and then it was straight to the powder room and off with the hair rollers. I've also heard that, in the 1940s, when stockings – or nylons – were scarce, the ladies would tint their legs with cold tea and get a pal to run a line up the back of their legs with eyebrow pencil to create the illusion that they were wearing silk stockings.

'And it wasn't just the girls who got all dressed up in their finery to go out to the dancing. Men would wear their best – or only – suit and tie. They would never dream of going out dressed like the young guys today, in casual gear. They would come in from their work, off with their boiler suit or dungarees, and head off to the public baths – tenements didn't have showers or bathrooms in those days – and they would pay to have a bath in a private cubicle. And their ma would have a clean white shirt ready for them.'

Barras patter

The Barras developed into more than a local street market. It was a hub of street entertainment. For almost a century, people have flocked to the Barras to enjoy the 'patter' and antics of the spielers, barkers, tipsters and buskers.

The sharp-witted banter that epitomizes that distinctive Glasgow humour is as alive today as it has always been (although some of the old-timers may disagree). Comedian Billy Connolly drew much of his material from his frequent visits to the Barras.

One of stallholder Frank Bennett's favourite stories involves the punter who took a liking to an old stag's head on Frank's stall.

'How much?' he asked Frank.

'Twenty quid.'

'But it's only got wan eye!'

'Aye, and if it had two eyes, Ah'd be wahntin' thirty.'

The punter found the solution immediately. 'Well, tak' oot the ither eye an' Ah'll gie ye a tenner fur it.'

Retired Freddie Bennedetti is another Barras stalwart who remembers only too well the showmen, such as Irish Paddy, the strongman who would 'miraculously' escape from yards of thick chains and half a dozen padlocks.

There was one story about Paddy arranging to be 'padlocked' by his friends using his specially designed locks. One day, after a minor dispute, his friends chained him up, swapped the padlocks and left him to his own devices. The comical image of a chained-up Paddy hopping along the street, trying to retrieve his dignity as well as his special padlocks, is a vivid memory for many.

There was no doubting Paddy's strength, however. In deep midwinter, lying in inches of snow, Paddy would perform tremendous feats of strength and endurance, inviting members of the public to smash giant sandstone blocks on his chest with a sledgehammer, balancing huge cartwheels and eating shoals of live goldfish while piercing his cheeks with six-inch needles.

Then there was the Snakeman, Chief Abadu from Nigeria, who claimed that his snake oil potion would cure a myriad of complaints, from callouses to baldness. As long-time 'grafter' Dick Lee put it: 'No one knows what it was made from, but one whiff of the stuff would blow yer bleedin' head off.'

Dick had come to the Barrowland market from London almost 35 years previously in the late 1950s, selling his goods from the back of his van, which, for many hawkers, serves as the modern day equivalent of the barrow.

He recounts many success stories of major High Street brands that made their early fortunes at the Barras, some of which went on to become plc giants from their humble beginnings.

Dick Lee remembers one of his contemporaries – Lou Wires – who laid on full-scale mannequin parades from his van, complete with models strutting up and down Kent Street, as though they were on the catwalk at a Paris fashion show.

Dick's distinctive East London accent earned him the nickname 'Cockney Jock', as he bombarded his audience with incredible stories of 'South Sea Island pearls' for 30 bob (£1.50), 'Roldini gold' brooches, 'stookie' (chalk) figurines and other 'swag'.

'You'd never get away with such fiction today,' laughs Dick, 'but the crowd loved it.' Then, as if he's still grafting at the back of his van, he falls into the familiar spiel: 'I'm not asking a tenner! I wouldn't even take a fiver, madam! Would you give me two quid for this magnificent piece of fine craftsmanship? Yes? Well, I don't want two quid, not even thirty bob. My treat to you, ladies and gentlemen – I'm giving them away today for 15 shillings!' he says, reaching a crescendo, with a flourish and a momentous clap of his hands. 'They snapped yer 'and off by the time you came to the bat [final knockdown price].'

Just along the road, there was Barnard the Herbalist, who sold potions out of the boot of his Rolls-Royce.

Not forgetting Mr Waugh, the former circus strongman with his own brand of miracle cures, with leftover crutches hanging round his stall, as if to prove his claims. His sideline in Barras-style entertainment of bending six-inch nails with his teeth was a real crowd puller.

Bargain hunters would often hear shouts of, 'Excellent value car radios and cassette players. Best prices in town – they're a' knocked off [stolen].'

And then there's the unforgettable Vickery, who, in order to emphasize the value of his wares, would lead eager shoppers to believe that the origins of his goods were, at best, questionable, intimating this with a nod and a wink and a tap of his nose.

Such were the bargains to be had at the Barras that punters just didn't believe it was the genuine article. So the grafters on the stalls had to resort to methods such as those employed by Freddie Bennedetti, who would sell his John White's brogues in the following fashion:

'Count with me, ladies and gentlemen, the number of

holes in this brogue' – and everyone would join in – 'One, two, three . . . twenty-three, twenty-four, twenty-five.'

'You see!' shouts Freddie. 'An extra hole. This means that there are twelve holes on one side and thirteen on the other. There's the defect. That's why we can sell these shoes so cheap. The "clicking machine" [a totally fictitious instrument] has missed one out!' In truth, there were twelve perfect holes on either side and one at the middle point to create the distinctive brogue appearance. So there was no defect.

'Let's face it,' Freddie continues with his spiel, 'it's not as if, when you meet your mates in the pub, they're going to say: "How you doin', pal. Did you know you've got twelve holes on one side and . . . ?" Sold!

As Freddie puts it: 'That's why they call us grafters, cos no one comes to the Barras to buy. And with some of the things for sale there, we really did have to graft to get rid of them. I had a crowd of people round my pitch one winter, standing in six inches of snow and queuing up to buy sunglasses from me – not just one pair but two! Now, that's salesmanship.'

Then there was Curt Cook, a real Barras character. He would auction jewellery at the weekend, with more gold on his hands than on his stand, and his favourite 'tiger's tooth' pendant hanging from his neck.

Curt arguably did more for the Barras than any advertising campaign ever could have done. Among his friends, he counted many politicians, as well as famed stars of stage and screen: Charlton Heston, Frankie Vaughan, Russ Abbott and many more, most of whom visited the Barras at Curt's invitation.

And, of course, the ubiquitous 'tipsters' would offer all-comers the winning horse for any race on the card, for the bargain price of a 'tanner' (sixpence, in old money).

One tipster, 'Wingy' Campbell, so named because of his only having one arm, was a favourite among the gambling fraternity.

Another well-remembered character would sell you a cigarette lighter and a coat hanger for a penny. A real bargain until you opened the bag to find you had actually bought a match and nail.

Polish Jack used to sell whole dinner sets, but you had to snap them up quick before he lost his patience and smashed the lot against the back of his stand.

And it wouldn't do to get too close to Johnnie 'Stick 'em'. Johnnie would mix a little powder with water, heat it over a bunsen burner and apply it to anything that moved – or, rather, stood still for a few seconds. Whatever the substance was, it would permanently bond together absolutely anything, a wooden walking stick to a sandstone brick, glass to metal, plastic to marble.

Johnnie's demonstration technique involved battering objects maniacally off the side of his stand to prove the strength of the substance.

And the most unlikely objects could be found at the Barras, from Capodimonte to a combined barometer, with clock and built-in humidity gauge, from canaries to elaborate musical cigarette dispensers.

Bud Pearson burned old gilt picture frames for their gold contents, no doubt reselling the charcoaled wood as barbecue briquettes.

There was even an old wireless 'volume expander', curiously named a 'stabulator' by its inventor.

Not to mention the plastic carrier bags full of tinned food. The only snag being there were no labels on any of the tins.

At Frank Bennett's, you could buy coffin handles, crutches, a dentist chair – all manner of crazy stuff – and it was all sold by the end of the day.

So many of the old characters are, sadly, departed now, but their memories are still a part of present-day Barrowland, as are their well-worn stories.

Stop anyone at the Barras and ask them about the old days and you will probably find that you are speaking to the friends, children or grandchildren of well-kent hawkers.

After the Barras outdoor marketplace was covered over in 1926, then completely enclosed by 1931, Maggie McIver hit on the idea of building a function suite for use by the traders.

She had reportedly come to regard herself as somewhat responsible for these traders who, while making their living at the Barras, were also contributing to her own sizeable fortune.

Every year she would lay on a huge party for the traders and hawkers, free of charge. For this purpose, the nearby St Mungo's Halls would be hired.

Official records show that Maggie bought a row of dilapidated tenements 'of the type which smudged the history of this great city of Glasgow'. She immediately had the sandstone buildings demolished and set about building 'a super Palais de Danse . . . on the site of evil slums'.

Not one to waste a single inch of space, Maggie's instructions to builders Messrs Hunter & Clark – Maggie had no time for excesses such as architects or designers – were that the ballroom should 'not encumber the ground'.

The dancehall was built on tall iron 'stilts', thus creating a ready-made roof for stallholders to trade their wares beneath. A canny business decision.

Another stipulation to the building contractors was that 'no one living beyond the precincts of the building should be employed in its erection and all materials [were] to be manufactured in Glasgow'.

By 1934, the Barras barkers had their own function suite, courtesy of the McIvers, and on Christmas Eve of that year, the Barrowland Palais de Danse was brought to life with the gaiety and colour of Barras traders on their Christmas 'night oot'.

Those were the days when the fashionable 'flapper' girls – so-called for the flapping of arms and legs required by the new racy dance craze, the Charleston – gave way to the more elegant waltz, foxtrot and tango. Every stallholder would attend 'aw done up in aw their finery', as Maggie put it. All the Barras traders would show themselves off at their best, bedecked in colourful silk shawls, taffeta dresses and bright jewellery, 'laughin', dancin' an' hivin' a rerr time', Maggie would say.

The Annual Barras Night Out became a tradition and many a romantic attachment was forged.

Reflecting the anticipation and excitement of concerts today, the emotional attachment to the place is summed up in a souvenir programme for Christmas 1935:

To view the outside of Barrowland Palais de Danse at night makes one impatient for the enjoyments within, the gay floodlighting and the last word in electric signs make you eager to join the happy throng of dancers and 'happy' does not adequately describe a company in Barrowland Palais. Imagine a hall aglow with cunningly concealed lights and a floor capable of holding a thousand dancers . . . the orchestra in scarlet uniforms of evening suit design, rendering their music, which is at once a pleasure and delight.

The booklet also praises the Barrowland matriarch, Mrs McIver, for managing to continue to play a prominent role in the social activities of the East End 'despite her 55 years'.

The New Year's Day matinee dance programme ran from 3 p.m. until 6 p.m., with ladies paying sixpence entry fee and gents paying ninepence.

Throughout the year, the ballroom was rented to bandleader Billy Blue and the Bluebirds, who held regular dances there. The rent augmented the McIver income, but, as Maggie's grandson Victor Cairns recalls: 'When grandmother saw the queues for those dance nights, she could see there was a lot of money to be made, so she approached a member of the band, drummer Billy McGregor, to form a big band of his own and work for her.' Billy Blue and the Bluebirds became Billy McGregor and the Gaybirds (a different Billy). Indeed, in a later line-up the band included Willie Rennie, Billy Mitchell and Billy McGregor.

The Barrowland dancehall had become so popular that regular dances were introduced and, by the time the Second

World War broke out, Barrowland was definitely the place to be and be seen, especially at weekends.

Up to 1,000 people could be comfortably accommodated; couples could waltz, tango and foxtrot the night away to the big band sounds of the Gaybirds, while American GIs introduced the less formal and livelier Big Apple, jive and jitterbug.

By the end of the Second World War, jiving had taken hold and the youth of the day made it their own, to the extent that the ballroom had a cordoned-off section just for the jitterbuggers, so that the traditional ballroom and cha cha dancers were safe from the more acrobatic antics of the GI Joes.

The years passed. Maggie's fortune grew and grew. The next generation of traders were taking up the reins, as were Maggie's own children, each with a different set of responsibilities. The third generation of the Barras Queen's dynasty was already in line for succession to the empire.

By the time of Maggie McIver's death in 1958, the Barras had already made her a millionaire. It seems incongruously appropriate that the same year saw the demise of the original Barrowland dancehall, which was totally destroyed by fire. Many saw these two unfortunate events as, indeed, the end of an era.

The success of the ballroom was in no small way attributed to Billy McGregor and the Gaybirds. Not only were they fabulous musicians playing all the popular tunes of the time, but also the emphasis for Billy was centred firmly on fun and entertainment.

After the reconstruction, the ballroom was reopened on

23 December 1960, the ceiling finished in 'midnight blue', the new design retaining the ceiling stars that had adorned the original, reproduced in a variety of bright colours.

It is rumoured that the new dance floor, made from imported Canadian wood, was 'sprung' using thousands of halved tennis balls to help cushion the dancers' feet.

Glasgow was dance crazy in the '60s and the city had an embarrassment of riches in various guises. There was Green's Playhouse, which hosted the world-renowned big band led by Joe Loss every year. The Cameo, the Astoria, the Tudor, F&F in Partick, the Locarno in Sauchiehall Street, Warrens in Bath Street, the Dennistoun Palais, the Berkeley, the West End ballroom, the Tower ballroom in Maryhill and the Plaza in Shawlands, to name only a handful, but what made the Barrowland Ballroom stand out was the showmanship factor among the band.

Barrowland resident bands were not only excellent musicians but also top-class entertainers, indulging the crowds with comedy skits and magic tricks.

Saxophonist Jimmy Phillips joined the band in 1959.

He remembers those days well: 'It was a totally different concept, which I had to take time to get used to. I had toured with Joe Loss and other top bands around the world. It requires a certain amount of discipline. The STV orchestra was the same. To leave that and join the carnival atmosphere at Barrowland was quite a shock. There was never a night when we didn't laugh our heads off at some of the antics. Billy even had comedy scripts specially written for our performances. Sometimes we could hardly play for laughing.

'I remember one night when [fellow Gaybird musician] John McGuinness was performing his usual stunt, the Indian rope trick, when the mechanism that pulled the rope up suddenly snapped. Johnny had already climbed quite high up before this and came thundering down, landing right inside the grand piano. The crowd loved it.'

Another popular feature of dance nights was the 'spot dance' competition. The band would play and couples danced until they felt the unwelcome tap on the shoulder that meant they had to leave the floor. The competition would continue until only one couple was left, and they were deemed to be the best dancers on the night. A variation of this competition was when the bandleader would ask all those couples who were, say, wearing red to leave the floor, then couples not wearing a tie, and so on until only one couple was left. The winning couple would then be asked to choose one of the boxes at the back of the stage with the chance of winning anything from a rotten egg to £500.

The band would also be expected to accompany any visiting singers.

Over the years, the Barrowland Ballroom has played host to many international stars, not least Dizzie Gillespie, Joe Loss, Henry Hall, Ray Fox and Jack Hilton – all among the greatest bandleaders of their time. Johnny Dankworth and his singer wife Cleo Laine also performed.

Stars such as Glasgow East Ender Lulu and local boy Allan Stewart were discovered there, and singer Lena Martell's early career began as the resident vocalist.

The Gaybirds and the Barrowland Ballroom also featured in the film *Floodtide*, starring the great Jimmy Logan.

Bible John

Barrowland Ballroom played a role in the case of another infamous serial killer who was never brought to book. On 22 February 1968, Patricia Docker became the first reported victim of the serial killer whom the press dubbed Bible John.

What began as a well-earned break, a girls' night out, was to end in the rape and bloody murder of a young mum. Glasgow had been spared the terror of a serial rapist and murderer for only a decade, following the trial and execution of Peter Manuel.

At the centre of the killings was the Barrowland Ballroom.

This became the killer's hunting ground.

On 5 August 1969, mother of three Jemma McDonald dropped off her children with her sister and headed out with her mates. She was found by children in a nearby building the next morning. She had been raped and strangled, and her body was badly beaten.

What little we know of the killer is a sketchy description from the sister of the third victim and a few regulars of the disco: a tall, thin man with sandy-coloured hair.

By October 1969, the killer had not been caught.

Women were encouraged to stay together and be vigilant and not to leave the dancehall alone with a man, whether they knew him or not.

Both of the first victims had been meeting friends.

On 30 October, two sisters were getting dressed up for a Halloween night out. Helen Puttock left her two children with her husband and went off to meet her sister, Jean McLaughlin. She would never see them again.

Helen's body was found in a garden near her home in Scotstoun. Again, she had been raped and strangled.

Jean was able to give more detail to the police about the man who was suspected of her sister's murder, as she had shared a taxi with her sister and the suspect on their way home. He was well-spoken, she said; well-dressed, tall, slim, with reddish hair, and he was teetotal. He quoted a lot from the Bible and explained to the two women that his father had told him dancehalls were dens of iniquity.

At this time, the forensic examination of DNA was in its infancy. Later, DNA evidence was inconclusive. So semen marks on Helen's clothing and a bite mark on her leg brought nothing new to the investigation.

In 2007, there was speculation that the convicted murderer Peter Tobin might have been the Barrowland killer, but, despite some uncanny coincidences, this theory was abandoned.

One striking fact that linked the three victims was that they were menstruating at the time of their murder, which some believe may have been a trigger.

It is also reported that menstruation was a trigger for Peter Tobin's violence. He met his first wife at the Barrowland dancehall and he left Glasgow soon after the third murder in 1969.

Bible John has never been identified and the murders remain unsolved.

Parkhead's 'Winning' ways

Few large industrial concerns, while significant, survived to see the millennium celebrations of 2000. In some parts, only the street, renamed after merchants and tobacco barons, holds a clue to certain factories' address. In others, not even a street sign is there to give away its secret – Papillon Street, named for the Turkey Red dye processor, no longer exists.

Many of the streets around the East End have vanished completely and are preserved only on some – but not all – ancient maps. However, some streets have been reincarnated in modern housing estates or in the names of modern business and industrial estates. It's a great pastime to walk around these estates with a notepad, taking down interesting street names. Obviously, all the caveats apply: daytime, not night time; don't go alone, bring a friend or set up an interest group; don't turn up looking dodgy – you don't want five screaming police cars screeching into the street.

Of course, if you'd take the couch potato route, there's a great website, parkheadhistory.com, that lists loads of street names and explains, as accurately as it can, their meanings. Fascinating stuff.

When Henry Winning of Parkhead started his twine- and string-making firm in 1880, he may have harboured expectations that his business would survive generations of Winnings – and he was right – but he would have no way of knowing just how much engineering and industry would change. And he could never have anticipated Google and the worldwide web.

Henry and his brother-in-law James Hamilton built their

impressive empire on Caroline Street in Parkhead 134 years ago.

It remains their headquarters in 2014, as they continue to produce a vast portfolio of string, twine and other packaging materials – up to 95 per cent in Parkhead. The business stayed in the family for four generations and is still family-run.

Parkhead Forge

Another key industry that is long gone is the Parkhead Forge, which continues in name only as a modern shopping complex, the old working forge having closed in 1976. At its height, the old forge employed more than 20,000 workers.

The Reoch Brothers & Co. established the forge around 1837 and sold the business only four years later to shipwright Robert Napier.

Napier had made his name in engine construction, having been apprenticed under his father from the age of 16, later working as journeyman to Robert Stevenson. This was an outstanding opportunity; Stevenson's was one of only three of the most renowned engineering firms of its day.

It was Stevenson who co-engineered one of the most celebrated lighthouses in history, the Bell Rock.

When I say 'co-engineered', his fellow engineer was the esteemed John Rennie. Stevenson didn't like the way Rennie questioned his decisions. After a visit from Rennie to the construction site off Angus, Scotland, Stevenson determined never to let him near 'his' lighthouse site again.

He made sure Rennie would be kept busy on his return

from the site visit. Rennie returned to the mainland to find a veritable tree-worth of letters from Stevenson asking technical and engineering questions in the utmost detail. He reckoned that would keep Rennie busy and out of his hair. He sent more than 80 queries by letter, including those discussing such minutiae as which putty to use on the lighthouse windows.

Even before the Bell Rock was finished, word of this pioneering feat of engineering was getting round and visitors arrived daily to this new tourist attraction.

It was a hugely dangerous job for engineering and construction workers, and there were a number of deaths during the project.

Those who survived accidents – at least one lost a finger and another was trapped under a falling crane – were offered other positions that suited their physical abilities. Others would be offered the job as a lighthouse keeper when the lighthouse was commissioned and working.

After one incident, in which a man had drowned after falling during construction, his brother was offered the job that had become vacant. It doesn't sound very sensitive, but the drowned man had been the family's only breadwinner.

Fallen engineers were also offered jobs as lighthouse operators. Although they would be thankful for the work, it must have been a difficult pill to swallow. These men were the engineering equivalent of a rock star's entourage.

And tragedy was not long in visiting Stevenson himself.

While on the Rock in January 1810, he received news that his twins were taken with whooping cough. Two weeks later, his youngest daughter died of the same disease.

One year later – four years after work began in earnest – the lanterns were lit for the first time on Bell Rock.

Even today, descriptions of Bell Rock are peppered with superlatives; it has been named one of the seven wonders of the industrial world.

There's no doubt that Stevenson considered Bell Rock to be his baby and he didn't want any interference. He claimed that he ignored most of the extremely detailed replies from Rennie during the construction period, but that is almost certainly not the case. Rennie was also a celebrated engineer and who would be so arrogant as to wave aside the advice of such a prominent engineering icon?

Stevenson was the founder of a dynasty of engineering greatness and his grandson, Robert Louis, was to make his name as one of Scotland's great writers and adventurers.

So you can imagine what a gig it was for Robert Napier to have the chance to work up close with Stevenson.

In 1815, Napier felt he was ready to go it alone. Early work was varied, but it helped pay the bills. The business steadily grew and he began to acquire contracts to build engines for shipbuilders.

Napier secured commissions to build engines for yachts and paddle-steamers and, at the 1827 August Regatta, the winner and runner-up in their class were fitted with Napier's engines, which certainly boosted his reputation, much to the chagrin of some rivals who dubbed him a mere 'tinkerer'.

He secured a major Royal Navy commission for HMS *Black Prince*. While Napier continued to be based in Govan, the Parkhead Forge would carry out much of the forging, plate and armour work.

It was his biggest contract to date and he was quite happy to work alongside locomotive engineer William Beardmore, who was invited in by the forge manager. This was a diversification for Beardmore and proved to be the beginning of a world-renowned shipbuilding operation.

Napier and Beardmore worked well together and, around 1860, Beardmore senior was made partner in the business, which would eventually give employment to upwards of 40,000 workers.

William Beardmore junior was apprenticed to his father at the forge from the age of 15. On the completion of his apprenticeship, young Beardmore pursued further education and was studying at the Royal School of Mines in London in 1877 when his father died. Beardmore junior was happy to leave the business in his uncle Isaac's hands until he completed his education two years later. He rejoined the firm in 1879 as junior partner.

Isaac retired in 1886, leaving William junior sole partner of the business.

The trustees of Isaac's estate weren't convinced that he was up to the task of running such a large operation. They knew little of his contribution to the firm and tried to rein him in on further investment, but to no avail. He had persuaded his uncle to invest in a new plant and a steel foundry, paving the way for further expansion.

He was experimentalist, open to new technology, ambitious and confident, all of which contributed to his driving Beardmore & Co. to greater heights.

His expansion included investment in other allied concerns. If he wanted to continue to expand, he needed more investment. He changed the operation from a partnership to a limited company, which made it a juicy investment opportunity, and Beardmore junior soon brokered a deal with the engineering firm Vickers (Son & Maxim) Ltd. And they were happy to let Beardmore continue with his expansions.

Sir Ernest Shackleton and Parkhead Forge

In 1906, Ernest Shackleton began working at the forge in a technical capacity, but by this stage he was already planning an expedition to Antarctica.

The Nimrod expedition in 1907 was funded mostly by William Beardmore junior, after whom he named one of the world's largest glaciers, the Beardmore Glacier. And, of course, Parkhead built the sledges and other iron and steelwork that was needed for the mission. On his triumphal return, Shackleton was already planning his next expedition.

But the bells of war were tolling and world leaders were gearing up for the mother of all wars.

Parkhead Forge was re-tooling to supply the irons of war and young Beardmore's expansion into steel really paid off. During the war years, the forge was running three shifts over twenty-four hours. Day and night, the whole of Parkhead could hear the earth-shaking thud from the mighty hammer, dubbed Samson.

One old timer I spoke to told me the forge worked all out, supplying the war effort. He remembered giant gun barrels the size of coffins forged from a single piece of metal.

The Parkhead forgers' expertise was known around the world and people would be sent from other countries to train there. He remembers one group of Japanese trainees.

To control the outflow of work, pieces would be sent out in batches to either of the forge depots with the foreman hailing: 'Awa Parkhead!' or 'Awa Camlachie!' The story goes that, not being great in the language department, the trainees used to make these calls randomly, believing they were some kind of mystical incantation influencing the quality of the work.

'My grandfather worked at the forge and, often, he would just leave his work clothes in the street because they were reduced to rags by the hot sparks and splashes thrown from the seething hot metal.'

It was during these tempestuous times that Shackleton had planned his most daring expedition. How could he take off on some Antarctic adventure when war was waging at home?

He and his whole crew decided to sign up to fight for Crown and country, but the then Prime Minister, Herbert Asquith, and the War Propaganda Bureau under David Lloyd George had other ideas.

The WPB recruited Britain's most influential writers to contribute to the country's morale and promote Britain's successes to the wider public.

The list of writers reads like a *Who's Who* of some of the world's finest penmen: Sir Arthur Conan Doyle, Arnold Bennett, John Masefield, Ford Madox Ford, William Archer, G. K. Chesterton, Sir Henry Newbolt, John Galsworthy, Thomas Hardy, Rudyard Kipling, Gilbert Parker, G. M. Trevelyan and H. G. Wells.

A heady line-up.

Everyone agreed that the best way that the brave and

honourable crew of Shackleton's *Endurance* could serve their country and keep its spirits up would be to go ahead with the expedition.

So, the Antarctic explorers set off on their own war mission: to raise the British flag and claim their own victory over some of the world's most treacherous terrain.

To cross the Antarctic via the South Pole – what an adventure! And now, what a mission to serve one's country! This expedition meant more than anything. The whole country needed it to be successful.

The modern day motto of the US Marines is 'Never leave a man behind'. This promise could have been inspired by the celebrated explorer, who first used those immortal words on the ill-fated yet legendary 1915 Endurance expedition to Antarctica.

It was an ambitious undertaking to cross Antarctica via the South Pole. Shackleton was an experienced Antarctic explorer and the Endurance expedition was considered the last of the great conquests.

Endurance never reached its destination but, far from being labelled a failure, this was to become an epic rescue journey of legendary proportions. The ship became entrapped in pack ice that eventually crushed its hull. It took ten months to sink after the men abandoned ship.

The tale of the gargantuan rescue mission in which Shackleton made good on his promise not to leave one man behind is truly awe-inspiring.

Talk o' the steamie

Well, heroics are all very noble, but life in the East End was business as usual.

To paraphrase the wisdom of the Holy Buddha: before Enlightenment – *dae the wahshin'*; after Enlightenment – *dae the wahshin'*.

Well, you couldn't get more down to earth than the Parkhead steamie.

It was a wash house, but also a central social hub for East End wifies.

It was a gossip store where friends and neighbours would meet and catch up on the local news and the latest fashions, a therapeutic release for women to let off steam, so to speak, about the trials and tribulations of married life: 'See that man a' mine . . .'

And an education, especially for the younger newlyweds, whose inexperience in the steamie protocol – and in life in general – left them vulnerable to light-hearted ribbing from the more worldly-wise among the wash-house wimmin.

Steamie protocol observed strict guidelines when it came to access to sinks and drying pipes. Diplomacy was all. Inevitably, equipment would pack up without warning and the skills of the steamie maintenance man would be sought.

'He was a good guy to be pally with if you wanted on one of the sinks in a hurry,' remembers one steamie stalwart. 'And all the women would flirt with him. It's true what they make oot in that play *The Steamie* [written by playwright Tony Roper].

'He was aye steamin' wae the drink and thought he was

God's gift. But ye had tae keep in wae um. Steamie day meant gettin' the wean's pram oot tae kert aw the wahshin'. Ye'd wrap up all the shirts and weans' claes in the sheets and pile it aw oan tap ae the pram and off ye'd go.

'There wiz even showers there, which were sorely needed after a half day sweatin' ower the sinks. Sheets are mair than just heavy when they're hingin' doon wi' wahter.'

But not everybody lived within the catchment area of this housewives' boon and washdays in the outlying areas were a soapy drudge.

In Tollcross, however, at the turn of the century and for years afterwards, Mrs Robertson, who ran 'the store' on Causeyside Street where young Cissie Smith lived, installed a huge industrial 'mangle', with its massive turning handle, and locals would take turns at wringing out the washing at Mrs Robertson's store.

Cissie Smith remembers what a boon the steamie was when she was growing up in the 1920s and '30s.

'The steamie was a wonderful thing. It really was. Up until then – and for years after – women would take their washing up to Glasgow Green to tread them in big buckets and then hang them out to dry on the hanging poles that the corporation had installed on the Green. Or they laid them out on the grass to bleach white in the sun.

'We didn't live close enough to the Parkhead steamie,' Cissie recalls, 'but I remember as a wee girl being sent down to Mrs Robertson's store with my big sister to wring out the sheets in the mangle, and ma da's and brothers' shirts, with the great long tails on them in those days.

'I also remember when I got married just after the war

and there was this great new thing which was a kind of early washing machine with an "agitator" no less.

'I couldn't wait to get one and, of course, with hire purchase being introduced, people felt as if they were getting things for nothing, virtually, because you could pay it up on the never never.

'Then, in 1951, I was walking up Union Street in the town and there was this big huddle around the Stuart Brothers furniture store and, in the window, was this new mangle: the Parnal, it was called. And instead of "cawing" the handle, which was heavy work and time-consuming, you just had to press a button. Well, I loved that Parnal! And I'll never forget when a friend of ours bought a twin tub with the automatic spinner, doing away with the mangle – the whole street turned up to see it. And she made tea and scones and sandwiches for everybody. It was the talk o' the steamie, right enough. It was so modern and swish. But I do remember she eventually took the scunner to it, as did many.

'Of course, there was always those who would say: "Spin drier? Ach, Ah widnae thank yea fur wahn." But it did turn out to be a mixed blessing, as there was so much more ironing to do, with all those creases spun into the shirts and sheets. The spin drier took a helluva lot more water out of the washing. You see, with the mangle, you folded the sheets quite neat and passed them through the roller like that and that helped to smooth them out.'

Parkhead can claim as their son William Miller, who gave the world 'Wee Willie Winkie', first printed in the cult anthology *Whistle-Binkie: A Collection of Songs for the Social Circle.*

Shettleston: mines, mills and ice cream

There are so many wonderful resources that go into the minutiae of how and why place names are changed; they also clarify misinterpretations of names and are worth seeking out. I tend to refer to the current nomenclatures for simplicity, but Shettleston is one of the most interesting cases, so I think it needs a special mention, having gone through almost 50 different spellings in medieval times alone and still its name continued to evolve.

Shettleston first appears in ecclesiastical record books in 1242, when the land was granted to Bishop William Bonnington by King Alexander II. The grant included huge swathes of land that became known as Tollcross. This estate was far more extensive than the comparatively small village of Tollcross of modern times.

In the 1700s, Shettleston was very much a mining village, with mines scattered around the outskirts, including Barrachnie, Sandyhills and Auchenshuggle. Around that time, it was known as Schedenstoun, but the village was also a hub for weavers and potters.

The weaver's shuttle was essential to the handloom process and so the village became known as Shuttleston for a while and the village church was recorded as Shuttleston Kirk, but this is a modern interpretation.

Another popular theory is that the village was named for the area the Sheddons at the toll, which local kids used as their playground. There was also a Sheddons coal pit. Some sources assert that 'Sheddons' was originally spelled 'sheddings', meaning parting, as in a middle shed in hairstyling means a middle parting. This makes sense because the toll was the end of the road, the point at which travellers had to turn right or left to carry on their journey.

I favour a different theory: that Sheddons relates back to an ancient family name of Sedin.

There are clusters of Sedins in the US, mainly around Washington and Illinois, but it is clear from US immigration and naturalization records that these were immigrants from overseas. There are also Sedins listed in the eighteenth- and nineteenth-century census records, located around London and Middlesex mainly.

The vast majority of Sedins, however, are from Sweden, which suggests the origin of the family name.

It appears that the oldest, and possibly only, Sedin in old Scotland lived in Shettleston as far back as the Middle Ages, prior to 1179. According to one reliable source, the Sedin family home was mentioned in correspondence to the Bishop of Glasgow and referred to a 'villam filie Sedin', meaning the house of Sedin's son, or Sedinson House. Actually, 'filie' strictly translates as 'daughter', so who knows?

The early settlement would have comprised 'clachans' of small dwellings, housing farm workers, pit workers or weavers, not the heavily tenemented thoroughfares of later developments.

Wages were low and often paid by the day. Some colliery owners paid no wages but allowed the pitmen provisions from the pit store instead.

Historically, miners from different collieries or villages had their own brass band, which travelled quite far afield to play. Championships were vigorously contested and

Shettleston had an enviable reputation as one of the best, even being invited to tour.

One may marvel at how men could be choking up coal dust and fumes all day in hard labour and then have the 'pech' to blow into a trumpet. Perhaps this was an effective way of 'clearing the tubes'. The band would practise in the Wee Seller pub.

Shettleston had no great need for a police station in the nineteenth century, but residents were induced to create an early 'neighbourhood watch' scheme to guard the graveyard at night.

Burke and Hare are the most notorious grave robbers, but they weren't alone. They were only really caught because, to keep up with demand from Edinburgh's medical students, they decided to cut out the middleman and nominate themselves the grim reapers of Edinburgh, carrying out at least 16 killings.

Grave robbers were so prevalent, in fact, that two sentry posts were built near the cemetery, with a running rota of villagers manning each one per night.

One of Shettleston's oldest sons and a great entrepreneurial character was Thomas G. Simpson. He moved to the village with his parents as a young boy.

Like so many successful self-made businessmen, Simpson wasn't that great at school. He was a natural and versatile opportunist who was always looking for a new venture from which to profit.

He certainly wasn't a johnny-come-lately.

His story goes that he dropped out of school at ten years of age – although that may be an exaggeration. He didn't want to recite poems and didn't see the need for the 'three Rs' – the historical essentials of reading, (w)riting and (a)rithmetic. He wanted to earn money and coalmining, at least at the seam, didn't have much need for the skills of reading and writing, although he would have at least picked some things up from school.

He continued down the mines until, at 45 years of age, which was the average life expectancy for a miner, he decided he'd done enough for the coal industry and wanted something new. His first business venture was an ice-cream and sweetie shop, which again he stuck with for two decades. Simpson's ice-cream shop drew folk from all over the county.

His next big investment, which he also worked at for 20 years, was running a billiard hall in his home.

In all his commercial concerns, he was fully invested and committed to offer the best quality standards.

He acquired land with permission to build a house that would be both home and business. He installed ten billiard tables on the ground floor on what he would name Simpson Street.

Simpson was not ostentatious; indeed, his politics were very much socialist. He was active in the Independent Labour Party and chaired the Shettleston branch.

Settled on the main road to Edinburgh, the village strategically punched above its weight and soon caught up with itself as it developed into the mid-1800s, when it was a busy stop on the Edinburgh/Glasgow route. At that time, the toll admitted six stagecoaches daily: 'the Express', 'Telegraph', 'Regulator', 'Enterprise', 'Red Rover' and 'Royal Mail'. It had its own rail stop by 1871.

Despite its strategic appointments, Shettleston was still a small village and had to fight the town council for every amenity.

Eventually, by the turn of the twentieth century, the village – which was growing into a small township – had street-lighting and proper paths and other essential amenities.

As with young boys who all of a sudden shoot up in height at puberty, Shettleston grew rapidly into something more like the town we know today. It had a Main Street (now Shettleston Road), shops and a new school, its own Shettleston Co-op, then the Co-op added a creamery on Pettigrew Street. It attracted large concerns eager for open space to develop factories, such as a large bottling plant.

Then came the stalwarts of a settled community: the Shettleston Boys Brigade, a football club, a bowling club and the gold standard Shettleston Harriers, a running and athletics club that is still revered around the world for its world-class and Olympian sporting heroes. World records were made and broken there.

But the incorporation of Shettleston as part of the City of Glasgow was the first sign that Shettleston truly had 'arrived'.

Carmyle

In the tradition of conveyancing since medieval times, Carmyle was brought under the jurisdiction of Bishop Herbert of Glasgow to the Newbattle Abbey in Midlothian.

During the 1500s, this was not occupied as one entity

by some bloated laird. It was feud to encourage community development and to raise some income in taxes and rents.

Around this time, it was the Bogles who were most associated with the estate. This was by no means a gentrified ancient dynasty. Theirs was new brass, worked from the muck o' the lands.

They had come through the ranks of 'rentallers' (or 'bunnetted lairds') as tenant farmers of Shettleston, eventually amassing enough in the coffers to purchase the land for themselves. That put the family on the first rung of the property ladder and the family fortunes progressed, with each judicious marriage another step up the social ladder – members of old baronial aristocracy weren't so daft as to sniff at the chance to augment their territorial portfolio further.

The Bogles were even beckoned to walk towards the light and partake of the many riches that the tobacco treasure chest bestowed.

In the 1700s, mainly through marriage or heredity, it was then the Dunlops who pretty much dominated the manor.

The land was highly prized, as lush and bountiful agricultural ground, which attracted wildlife in abundance, who enjoyed the shelter of the forest. The luscious lands along the riverbanks were fertile and giving. But it wasn't the flora and fauna that attracted ambitious merchants to the place.

James Dunlop, together with his friend James Corbet, was after the quarrying and mining privileges, and would use the fertile land for agriculture.

When whispers of the opening of a canal started circulating in the corridors of power, any merchants in the know invested in the project. They knew that, by the time the

Monkland canal was opened, their multiple estates would have shot up in value and the new waterway would have eased the transportation of minerals, coal, slate and even livestock.

James Dunlop pretty much bought into the whole of Carmyle. It was a substantial estate that Colin Dunlop inherited on his father's death only a few years later.

Colin was to take his family name to greater heights in the field of commerce, not least in co-founding the Ship private bank, which funded much of the tobacco trade's expeditions. Colin Dunlop & Sons was a giant concern.

It seemed impossible that such a hulking commercial concern could be brought to its knees, but Glasgow's tobacco merchants suffered a veritable bankruptcy epidemic as businesses and their funding banks went down with the American War of Independence. There were three generations of Dunlops involved in businesses and holding property in the East End. Whole estates had to be sold off to avoid total bankruptcy and it was the grandfather, James Dunlop of Garnkirk, who would lose most of his assets in a financial rescue mission. He did not live long after the Garnkirk estate, among other assets, was sold, but his two sons managed to finesse a deal with their sympathetic buyer whereby the brothers held on to the mining and quarrying rights. Thus, the Dunlops could continue mining.

Possibly the best known Dunlop today is Colin, who was born in 1775. It was he who bought the sputtering business of the Clyde Ironworks and raised the firm to new heights. He was also very active politically and a prominent leader of the new Reform Party in Glasgow.

The Dunlops of Carmyle and Tollcross, and the Corbets of Tollcross, were almost inextricably linked over some few generations, either through marital connections or as friends and business colleagues.

Tollcross

I mentioned earlier that 'Little Hill' – which became Janefield Cemetery and was renamed the Glasgow Eastern Necropolis – is known variously as Little Hill of Camlachie and Little Hill of Tollcross, etc.

This may simply have been according to geographical perspective: if you lived on the Camlachie side of Little Hill, then what else would you call it?

Similarly, the (boundary) lines were blurred between many estates because they were sectioned off to different owners. So more than one family could claim to be, for example, the Walkinshaws of Camlachie or the Buchanans of Camlachie in the same generation.

So why, when we read about Tollcross, do we first learn about Shettleston?

Perhaps because, when the lands of Shettleston were conveyed to the bishopric of Glasgow, they included the whole of the lands of Tollcross, if I'm understanding this right.

It would appear that Tollcross was wholly a part of Shettleston and not just its geographical neighbour. It is accepted that the original Shettleston Cross was actually situated some way away from the later village cross-road and within the boundaries of Tollcross.

And originally Camlachie was wholly part of Tollcross,

although that might be over-simplifying matters.

But such detail is not for this book. This is a book of stories, so let's get on with some more . . .

Possibly the oldest landowning family in Glasgow is the Corbets of Tollcross, whose predecessors were the MacKerstens, known to have resided in the East End for centuries – even before mention of Baron Roger Corbet in the late thirteenth century.

Gabriel Corbet (sometimes spelled Carbart) was already occupying Tollcross (or Towcorse) before it was formally feud to the family by Archbishop Boyd in 1580.

In the early 1600s, records name James Corbet of Towcors.

The Corbets were still in residence by the end of the century and continued to woo the land until 1810 and the last of the Corbet line, brothers Major James and Cunningham.

The Dunlops of Shettleston inherited the Tollcross estate. Population figures shot up with the establishment of the Clyde Ironworks in 1786, the sister company of Carron Works, and new businesses moved in. The Clyde Works almost exclusively fed the troops with armoury during the Napoleonic Wars.

The Clyde Works manager, Joseph Outram, was to become the proud father of George, who would grow up to become founder and editor of The (then 'Glasgow') Herald. He was also quite an accomplished poet and satirist. History has never before offered such a satirical social commentator, who could not just cleverly highlight the peculiarities of old Scots law, served up in a dish that would be palatable to the lay reader, but also employ the vernacular of ancients Scots to boot – well, it's just sheer genius.

If you get a chance, have a go at a few of Outram's works: 'The Annuity', 'The Multipoinding', 'Souman an' Rouman' or 'The Process of Augmentation'. Indeed, if you can get hold of it, *Legal & Other Lyrics: Containing a Number of New Pieces*.

Outram's father, Joseph, would still have been works manager when, in 1829, Clyde Works was approached by a funding syndicate to carry out a series of trials and experiments that would completely transform iron production and spark the exponential rise of the Scottish iron industry worldwide.

I have to keep repeating myself, but so many inventions and innovations across history were incubated in Scotland and a large proportion in Glasgow and the East End. What can I say? We're a country of geniuses.

Shettleston-born James Beaumont Neilson invented hot blast technology, which improved the efficiency of iron furnaces and reduced processing costs significantly. Not having the funds or facilities to carry out trials to prove this new hot blast process, he approached local men of substance – Charles Macintosh (of raincoat fame); Colin Dunlop (of the rubber tyre family) and John Wilson of Dundyvan – to invest in his brainchild. This syndicate of business angels were to be repaid for their convictions rather handsomely.

Ask not what your creditors can do for you, but . . .

Colin was succeeded by his son, James of Tollcross, in 1837.

It was James who built Tollcross and founded Tollcross public park. His meticulous attention to the gardens and personal selection of all its flora laid down a marker in estate management that would endure. Tollcross Park has long been associated around the world with excellence and, for many years, hosted the hugely prestigious World Rose Trials.

James, while possessing many of the traits and qualities of a business magnate so prevalent within the family genes, didn't have in his armoury the quality of ruthlessness that goes along with the traits of sound judgement and entrepreneurship. He wasn't quick to ask: 'What's in it for me?'

Indeed, had his bank's fellow directors possessed just a modicum of his sense of fairness and justice, they may have been able to save their business from bankruptcy.

James had the misfortune to be chairman of the Board of Directors at the Western Bank when, in 1857, it experienced a totally epic fail.

His response was to attempt to honour as many of his bank's creditors as possible rather than to walk away wiping his hands of the whole sorry affair and liquidized all of his personal assets to pay creditors off. He managed to raise upwards of £100,000 (again, squillions in today's money).

His fellow directors were not of the same mind and the case was taken to court. The court judged that directors had no further obligation to their creditors than to meet their limited responsibilities as ordinary shareholders.

In a rare example of benevolence over greed, had the story played out to James's script, and others followed his example, the bank may well have been saved.

The Tollcross Park of today, which was taken over by the then Glasgow Corporation (town council), has a stunningly beautiful centrepiece within the district of Tollcross free and open to all visitors.

Tollcross can claim as their son William Miller, who gave the world 'Wee Willie Winkie', first printed in the cult anthology *Whistle-Binkie: A Collection of Songs for the Social Circle*. As their son, he was buried in the grounds of a church, which was devastated by fire and, soon after, demolished. No one knows exactly where his grave would have been.

Mount Vernon – what's in a name?

Now, this is an interesting one. All ye who thunk for generations that Mount Vernon was named after the Virginia tobacco plantation, think again.

The popular version of how Mount Vernon got its name is embedded in the golden years of tobacco trading.

According to generally accepted theory, the lands a few miles east of Glasgow were originally named Windyedge and were bought from Edinburgh merchant Adam Fairholm by Glasgow tobacco merchant George Buchanan, son of Andrew of Drumpellier.

Buchanan was a junior partner in a syndicate set up to rake in a fortune in tobacco, as did many syndicates and a few individuals who invested in plantations, mainly in Virginia, to corner the supply route from source.

To make the story uber sexy, we are informed that George Buchanan's syndicate had bought a plantation neighbouring that of Lawrence Washington, half brother of George, who would go down in history as the first President of the United States, following the War of Independence, which spoiled the party for everyone by fighting a silly war while they were trying to make a killing in a far more cut-throat war of Profit and Loss.

Lawrence's property was originally known as Hunting Creek, before he renamed it in favour of the celebrated naval campaigner Admiral Edward Vernon, whom Lawrence had served under during the Spanish war of 1739–42. Most sources say that Buchanan named his East End estate Mount Vernon after his neighbour's plantation in the US.

Though, according to a feature in the *Glasgow Herald* as late as 1861, the name was changed from 1743. It suggests that Buchanan's tobacco imports were not from his own plantation, but bought directly from Washington's renamed Mount Vernon estate, which prompted Buchanan to alter his Glasgow estate.

This is the recurring version: that Buchanan simply named the estate Mount Vernon because George Washington's brother, and Buchanan's Virginia neighbour, called his that.

Dates vary as to when Buchanan acquired the property from Fairholm, but 3 April 1758 looks like the frontrunner.

So the main and possibly only conflicting view, backed up by what looks like original documentation and facsimile, is that of local historian Robert Murray, who contests that Buchanan could neither have named Mount Vernon as late as 1758 for either Washington or Admiral Edward Vernon, nor in 1743, since Buchanan hadn't bought the Windyedge estate as early as that.

It would appear that the estate was named Mount Vernon in December 1741, before Fairholm or Buchanan were even in the pie, by one Robert Boyd, who had acquired the land from the trustees of the estate of a certain John Pitcairn. One argument asserts that it was mere coincidence and that, well, the world's full of Mount Vernons.

Another theory is that it was Boyd who had named the estate Mount Vernon after the decorated Admiral.

Mount Vernon was the motherlode from which more modern villages were created.

Baillieston Baillies

Baillieston appears to have evolved as a piece of land annexed from Mount Vernon, or Windyedge, as it was known in 1732, when the village name was first used. It therefore shares its history with Mount Vernon.

I'm grateful to the meticulous historian Robert Murray for pointing me in the direction of fellow detail-driven historian the late Scott Maxwell, who put so much work and time into identifying the original purchaser of the quaintly appointed village and who owned the estate from 1899 until 1951.

I think the presumption is that, when we see a buyer has purchased a piece of an established estate, they'll want to lay down roots there, which can leave one drawing blanks all over the shop, trying to find out more.

Maxwell's determination to get to the bottom of who

Ballie of Baillieston was led him to a modest little gem that may well have been lost in the annals of time, never to have been discovered, were it not for a man with the detective skills of some of the country's greatest sleuths.

A single entry in a Court of Session record concerning a financial dispute involving Robert Boyd of Windyedge/ Mount Vernon fame threw up the missing clue. There was a John Baillie, who had purchased the land and named it for himself, in the time-honoured fashion.

The other red herring in researching local history is the popular presumption that someone who buys himself an estate is doing so with the purpose of dynasty-making, building the ubiquitous manor house. But many landowners acquired their estates solely to reap rewards in mining or quarrying revenue.

Often the 'big hoose' was built to make the property more attractive to potential buyers after the natural resources had been depleted or became too expensive to pursue.

Such, it seems, was the intent of John Baillie. He never took up residence in his Baillieston estate because he was playing with the big boys in London as a successful merchant. Baillieston, it turns out, was just another investment.

And it's understandable that so many other worthy historians and academics would make the connection with the baillies or provands of Glasgow by dint of the various definitions of baillie – is it a name? Is it a public office?

This is the difference between a true historian determined to seek out for posterity the fine details of life in the past and those who simply want a good story.

For a real insight into the day-to-day lives of Baillieston's miners and weavers, you could do worse than read a very well-written piece published in the *Scots Magazine* in 1980 entitled 'Baillieston is Beautiful' by Elizabeth Sutherland.

Scott Maxwell inherited Baillieston lands in 1899. While Baillieston developed into mainly a mining and weaving community, the area that became known as Garrowhill originated from the estates of Barrachnie. In contrast to the coalmining concerns that dominated Baillieston, Garrowhill – still owned by Scott Maxwell – was designed as a 'garden suburb', with its pretty Garrowhill House on the hill in around 1810.

Carntyne

Carntyne, for the most part, was one massive coalpit, mined for its copious fuel output by generations of the Gray family, who owned the whole estate – among many others, including most of Tollcross, Shettleston and Dalmarnock – since the late 1500s.

The expression 'as deep as Carntyne Heugh' speaks to the seemingly inexhaustible resource in that area.

Despite the fact that Glasgow as a whole was rich in such an essential resource, colliery owners across the city formed a cartel between 1813 and 1817 that sought to keep the price of coal at a premium.

The safety of the mines and miners was not held so dear and working conditions were hard and dangerous. Many died in accidents or cave-ins. The lucky ones took longer to die of the fumes and coal dust ingested over years. Few men were expected to live beyond 45 years. And the Gray family didn't take too kindly to the men downing tools in 1833, protesting at the poor working conditions. Family archives even retain lists of those workers who took part in the strikes.

Collieries were under constant threat of flooding and miners relied heavily on wind power to drive the mills that extracted water from the shafts. Older mines used horse-power. However, having to rely on the weather to blow the blades of the mill was a fickle affair. In fair weather with little wind, mines just couldn't be worked, as water accumu-lated, which meant no work and no pay until the water was raised.

But too much 'weather' could be equally debilitating, as John Gray found to his cost during his tenure as coalmaster.

In Carntyne, the Westmuir colliery was fitted with a new windmill in 1737 and, during unusually heavy storms in January 1740, the huge construction was reportedly 'blown to pieces and never again refitted'. The fateful night of 13 January became etched in local history as 'the Windy Saturday'.

Gray was forced to install what is believed to be the first steam engine in Scotland, certainly in the west of Scotland mines, for water extraction.

The Reverend John Hamilton Gray succeeded to the estate in 1833 after his father, Robert, died.

While he enjoyed profits from the mines, this Gray was an absentee landlord made of gentler stock who carried on his ministry as vicar of the market town of Bolsover, a picturesque village near Scarsdale a few miles east of Chesterfield. John Hamilton lived in the town's castle, which was once the home of William Peverel, believed to be the illegitimate son of William I, the Conqueror. This link with the Norman king becomes more significant when we explore the auspicious ancestry of this ancient family. The Grays were certainly not originally of coalmining stock.

The Grays were an old, old family. Fully eight generations worked the mines over more than 300 years until the colliery was forced to close in 1875. But their lineage stretches back to the thirteenth century, when the de Grays of France first made their way to Scotland. The Grays have been linked with the town of de Gray in Haute Saone, in Normandy, which some sources suggest gives credence to the school of thought that the family may boast credentials stretching further back to the middle of the eleventh century and close links to William the Conqueror.

Indeed, one John, Lord de Gray, appears in the Domesday Book, the census that was commissioned by King William in 1085. Lord de Gray's son was at the Normandy king's side at the Battle of Hastings, which put William on the English throne.

Certainly, the Grays picked their friends carefully and their fights even more so, making alliances with English and Scottish royalty, who bestowed great wealth, with lands gifted throughout the country.

Future generations were highly favoured by King Richard I (and IV of Normandy), whose military prowess earned him the informal title Lionheart. He ruled England – and a fair swathe of French real estate – until his death in 1199. He was succeeded by his brother John, who pretty much made a dog's dinner of his reign: it eventually led to the siege of London and his reluctant signature on the fledgling human-rights manifesto the Magna Carta; England's excommunication from the Vatican Church; supremacy of the Pope over monarchy; and the virtual fiefdom of England to the Catholic Church.

So when I say the Grays picked good neighbours, goodness knows what they were doing currying favour with the man who virtually sold the royal jerseys for a song. Still, the Grays' wealth and landholdings spilled out across the land.

Across the border, the dynasty continued, initially under the Scottish king Alexander II, who gifted lands by Royal Charter across Roxburgh. This may be the first mention of the Grays of Scotland. Later generations were rewarded for their allegiance to King Robert Bruce in the early fourteenth century, with the gift of lands known as the Carse of Gowrie.

The genealogy of the Grays, including Lady Jane Grey – who ruled as a child monarch for just nine days before being introduced to the executioner's much-polished axe – is rich with tales of murder, mayhem and intrigue, and it very much warrants further investigation.

Carntyne was also noted for its arable and dairy farming. Between the wars and after the Second World War, the farms were given over to one of the city's most ambitious housing projects, particularly after the Social Housing Act of 1924, which moved thousands of families from overcrowded Glasgow tenements to the promised land of Easterhouse, Sandyhills and Carntyne housing schemes.

Carntyne Stadium was the social hub from the early 1920s, running regular dog races and later speedway or dirt-track car-racing events. It rivalled the better-known Shawfield Stadium, boasting a crowd of up to 40,000 in the summer of 1928, who came to see boxing hero Tommy Milligan duke it out for the British middleweight title with defending champion Frank Moody, who also held the British light-heavyweight belt in the same year. It was an outdoor event, so no doubt a few non-paying guests managed to sneak in, but official attendance in *Boxing Magazine* at the time was capped at 35,000, according to sport historian Miles Templeton, who co-runs the well-worth-a-gander website boxinghistory.org.uk. Milligan was knocked out in the first round.

After that fight, manager Jack Nixon-Browne quit the stadium after only six months in the job, believing he would make a better politician than promoter. He was no A. E. Pickard, he would be the first to admit, but he was right to jump ship, as he went on to carve out a notable career in politics.

He won a seat at Westminster, representing Craigton as a Tory MP, and would eventually take his place in the House of Lords as Lord Craigton. Yet, while he was Scottish Office Minister of State, he betrayed a long-held love from his youth, one that he nurtured for a short time at Carntyne Racecourse: speedway racing. He would speak out vociferously against the proposed levying of an Entertainment Tax on this sport.

During the 1970s, actor and comedian Billy Connolly put the town firmly on the world map with his song 'Three Men from Carntyne'.

Easterhouse

Discovering Easterhouse was probably my favourite part in researching some of the larger districts of the East End. I'll fess up to being apprehensive that I would have a dearth of material to draw on from ancient times. Wasn't Easterhouse a manufactured solution to the problems of decaying housing and overcrowding in the city?

Easterhouse, to my limited knowledge – nay, my own ignorance – was a quick-fix solution to social housing that had whole urban communities farmed out to the outlying countryside with the promise of state-of-the-art design, land to roam, hot running water, modern heating and an inside loo. All of which is true and, reading East Ender James Doherty's foreword, was manna from heaven.

But what else can be discovered about the history of such a contemporary township?

Loads, as it happens.

That's not 'modern' Easterhouse. Modern Easterhouse was back in the 1100s, when Glasgow was officially designated an ecclesiastical bishopric.

Easterhouse and its neighbouring communities were on the quite extensive lists of grants by King Malcolm IV to the monks of Newbattle Abbey way back to the mid-thirteenth century via Bishop Herbert.

The village of Easterhouse was founded in the late 1800s, beginning with a farm of that same name somewhere near where the old Easterhouse train station stands today. It was an agricultural community and was possibly originally named Conflattis, describing the cornfields that were farmed in those parts. The first tenant farmer (or 'rentaller') appears to be a certain farmer John Wood, thanks to those old diocesan rent books. Wood would have worked the land there from around the middle of the 1500s.

While mainly a farming community, many of the growing hub of villagers were also to find work at Auchinlea quarries or local mines, and on the nearby and crucial Monkland canal.

There remain many aspects that date the area back to medieval times. The restored Provan Hall, originally set within Auchinlea Park, would have been the Bishop of Glasgow's summer retreat.

Provan Hall is now an A-listed building, preserved for posterity by the National Trust for Scotland, which proudly proclaims it as the 'best-preserved medieval fortified country house in Scotland'. That's quite a boast.

Of course, every ancient building likes to lay claim to a queen in its bedroom or a king on its commode.

Provan Hall may well have hosted Mary, Queen of Scots – who else? She was travelling with her husband, Lord Darnley, who allegedly was taken into St Nicholas hospital in the late 1500s.

That may be a fairy tale, though, because first, the afore-mentioned was a charity for the poor and the unwashed of Glasgow. And, if she was going to stay in a prebendary house, why not the one right next door to the hospital, Provands Lordship?

Nearby Blochairn House was taken over in 1760 by John Buchanan, who wanted to transform it into his plantation house in Jamaica.

But Easterhouse history stretches way back before the bishops.

An archaeological dig of 1898 – so de rigueur from Victoria's reign onwards – discovered in Bishop's Loch ancient forms of buildings known as crannogs, dating back to 700 BC during the Iron Age. These were mainly wooden structures built on stilts embedded into the loch, forming small man-made islands. These outdate St Kentigern's church by a Roman mile.

Education of the masses has long been one of the pillars of Red Clydeside socialism – and anathema to the autocratic leadership that dominated Victorian and pre-Victorian societies.

Teach a man to read, to learn, to understand – to question – and he can change his world. What autocracy wants to be answerable to their minions and have their policies exposed for the mutual back-scratching, self-serving, coffer-filling, fiscal-pillaging manifestos that seek to widen the gap between rich and poor, both in economic terms and in terms of social justice? Equality was not an option in a class-defined society.

The Communist dictator Chairman Mao Tse-tung was so afraid of education of the masses that he ordered the mass burning of books and works of art, and encouraged the persecution of anyone found reading books or discussing serious issues. Neighbours and family members had a duty to seek out and attack anyone suspected of learning.

In a fair, free and just society, education is essential for the inclusion of all the people in the running of their own lives. The name that identifies one of the country's first exponents of justice, equality and education is John Wheatley.

John Wheatley College, or Campus, in Easterhouse commemorates a local hero who stood up for the rights of workers, led strikes and campaigned for just these values. He and fellow activists were ready to go to jail for their convictions.

John Wheatley was badly injured during the 40-hour working week demo; he stood fast beside the women protesting extortionate rent increases; he stood shoulder to shoulder with suffragettes; and was in the frontline in the campaign against conscription. He was fervently anti-war.

Wheatley was as at home on the picket line as he was in negotiations with council leaders and influential benefactors.

He also wrote the blueprint for housing reform that led to a massive re-housing initiative that transformed its provision for the working classes.

Born in Ireland in May 1869, Wheatley came over to Scotland with his family in 1876 and settled in Braehead, Lanarkshire. The son of typically devout Irish Catholic parents, he was one of ten children who were all educated at St Bridget's in Baillieston. He followed his father down the pits when he left school.

When his shift was over, he would wash and change and head off on foot to Glasgow and the Atheneum Commercial College, which had been recently set up with grants and funding to provide subsidized part-time courses for working-class adults on a wide range of subjects. This would be his route out of the pits, but he never forgot how life was down the mines and wrote a number of pamphlets about the miners' plight.

He later ran a grocery shop in Shettleston with his brother, but moved on to find work as a reporter on the *Glasgow Catholic Observer*.

As his political views took shape, he founded the Catholic Socialist Society in Glasgow and in 1907 joined the newly formed Independent Labour Party, where he would meet the socialist heroes of Red Clydeside.

Around the same time, he invested in a printing press and quickly secured bread-and-butter contracts to service the printing needs of the Catholic Church and the Labour Party. It served as a medium for pamphleteering, Wheatley being as prolific a writer as he was an orator.

He published in succession *How the Miners Are Robbed*, *The Catholic Workingman* and *Miners, Mines and Misery*. He was elected to the town and county councils, where he immediately pursued the issue of decent housing for workers.

Far from shunning the benefits of industrial capitalism, Wheatley proved that socialist views and profit from commercial business could sit at the same table.

His main regular publication, the *Glasgow Eastern Standard*, contributed greatly to the more than £70,000 turnover by 1921. He could afford to pay for public schooling for his children and take over a substantial stone building in Shettleston as the family home.

For Scottish politics, 1922 was a landmark year. It saw the return of ten leading Red Clydesiders to Parliament in Westminster, people that would inspire and inform the fight for rights through many generations to come: Wheatley,

David Kirkwood, Manny Shinwell, Jimmy Maxton, John Muir, Tom Johnston, Jimmie Stewart, Neil MacLean, Keir Hardie's brother George, James Welsh and George Buchanan.

Wheatley was appointed to Ramsay MacDonald's Cabinet as Health Minister in January 1924, but his most outstanding contribution in his first years at Westminster was the Housing Act of 1924, of which he was chief architect. His powers of persuasion and organization came to the fore when it came to implementing the Act. He had a bit of a juggling act to perform in bringing together a group of disparate organizations and getting them to work with one another. For the Act to work, Westminster committee members and local councillors had to sit comfortably at the table with construction firms and trade unions.

The aim was an ambitious one: a ten-year plan to build 450,000 council-owned houses at a fair rent, starting with 190,000 houses to be completed within the first year of the scheme.

So far, Wheatley's religion and politics were an easy fit and one had not encumbered the other. This was to change, however, when only months into his role as Health Minister his faith would come into conflict with the rights of women to exercise birth control.

In May 1924, Wheatley was faced with a delegation led by the writer H. G. Wells that sought to enshrine in law a woman's right to birth control. To Wheatley, this was just unthinkable and he refused to give the campaign his support.

Wheatley fell out of favour with his Westminster colleagues and was losing the support of some of his ground floor supporters. He was also in poor health himself and on 12 May 1930 he died of a cerebral aneurism.

Dalbeth Cemetery had never seen such crowds as at his funeral, with huge numbers coming to pay their respects to a fallen socialist brother.

Wheatley II and III

John Thomas Wheatley junior was still a babe-in-arms in 1908 when his uncle entered the arena of politics, but it wouldn't be long before he was awarded honorary membership of the Independent Labour Party – at the age of eight.

John Thomas was the youngest child of John Wheatley's brother, Patrick. He was an exemplar of new unbunnetted socialism, the result of the fights of the first generation, who demanded improvements in health, housing and education so that their children would develop a better quality of life and lay further groundwork for generations to come.

John Thomas did this in spades, carving out an impressive career in law and in the military. Patrick was pleased that his son didn't have to go down the mines as a young boy. John Thomas had more options growing up.

After university, and having spent time as an 'articled clerk' in the apprenticeship of a Glasgow legal firm, he qualified as an advocate in 1932.

Being submersed in a strong family connection with the Labour movement was somewhat off-centre with the lofty heights of the judge's chamber, but his background would inform many of the cases that he would argue as an advocate after being called to the bar in Edinburgh early in his career.

Under Churchill's government of 1940, John Thomas prosecuted cases as Advocate-Depute to the Sheriff Court.

Not long after his appointment, war broke out in Europe and he was called to service in the Royal Artillery.

According to tradition, members of the advocacy were entitled, during times of conflict, to lay aside their gown and wig and prosecute cases in military uniform.

John Thomas was said to have been very proud to become the first as yet non-commissioned officer to appear in court in uniform without wig or gown.

Now, this is another road that deviates from the Wheatley family core values. John Thomas was happy to serve king and country, but that was in total contrast to the pacifist position adopted by the Independent Labour Party of his elders.

It was with a sad heart that John Thomas resigned his almost lifelong membership of the Party.

Still working as court prosecutor, in the post-war years he stood unsuccessfully as Labour candidate in two elections.

Where his political ambitions faltered, his legal career was on a fast train to the top of the hill. In 1947, he was first appointed Solicitor-General for Scotland and, soon after, Lord Advocate, while still only 39.

He finally found electoral success as MP for Edinburgh East. Seven years on, he was called to the bench.

His legacy to the working-class struggle lay in the two big transformations of the post-war government: the nationalization of key industries and the introduction of free health care in the new National Health System.

He was involved in setting up the Law Society of Scotland

and in formalizing legislation that introduced free Legal Aid.

As Lord Justice Clerk, he laid down guidelines on bail and sentencing that are still followed today and his judgements set precedents that are often quoted in legal arguments.

Wheatley's daughter Kathleen was to marry the future Father of the House of Commons and poser of the ubiquitous 'West Lothian Question', Tam Dalyell, many years before Scotland's devolution.

John Thomas's wife, Nancy Nichol, outlived him by 15 years. They had met in the Independent Labour Party, where Nancy played key roles as treasurer and social convenor, running a socialist Sunday School and organizing speakers to come to social functions.

She once got Ramsay MacDonald to turn up and speak at one of the regular Monday night 'hops' (dances) at the Wellshot Hall in Tollcross, where she was brought up. She had been among the throngs as a little girl when the quasi-military battle took place on George Square in 1919.

John Thomas's funeral in July 1988 was clouded by controversy, when his lifelong friend and, at the time, Lord Chancellor, Lord Mackay of Clashfern, was banned by his church, the Free Church of Scotland, from attending his friend's funeral, it being held in a Catholic church. Lord Mackay ignored the ban and went to pay his respects to Wheatley and his family – a move that resulted in his suspension from the Church and of his right to take Holy Communion.

At the disciplinary synod, Lord Mackay was accused of 'showing support for the doctrine of Roman Catholicism', which Lord Mackay denied, asserting he was merely paying respect to a dead friend and colleague.

He refused to bow to the synod's insistence that he vow never to attend another Catholic service and withdrew from the Church.

The whole sorry business was so fractious as to cause a schism within the Free Church.

John Thomas's son, John Francis Wheatley, followed his father into the law and blazed a similar trail to the top of his profession. Born in 1941, he was boarded out to the same Jesuit school attended by his father, Mount Saint Mary's College, Derbyshire, and studied law at Edinburgh University.

Admitted to the Faculty of Advocates in 1966, he was appointed advocate-depute in 1975. His career followed similar lines to that of his father, including an appointment as a Senator of the College Justice, leading to Court of Session, where he took the title Lord Wheatley. He also served on the Privy Council.

The Wheatleys became a dynasty of a different sort to those who simply inherited their merchant father's estate and mansion house. The rise of the Wheatley family from miner, to Baron, to Lord was certainly not one of privilege, but one firmly rooted in a foundation of faith and social justice.

No matter the heights future generations rose to, they never turned away from the core values of access to education, to healthcare, to legal representation for all.

A gauin' fit's aye gettin'

I often find that the soundest advice comes in the vernacular in any language and none more than guid auld Scots. The recently resurrected wartime mantra Keep Calm and Carry On is another little gem that has been paraphrased all over the place. But I prefer the Barras queen Maggie McIver's couthy version: 'Work hard an' keep the heid.' In my view, she said it first and she said it best.

Another favourite is 'A gauin' fit's aye gettin'', meaning we always pick up something of value when we're on the hoof.

It's particularly appropriate on the many walking tours around the East End, where one's guaranteed to learn something new about the city and its many unsung heroes.

Here, I've compiled some interesting walks to include in any travel itinerary and I'm sure some of Glasgow's long-term residents would benefit from checking some of them out.

There are many websites that list heritage trails of interest, from Frommer's travel guides to What's On in Glasgow.

Historic Glasgow runs a handy website and has created PDF documents that outline various walks, including the Glasgow Necropolis Heritage Trails and Tollcross Park Heritage Trail, and nature walks with the park's historic rose garden, the mansion house and children's city farm.

Merchant City Women's Heritage Trail is well worth donning one's walking shoes for, as is Calton, Bridgeton and George Square. There are archaeological digs and tours of famous feats of architectural genius, including buildings by esteemed architects Charles Rennie Mackintosh, Alexander 'Greek' Thomson and Robert Adam.

The history of the grand old Barrowland Ballroom and market is a story worth the telling and staff are happy to show visitors around by appointment.

Student Tours Scotland (STS) also has a website listing various tours aimed at students from outside the city and from overseas who are coming to Glasgow to study. These include Parkhead and Tollcross; the Commonwealth Games village; City of Light tour; City of the Dead; Dalmarnock and Cuningar Loop, and loads more.

The Women's Library in Bridgeton also runs tours where visitors can find out about female pioneers, suffragettes and Red Clydesiders among others.

People Make Glasgow also run tours, some of which may charge a fee. One I would highly recommend is the City Sightseeing Bus tour.

Many of these tours are free, so don't book with an organization that charges a fee if you don't have to, unless you want to contribute to a particular historic or charitable organization. Most of the free ones can be accessed from the Glasgow City Council website and that of Glasgow Life.

Recommended Further Reading

Obviously, I'd recommend *Barrowland: A Glasgow Experience*, since I wrote it. In fact, anything on Glasgow from Mainstream Publishing, now an imprint of Random House, is well worth looking at.

For those who are lucky enough to live or work within commuting distance of the Mitchell Library in Glasgow, there is a richness of gargantuan proportions within its walls. The Glasgow Room is a must-go-to, but there are many more books and archives, including microfiche storage, that offer a veritable banquet of information on the East End and its characters. 'Virtual Mitchell' is an extensive digital archive which hosts the library's digital content for those further afield. National archives – governmental, civic, religious and academic – are also marvellous hubs of information.

Books I found useful include: *Glasgow East* by Gordon Adams; *A History of Bridgeton and Dalmarnock* by Gordon Adams; *A History of Tollcross and Dalbeth* by Gordon Adams; *Recollections of Bridgeton* by William Guthrie; *A Tale of Two Towns: A History of Medieval Glasgow* by Neil Baxter; *The Glasgow Almanac: An A–Z of the City and Its People* by Stephen Terry; *Glasgow: The Forming of the City* by Peter

Reed; *The Hidden History of Glasgow's Women* by Elspeth King; *A Grim Almanac of Glasgow* by Lynne Wilson; and *Pre and Post-Industrial Bridgeton* by Raymond Thompson, with the Bridgeton Local History Group.

If you can get a hold of anything by Bob Currie, it is well worth reading. Bob's memory of who lived where and when in Bridgeton is legendary, as well as his knowledge of shops and trades changing hands over generations.

All that said, there's really nothing like being in Glasgow: smelling the smells, hearing the echoes from the acoustics that seem to be unique to cathedrals and churches; marvelling at architectural magnificence while standing in its midst; leafing through precious, meticulously preserved registers and record books.

Useful websites

Listed below are useful websites to whet the appetite and help with planning a trip or simply for further research. Word of warning, though, some of these sites run very informative forums and blogs, but the language can sometimes be somewhat colourful:

historictownsatlas.org.uk;
glasgowhistory.com;
theglasgowstory.com;
glasgowhistory.co.uk;
scottishbanner.com;
gdl.cdlr.strath.ac.uk;
catandmouse.org.uk;
universitystory.gla.ac.uk;

suffragettes.nls.uk;
sites.scran.ac.uk;
glasgowguide.co.uk;
hiddenglasgow.com;
redflag.org.uk;
gcu.ac.uk/archives;
glasgowcathedral.org;
parkheadhistory.com;
glescapals.com;
glasgownecropolis.org;
glasgowarchitecture.co.uk;
greetinglasgow.com;
urbanglasgow.co.uk;
britanniapanopticon.org;
monklands.co.uk;
boxinghistory.org.uk.

Things to Do and Places to See

Here is a list of places to visit in Glasgow in no particular order. OK, they're not all in the East End, but most of them are and it's all right to venture further west, as no visit to Glasgow would be complete without a trip to the Kelvingrove Museum and Art Gallery, for example. Many of these have websites.

The Barras; Barrowland Ballroom; Blythwood Square; Botanic Gardens and Kibble Palace; Brittania Panopticon Music Hall; Buchanan Street; The Burrell Collection; City Chambers; Glasgow Cathedral; Glasgow Film Theatre; Glasgow Green; Glasgow Police Museum; Glasgow School of Art; Hunterian Art Gallery; Hunterian Museum; Kelvingrove Art Gallery and Museum; Kelvingrove Park; Merchant City; Museum of Modern Art; Museum of Religion; The Necropolis; Òran Mór for A Play, a Pie, and a Pint; People's Palace and Winter Gardens; Pollok Country Park; Provands Lordship House; Riverside Museum of Transport; Royal Concert Hall; Royal Exchange Square; Sharmanka Kinetic Theatre; Trongate; Tron Theatre; University of Glasgow.

Heartfelt Thanks

All that remains is for me to thank the many people and organizations that gave me their valuable time and the individuals who allowed me to use some of their photographs. If I've missed anyone out, I can only apologize most sincerely.

Special thanks go to my good friend, mentor and killer researcher Monty Bryden. Monty also offered me historic family heirlooms of books of etchings by the respected lithographer and architect Robert Bryden, which I think deserve to reach a wider audience.

Thanks to Bill Campbell, of Mainstream Publishing, for his patience, which I tried to almost criminal extremes; and to editor Debs Warner, whose attention to detail and fine-toothed comb transformed my random ramblings, dotting every i and crossing numerous t's. And to Brenda Kimber and Shiela Lee of Transworld.

We are greatly indebted to the curators and researchers of Glasgow's Museums and Libraries for their extensive work in preserving the remembrances and experiences of the people of Glasgow in extensive projects that will inform present and future generations in old Glasgow, not least the 2000 Glasgow Lives project.

My thanks in particular to Fiona McLeod, commissioning editor of Museums and Libraries, for introducing me to so many people whose input and advice have been invaluable. Also to Fiona Hayes, Glasgow Museums; Tracey Hawkins, Glasgow Museums Resource Centre; Dr David Walker, Glasgow Museums Oral History Project; Simon Biggam, the Olympia Theatre, Bridgeton Cross; Sally Clegg, chief librarian, Glasgow Life; Professor Irene O'Brien, senior archivist, the Mitchell; Mark Roberts, Glasgow Museums Resource Centre; Tom Joyes, Willie and Linda at Barrowlands; Miles Templeton, boxinghistory.org.uk; Dr Charles Doyle; Kevin Buchanan, STUC; Fiona McLeod, publishing editor at Glasgow Life; James Doherty, head of media at Glasgow Life; and Gordon Boag, Glasgow Life.

And to the wonderful Elspeth King, museums curator, just for being. A wee gem of a booklet, *Barrapatter*, is compiled by Elspeth in her role as curator of the People's Palace.

Finally, special thanks to my gorgeous husband David Shepherd, with all my love.

Picture acknowledgements

Every effort has been made to get in touch with copyright holders. Any who have been overlooked are invited to get in touch with the publishers.

Images in the text

26, 31 both, 59 both, 64: from *Glasgow Etchings* by Robert Bryden R. E., 1914; 49 all: from *Workers Etched* by Robert Bryden R. E., 1912

Picture section

Pictures are listed clockwise from the top left of the spread
Cathedral Square fountain: © CSG CIC Glasgow Museums and Libraries Collection, The Mitchell Library, Special Collections; Joseph Lister, engraving from *Antiseptic Surgery: Its Principles, Practice, History and Results* by William Watson Cheyne, 1882: Wellcome Images

46 Saltmarket: Science and Society/Superstock; Glasgow Corporation tailoring workshop; women factory workers making Jewish skull caps; Barras market: all © CSG CIC Glasgow Museums and Libraries Collection, The Mitchell Library, Special Collections

Juvenile Delinquency Board; Dennistoun School: both © CSG CIC Glasgow Museums and Libraries Collection, The Mitchell Library, Special Collections; tank, George Square, 1919: courtesy of the Herald and Times Group, Glasgow

Mother nursing her baby; well-to-do mother and baby; conductresses, 1939; workers, R. White's: all © CSG CIC Glasgow Museums and Libraries Collection, The Mitchell Library, Special Collections; Cissie Smith: courtesy the author; girls on Glasgow Green, 1955: courtesy of the Herald and Times Group, Glasgow

Cinema queue; Modern Homes Exhibition: both © CSG CIC Glasgow Museums and Libraries Collection, The Mitchell Library, Special Collections

Index

Page numbers in *italics* denote an illustration

321

Index

Index

Index

Index

325

Index

Index

Index

Index

Index

Index

Index

Index

Nuala Naughton is an award-winning journalist, editor, lecturer and trainer. She has worked for national and international newspaper groups in news and features across the spectrum, from main section to business, life-style, entertainment and obituaries. Her previous book, *Barrowlands: A Glasgow Experience*, which allows readers to take a trip down memory lane and remember their favourite gigs at the world-famous venue in Glasgow's East End, was published in 2013. She lives in Glasgow.